CRUISING BULGARIA & ROMANIA

NICKY ALLARDICE

Imray Laurie Norie & Wilson

Published by
Imray Laurie Norie & Wilson Ltd
Wych House The Broadway St Ives
Cambridgeshire PE27 5BT England
☎ +44 (0)1480 462114
Fax +44 (0)1480 496109
Email ilnw@imray.com
www.imray.com
2007

All rights reserved. No part of this publication may be reproduced, transmitted or used in any form by any means – graphic, electronic or mechanical, including photocopying, recording, taping or information storage and retrieval systems or otherwise – without the prior permission of the publishers.

1st edition 2007

© Nicky Allardice

Nicky Allardice has asserted his right to be identified as the author of this work in accordance with the Copyright, Designs and Patents Act 1988.

© Plans Imray Laurie Norie & Wilson Ltd 2007

ISBN 978 0 85288 910 7

British Library Cataloguing in Publication Data.
A catalogue record for this book is available from the British Library.

PLANS
The plans in this guide are not to be used for navigation. They are designed to support the text and should at all times be used with navigational charts.

CAUTION
Whilst every care has been taken to ensure accuracy, neither the Publishers nor the Author will hold themselves responsible for errors, omissions or alterations in this publication. They will at all times be grateful to receive information which tends to the improvement of the work.

CORRECTIONAL SUPPLEMENTS
This pilot book will be amended at intervals by the issue of correctional supplements which will be published on our website www.imray.com and may be downloaded free of charge. Printed copies are also available on request from the publishers at the above address.

Printed in Croatia by Zrinski

Contents

Preface *iv*
Acknowledgements *iv*

I. **INTRODUCTION**
   General *1*
   Preparation *2*
   Essential equipment *4*
   Navigational information *6*
   Using this guide *7*
   Bulgaria *8*
   Romania *14*

II. **THE BLACK SEA**
   Sea and weather *18*
   Turkey, Thrace
   Bosphorus to the Bulgarian border *21*
   Bulgaria
   Turkish border to Burgas Bay *25*
   Burgas Bay *31*
   Nos Eminie to the Romanian border *45*
   Romania
   The Black Sea coast *60*
   River Danube-Black See Canal *63*
   Sulina Canal entry *67*

III. **THE RIVER DANUBE**
   General *68*
   Navigation *68*
   Navigational dangers *71*
   History *71*
   The Danube Delta *75*
   River Danube navigation *75*
   Bulgaria *78*
   Romania *97*

   Appendix *103*
   Index *104*

PREFACE

The journey was started with no pilot or guidebook. When we left the UK there was no plan as to where we were going to go: the only plan was to escape the rat race. Destiny took us to the River Danube. There were all the notes in the logbook and the story of the journey started to be written up. Only after this was completed did I read Rod Heikell's *The Danube, A River Guide*. Although written in 1991 his is still a very useful book, and it was very gratifying to note that much of what I had written corroborated what Rod Heikell had written. Before going to the Black Sea I had purchased *Black Sea Guide* by Rick and Sheila Nelson, and my journey confirmed my belief that I could supplement and update their information. I then contacted Imray Laurie Norie and Wilson, and am very grateful to Willie Wilson for agreeing to publish this book.

Nicky Allardice
February 2007

ACKNOWLEDGEMENTS

Thanks to those who acted as crew, and (as in the movies) the cast in order of appearance: Ewan Cameron, Mark Korad and friends, Karol Vlasak, Voita Saman, Ulf Drechsel, Peter Manchev, Irina Trandafirescu, Diana Toulin, Saso Alexander and friends, Bill Mitchell, Todor Slavov, Sorin Lacurezeanu and Iamut Ionescu Dragos.

Thanks must also go to Gosho Tochev for providing many facilities and solving problems in Bulgaria, Saso Alexander for his knowledge of the Black Sea and showing us places we would never have found by ourselves, Paul Popovici for assistance in Romania, Diana Toulin for typing and sending out spare parts, Bisser Galabov for solving many problems in Bulgaria, Momchil Bashev for photographs, Paro Artemov for assistance at Nessebar harbour, the many individuals that I sat and had a beer with while I asked them for local information, and the staff of the tourist information offices where I picked their brains and gathered the tourist leaflets. Billy Wolfe for doing some proofreading and adding comments as a non-sailor. Last but not least, Willie Wilson and the staff at Imray, Laurie, Norie and Wilson who produced this book.

I. INTRODUCTION

GENERAL

For the visiting yachtsman, the cruising areas of Bulgaria and Romania – the River Danube, parts of the Black Sea coast, and (in Romania) the Danube Delta, a special area in its own right – offer a fascinating diversity. Despite being close geographical neighbours, Bulgaria and Romania are culturally very different. It was two Bulgarians, St Cyril and St Methodus who invented the Cyrillic alphabet which was adopted by other Slavic nations showing their close historic links, whereas Romania is, as it name suggests, a country with Latin cultural traditions similar to other western Mediterranean countries, and a Romance language written in the Roman alphabet. For anyone interested in history, archaeology and cultural heritage there is ample evidence of many influences – Thracian, Celtic, Dacian, Greek, Roman and Turkish – wherever you travel within the two countries.

Another strong attraction is the wide diversity of flora and fauna (birds and fish as well as animals), especially in areas such as Srebarna Lake, the North Romanian Black Sea coast, Ropotamo, Kamchia, Strandja and the Danube Delta, which are internationally important as nature reserves and as homes to some rare and endangered species.

The River Danube, one of Europe's most ancient thoroughfares, has formed a trading route and a boundary between north and south for thousands of years, but the east-west political divide within Europe after 1945 has also left its legacy for those wishing to visit the area by boat. In places on the river it is almost as if the Iron Curtain still existed: between Vienna and Bratislava the number of vessels on the river drops dramatically, after Mohacs on the Hungarian border there are almost no pleasure boats or associated facilities, and the area is still relatively unknown to foreign boats. However, in January 2007 Bulgaria and Romania joined the EU, and it is hoped that a relaxation of the old (and often complex) rules and regulations for boats will make visiting the waterways of the Danube and the coasts of Bulgaria and Romania easier than ever before.

Cruising Bulgaria and Romania aims to encourage many more yachtsmen to discover the pleasures of cruising the Lower Danube and the western Black Sea, and to visit the ports and harbours (both antique and modern) and the miles of unspoilt beaches in these fascinating areas. The chapter format reflects these naturally defined areas, as well as including additional information to cover the Turkish Thrace coast from the Bosphorus to Bulgarian border, since this area has to be transited on the way to and from the main area described in this guide.

Ropotamo River

INTRODUCTION

PREPARATION

Charts

British Admiralty Charts purchased from Imray Laurie Norie and Wilson were found to be adequate and should be obtained in advance. Turkish Charts from their Hydrographic Institute of the Navy were also recommended. We could not find anywhere in Romania to buy charts, and in Bulgaria one place selling Admiralty charts is noted in that section. Several inaccuracies were found on the charts. Where we have found rocks and reefs not plotted on the charts, they are mentioned in the texts. The charts that cover each individual area are specified at the beginning of each text.

Courtesy flags

These should be bought in advance. Flags are available in the tourist resorts but difficult to find elsewhere, the exception being the ship chandler in Varna who stocks flags for other countries as well. Both flags have been changed since the Communist era, so it is not diplomatic to have an old one.

Visas

Visas for Romania and Bulgaria are not required for European Union nationals for short visits. Other nationalities should check with embassies well in advance. There are more details in each individual section.

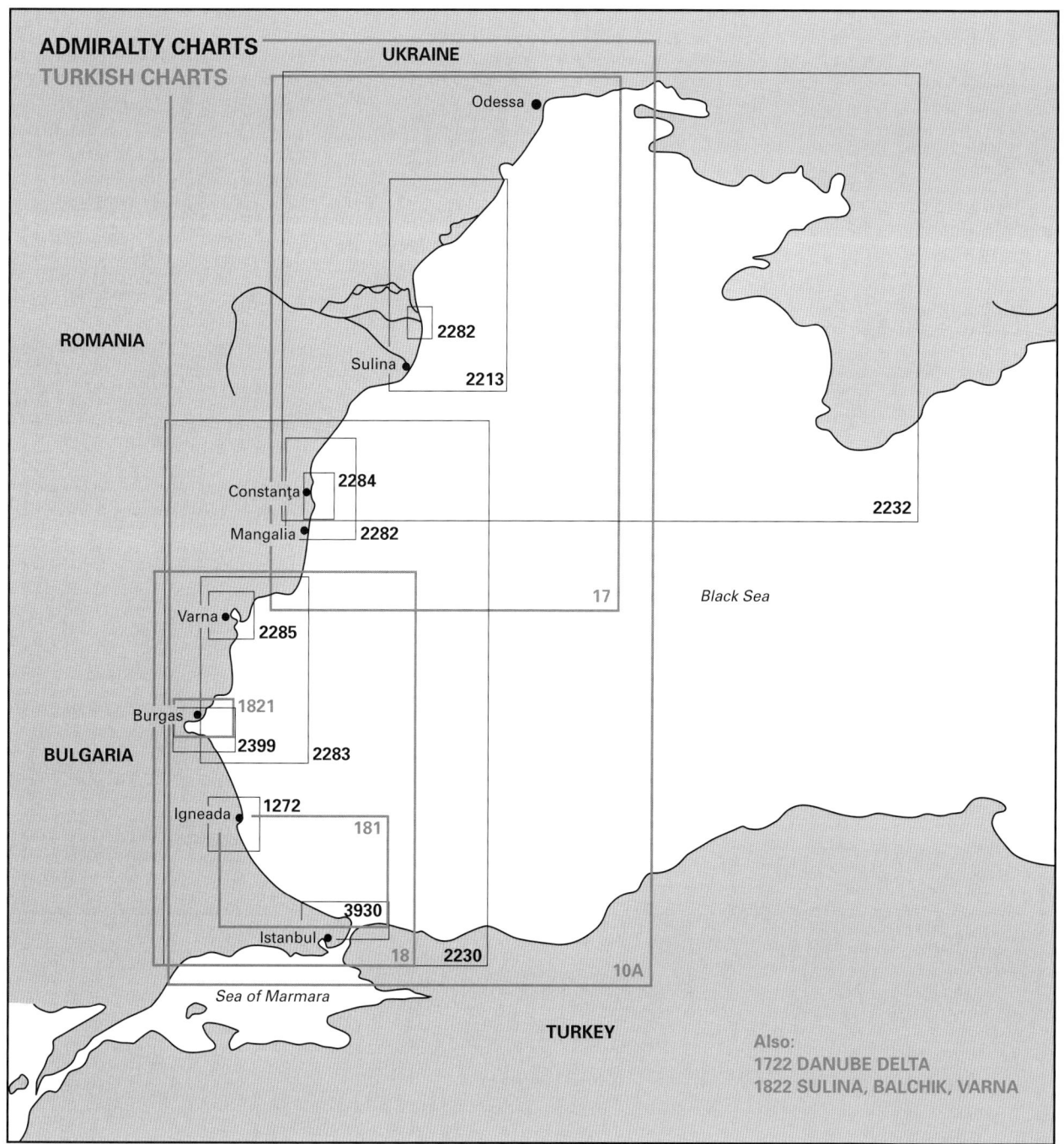

Money

There are banks or exchange offices in most towns, but be prepared for a stopover in smaller towns or villages where there are no exchange facilities. Traveller's cheques can be cashed in larger towns but have a commission charge. Credit cards and ATMs are becoming more popular but don't rely on finding one when you need it, except in major holiday resorts. Credit cards are not widely accepted yet. Defaced, old or marked notes will probably not be accepted even if there is only a slight mark on them. Some restaurants and shops will accept payment in dollars or Euros. Bring a supply of small denomination notes since sometimes large denomination notes are not accepted. Shop around when exchanging money there can be as much as 20% difference even between two neighbouring exchange bureaux. The main banks generally give a better rate than kiosks. If taking large amounts of money into the countries, complete a currency declaration at the border. It is illegal to take out more than you have taken in, unless proof of where the money was obtained can be produced. Keep ATM and credit card receipts in case they are required. Only dollars are acceptable for some payments and this is specified in the text, but there is a gradual change to Euros.

Prices, where given, are converted to Euros and are for guidance only.

Crew lists

A sample of the one we prepared is shown below. Take plenty of copies: in one port 7 copies were required. Pieces of carbon paper would be useful, as we then used about 60 copies to cruise round the two countries.

Declarations

We were asked for different types of declaration at different ports. It was decided to combine them all on one form which we show below. Officials seemed to like it and it saved us handwriting many declarations.

Rubber stamp

Very beneficial to have, but not essential. Put on the stamp: Ship's Name; Registration Number; Home Port; Owner's Name. (This can be arranged in many local stationery shops.)

Registration document

This is absolutely essential; photocopies are not acceptable. One official complained at us for two days because, amongst other things, our Certificate of British Registry did not have a rubber stamp on it and 'must therefore be false'.

Insurance

Leave plenty of time to communicate with your insurance company to make sure that your insurance covers this area. Some port officials may ask to see it; we found the English version was acceptable in both Romania and Bulgaria.

Qualifications

A document such as the RYA International Certificate for Operators of Pleasure Craft, or something similar, may be requested at some harbours.

Radio licence

The necessary licences are required for the marine band radio(s) themselves and for competence to use them.

Proof of engine specifications

We were twice asked for proof of this information. A photocopy of the general data page of the workshop manual was sufficient for this purpose.

Gifts

It is traditional to give and receive a gift; sometimes these can be rather unusual. We received Ukrainian herbal tea, socks, eggs (from a barge which kept chickens on board), and local home-made drinks (*rakia, tsuika, slibovitz*).

In return we gave national flags, badges, boat club T-shirts and tops, whisky, old boat magazines, fancy keyring holders, cassettes, CDs and gloss paint. Bring a supply of small items to give as gifts. What is useful is a business card with your boat's name, your name, email address and any other information you wish to supply.

CREW LIST

BOAT NAME   LENGTH   BRITISH REGISTRY №
SPORT BOAT FLAG   WEIGHT   PORT of REGISTRY

№	Name	Passport №	Nationality	Place of birth	Date of birth	Arrival port	Departure port

Crew list

GENERAL DECLARATION FOR ARRIVAL OR DEPARTURE

SPORT BOAT   FLAG BRITISH   BRITISH REGISTRY
WEIGHT TONS LENGTH METERS BEAM METERS DRAFT METERS

PORT OF ENTRY OR DEPARTURE……………………
ARRIVED FROM /DEPARTING TO ……………………

THERE ARE NO FIREARMS, NARCOTICS OR OTHER DANGEROUS SUBSTANCES ON BOARD
THERE ARE NO STOWAWAYS ON BOARD

PROVISIONS, SPIRITS AND CIGARETTES ARE TYPICAL FOR PERSONAL USE FOR ONE WEEK

DATE OF DECLARATION……………
CAPTAINS NAME……………   OFFICIALS SIGNATURE……………
SIGNATURE AND SHIPS STAMP……………   OFFICIALS STAMP……………

Declaration for arrival and departure

ESSENTIAL EQUIPMENT

Fuel

Almost everywhere fuel can only be obtained from garages, so it is necessary to find a friendly local or hire a taxi and carry it in cans. The bigger the capacity of cans you have on board, the fewer trips you need to make to the garage. The only places with quayside fuel are in Romania at Mila 23 and Tulcea, in Bulgaria at Nessebar and in Thrace at Iğneada. At major harbours, particularly those with larger fishing boats or tourist cruise boats, a fuel tanker can be arranged to visit the boat. Ask the locals for the telephone number, or ask them to arrange it for you. The price of fuel is the same as for motor vehicles except when being delivered to the boat, when there may be a higher charge.

Water

This will also have to be carried in many places so water containers are essential, as is a hose with various adapters, since often you are filling them from a sink. If space permits and you have large water tanks a long hose could be beneficial since you may be moored some distance from the tap. (It is sometimes possible to borrow a hose from the locals.) On the River Danube the main pontoons will have a water supply, but in the more remote backwaters you are dependent on the goodwill of café owners and households to fill a container. At the Black Sea most major harbours will have a supply, otherwise it is a visit to a café or restaurant to fill a container. Bottled water is available almost everywhere.

Gas

Since many households use bottled gas for cooking it is relatively easy to find. The Bulgarian and Romanian gas cylinders are a different size to those obtained in the UK and may not fit into the gas locker. The size is 60cm high x 28cm diameter, compared with the UK size of 55 or 58cm high x 33cm diameter. If a new gas locker has to be fitted before departure, taking into account this additional height could be an advantage. The regulator fittings are different and a new one will have to be obtained. The people supplying the gas should be able to supply this as well, otherwise hardware stores and garages selling gas also stock them. The small camping gas cylinders are almost impossible to find, but in some places the people can refill the ones you have from a large gas cylinder.

Refuelling by tanker

Electricity

In places that do offer shore power it can sometimes be a long distance from the mooring, so a long cable is required along with a selection of electrical plug tops or adaptors. The two-pin round schuko plug is popular. Solar panels or a wind generator are useful accessories to keep the batteries topped up. The battery charger we had on board was used on several occasions, but the generator that was there for a final standby was never used.

Service and spares

The engines should have had a good service before departure.

A good supply of spares specific to your boat should be carried since they may not be available locally. Any maintenance handbook and service manuals should be on board. Carry more filters than you normally would, since fuel could be dirty. In some towns there are general hardware and electrical shops and it is amazing what parts can be found. Their diverse stock could include stainless steel fixings, hoses, ropes, paints, adhesives, chain, cables, switches, etc. We obtained some unusual things which generally were not on display; the shop owner had boxes of bits and pieces under the counter or in the back shop and if we took the faulty part and showed them we found everything required during the trip.

There are a few ship chandlers but stocks are limited. They have the franchise for major international supplies and items can be ordered, but this takes time for delivery. It is worthwhile paying a little extra to leave the ship chandler with the problem of clearing customs and getting the goods into the country. Couriers may get the goods to Bucharest or Sofia airport but leave you to fight with customs over clearance, which might take days.

Specific spare parts Prepare a list of addresses, email and telephone numbers of all your favourite suppliers for spare parts. If you have to order from them most international courier companies can deliver, but clarify that they will do the customs clearance, and exactly where the delivery point will be. A local address is needed for delivery, and we found local restaurants, shops and harbourmasters willing to accept the delivery.

Repairs

In most main harbours there will be someone who knows someone who has a lathe and other equipment in their garage or cellar, or they can reproduce small metallic parts at work. We have had several modifications to the engine and cooling system thanks to local production. Since there are few original spares, the locals have had to be creative and improvise to keep their own boats running.

Engine cooling water intake

This should have a filter in the line. If it is practical this should be located above the water line of the boat and have a shut off valve, so that it can be cleaned without taking the boat out of the water. The River Danube has weeds and the Black Sea, particularly in some harbours, has a sea grass that can block the filters, as well as other rubbish such as polythene bags.

Toilets

Sea toilets should not be used on the River Danube since millions of people depend on this as a source of drinking water. However, we did not find any facilities for pumping out holding tanks, and very few moorings had toilets ashore. We asked the locals about this facility at several places and we received the same answer, 'we just discharge it into the harbour, or river'. A holding tank should therefore be capable of being pumped out well out at sea even if the locals do not understand why. Whenever possible we used a portable chemical toilet and emptied it at toilets or in the woods. The Marpol *73/78* regulations covering the disposal of waste at sea are as follows and apply to all vessels including pleasure craft.

- Up to 3 miles offshore, all disposals prohibited.
- 3–12 miles offshore, food waste ground to less than one inch.
- 12–25 miles offshore, paper, rags, glass, crockery, metal and food not ground down. Forbidden for disposal here are plastic and anything that floats.
- Over 25 miles offshore, forbidden for disposal are plastics, man-made ropes, fishing nets, bin liners.

Bulgarian law on environmental regulation from July 1987 states that it is forbidden to introduce or dump any pollution in internal waters and territorial sea, which is 12 miles.

Showers

There are very few available in the harbours. If your boat is not equipped with a shower there are other compromise solutions. A solar shower is like a plastic bag, which when filled with water is hung up in the sun to heat. It has a spray unit fitted on the end of a hose. We left this heater with a hose leading to the sink and it was useful for washing dishes. Another option is a pressurised spray unit that you fill with water, pump up, and have a shower head fitted to the end of the hose. Other solutions are to use a hotel swimming pool shower, beach shower or negotiate for a small fee the use of a shower in a guesthouse.

Refrigerators

We found a refrigerator could run down a battery overnight. If you found it essential to have a refrigerator operating all the time, it would be necessary to fit solar panels and/or or a wind generator. Gas was ruled out for operating the refrigerator, which left us the last option: we only used it when mains power was available. This was adequate, except for the occasional inconvenience of having no ice cubes for the drinks.

Fenders

A good supply of large fenders is essential. Some moorings have little shelter and you can get a lot of buffeting from passing large commercial and military ships. Most mooring places are also not well prepared and have many spikes and jagged edges. This also means you wear through mooring ropes, so many spares should be on board.

Anchor chain and rope

Pontoon moorings are almost non-existent. In some areas continental moorings (going bows-to or stern-to the jetty and an anchor offshore) is the practice. A good anchor is therefore essential and a second one is beneficial. Anchor chain should be preferred to rope, but a good selection of rope should be on board.

Anchor

The merits of different types of anchors are given in many books and magazines, and we will not repeat them here. A unique one that was very useful is 'The Flying Anchor' from Australia. It is designed to fly at an angle of 18 degrees to the surface and should land on the seabed a distance forward 5 times the depth. Being lighter and only using rope, it is easier for a smaller crew member to use. It is launched with a forward motion horizontal to the water. It was very useful when mooring Mediterranean-style or holding the boat clear from wharfs with rough edges. A drogue anchor is useful on the River Danube when mooring bows-to on the downstream side of a pontoon.

On the Black Sea there are no fixed rules for mooring. It could be alongside a jetty, or against another boat, or Mediterranean-style with the bow or stern into the jetty.

Winch

When sailing single-handed it soon became apparent that a winch, which could be operated from the cockpit, was essential, and this was soon fitted.

Other equipment

A shade from the sun is necessary, but if you forget it many kiosks in the Black Sea resorts sell them for a very modest price. A second boat-hook was useful in some tight corners. Bicycles are very beneficial for exploring or going to the shops.

Don't forget the binoculars and cameras.

Mobile phones should have international roaming activated before leaving home. In a few of the more remote areas there is no coverage for mobile phones.

Medicines

Adequate supplies of any prescribed medicines should be taken. General medicines are available in all but the smaller villages. A supply of suntan lotion and insect repellent should be carried on board.

INTRODUCTION

NAVIGATIONAL INFORMATION

Sailing season
From April to early October.

Buoyage
IALA system A is used in Romania and Bulgaria.

Navtex
Navtex is useful and operates in the area, transmitting on 518kHz in English. The stations that were received in various places covered in the book are:

Varna	J
Odessa	C
Istanbul	D
Limnos	L
Izmir	I
Novorossiysk	A
Samsun	E

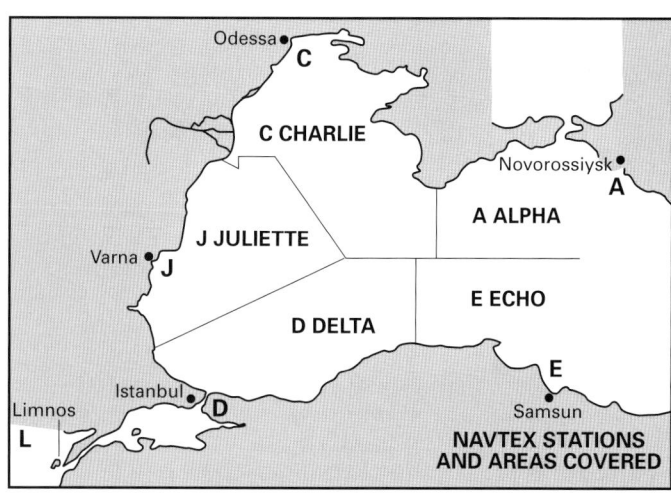

NAVTEX STATIONS AND AREAS COVERED

The strength of the reception from different stations varies at different locations and sometimes the more distant ones are broken.

Message priorities
Vital: for immediate transmission
Important: for transmission at the next available time
Routine: for the next transmission period

Message types
Type
identity   Description of message type
A   Navigation warnings covering the stations area
B   Gale warnings
C   Ice reports
D   Search and Rescue information (Distress messages), Pirate attack warnings
E   Weather forecasts
F   Pilot messages
G   Decca information
H   Loran-C information
I   Omega information
J   Satnav information
K   Other electronic navaid messages
L   Rig lists, submarine and gunnery information
V   Rig movements, Amplifying messages from A
Z   No messages on hand.

Weather forecast internet sites
www.bbc.co.uk/weather
www.cnn.com/weather
www.weather-forecast.com
www.wunderground.com
www.rssweather.com
www.weather.digsys.bg
www.weather.yahoo.com

Weather forecast in English
Bulgaria: Varna Radio Ch26 10.30, 16.30
Romania: Ch12 just after 10.00, 22.00

Anchoring and mooring
In Bulgaria and Romania Black Sea moorings were alongside and Mediterranean-style. Although there was space alongside, many harbours had rough sides or were shallow at the edge, so bow-to mooring is essential. If there are other boats round about, it is advisable to put out many fenders before starting the mooring operation. In some Bulgarian harbours you may be about the only one in the area so the minimal number of fenders may be required. For Mediterranean-style mooring the anchor should be dropped about 5 boat lengths from the jetty (see *Anchor* above) before manoeuvring into position. Apart from taking into account the depths and rocks, whether to go bow-to or stern-to in is personal preference. If the side is shallow or there are other obstructions in the water, it would be necessary to go bow-to in to the shore to eliminate damage to the steering or the propellers. This could also give more privacy. If an electric winch were fitted going stern-to would be preferable, since the main anchor would be utilised. Other advantages are that the ropes from the transom are probably easier to take to the shore, and the boat may have a passerelle or a plank that can be utilised for going ashore. By mooring Mediterranean-style there is less chance of vermin coming aboard than when mooring alongside. Berthing in the River Danube is generally alongside a pontoon, with the bow upstream. In some places you are asked to moor on the downstream side of the pontoon with the bow into the pontoon, and both stern ropes back to the pontoon, or perhaps one of them onto the shore.

Lights
All known lights are mentioned in the appropriate sections of the book. Particularly in Bulgaria, many of them do not work for considerable periods of time. They may also not be switched on until well after sunset, or switched off long before sunrise. They are not to be relied on. Navtex may not give a warning that a light is not functioning, so it makes sense to plan for an arrival during daylight.

Rescue services
In Bulgaria this is undertaken by the border police, who have fast patrol boats. In Romania there is a rescue boat manned full time at Port Tomis

In Turkey the coastal safety service is known as Kiyi Emniyeti. One of the lifeboat men told us that they are full-time employees and the staff rotate during the day doing various jobs such as being beside the lifeboat, on lookout, and manning the lighthouse.

Trailer-sailers
With new roads under construction in Romania and Bulgaria, the River Danube and the Black Sea will become more accessible for those wanting to tow a boat, particularly with the two countries now in the

Mediterranean-style moorings at Balchik

EU. Included in the book are many small harbours that may not be suitable for large cruising yachts, but might be of interest for small boats to explore. Where there are slips these are indicated on the charts; however, in many places it is possible to hire a crane, and prices vary from approximately €5 to €60. (For a lift in or out and for a 140-ton crane the cost was about €75.)

Seamanship
Seamanship can be abysmal, particularly on fast boats. In Bulgaria it is necessary to get a captain's certificate by taking a test consisting of 14 multichoice questions (for which the answers can often be bought in advance). It is not necessary to have ever been on a boat, and after this paper test you have permission to be in charge of a boat up to 30 tonnes, including one taking fare-paying passengers.

In Romania you join a boat club and it takes about three months to obtain a captain's certificate which is essential for all types of boats.

Swimming
Since both countries have many fine beaches, swimming is a natural thing to do. The beaches at the tourist resorts are covered by lifeguards, and they display flags to give the safety conditions in the water. Green flag: swimming allowed. Yellow flag: swim with caution, no airbeds allowed. Red flag: swimming forbidden. A few of the beaches can have bad undercurrents and people have drowned.

USING THIS GUIDE

Format
If you intend to sail the whole area, then irrespective of the direction from which you approach, half of the book is written in the direction in which you are travelling. The section on the River Danube is written starting from the upstream side towards the Black Sea. The Black Sea section starts at the Bosporus and goes north towards Romania.

Plans and positions
The plans in this guide are for illustration purposes only, and not to be used for navigation. The author has drawn them to the best of his ability after visiting the various sites. The depths are in metres, and should be used for guidance only, since depths change either by silting or dredging.

The latitude and longitude readings were taken from the GPS and will be to WGS 84 standard. This is shown in degrees, minutes and decimal places of a minute.

Where we passed a hazard such as a cape, rock, or fixed fishing nets, the position is given only to highlight that a hazard exists and this was the point we came closest to it. It may be possible to go closer, but the more prudent would stay further away. It is the responsibility of each captain or navigator to assess all information available to them and plot their own course.

Place-names
Many places can have their names spelt in different ways; this partly arises because Bulgarian is written in Cyrillic letters and this has to be transposed into Latin letters: Burgas, Bourgas, Burgaz. A Romanian example of different names for the same place is: Hirsova, Hârsova, Hrsova. Sometimes an old name is added to a new name, hence Turnu Severin became Dobreta Turnu Severin. The Communists renamed many places and, after they lost power, some places reverted to their original names. The Admiralty charts still use the name Micurin, whereas everyone else knows the town as Tzaravo; and Drojuba (Friendship) and St Konstantin and St Elena are the same place. The Bulgarians also translate some of their place-names, so Slanzi Breg or Slunchev Bryag is known as Sunny Beach. In this book we try to always use what is the most modern and popular format in use and give other popular variants in brackets. Trying to connect some of the historic places, with Greek or Roman names, to the modern names took a lot of research. For those interested in history, where we have identified the ancient names these are also included.

Restaurants
We deliberately have not mentioned specific restaurants except in exceptional circumstances as owners and the names of the establishments frequently change. You can assume that if at any town there is no mention, there is something ranging from adequate to excellent. The only exception to this is in the Danube Delta where there are only small fishermens' hamlets and tourism is not well developed. In places here, you should have supplies and be prepared to cook on board.

INTRODUCTION

BULGARIA

GENERAL INFORMATION

Time
GMT +0200.

Communications
Telephone The code for Bulgaria is +359 and for the UK +44. There is coverage for mobile phones in all areas except at remote parts of the coast where there are no towns.

Police 166
Ambulance 150
Fire and emergency safety service 160
Free from all phones.

If you intend to be in the country for a while, it may be advantageous to get a local number with prepaid cards. These cost 20 leva (about €10) and sometimes, with special offers, this includes 10 leva worth of calls, effectively giving you a local number for €5 and phone calls are a lot cheaper than paying for international roaming. The top-up cards come in different denominations from 15 to 120 leva and are available at many kiosks.

In main towns and tourist resorts there are kiosks offering cheap phone calls worldwide, and this is the cheapest form of calling.

Internet Most towns and resorts have internet cafés and clubs. Facilities can also be found at some post offices and hotels. The internet code for Bulgaria is .bg.

Charts
For the River Danube the same charts as for Romania (see below).

A good road map (such as the series from the Bulgarian company Domino) is available from kiosks, newsagents and bookshops.

Admiralty Charts

2230	Black Sea Constanţa to Kefken Adasi
2238	Kefken Adasi to Inceburun
2399	Burgas and Approaches
2283	Black Sea Maslen Nos to Nos Kalriaka
2285	Varna and Approaches

Turkish Charts

10A	West Black Sea
17	Mis Kinburn to Nos Kaliakra
18	Nos Kaliakra to Istanbul Boğazi
1821	Burgas bay
1822	Balchik and Varna

The official Bulgarian agent for Admiralty Charts and Nautical Publications in the Black Sea, including correction service and Admiralty weekly *Notices to Mariners* is Naviagent at the following addresses.
Port Varna (including Port Balchik) 1, Primorski Blvd, 9000 Varna
☎ +359 52 632 863; 632 945
Fax +359 52 600 363; 632 916
Port Burgas (including Nessebar) 1, Kniaz Alexander Batamberg, 8000 Burgas
☎ +359 56 879 716
Fax +359 56879 738
Numbers specifically for charts
☎ +359 52 683 580 Fax +359 52 683 033
Email chart@navbul.com

Navigation Maritime Bulgare (part of the same organisation) provide a Liferaft Service Station at
13, Kuay Place, Varna East
☎ +359 52 683 762
Fax +359 52 632 948
They are Lloyds Register and Germanischer Lloyd approved.

Weather
The climate is temperate continental, with long hot summers and cold winters.

Northwesterly and westerly winds can increase the warming effect in the spring, and during the summer can bring rain which is often accompanied by thunder and lightning storms, which can be severe but generally do not last long. The autumns are mild and pleasant, but rain is more frequent in the spring. During the winter the northeast wind brings dry cold continental air masses. The winters are colder in the north and milder in the south.

On the Black Sea coast there is often a sea breeze which can moderate the extreme heat found further inland. The southern end of the Black Sea can have some influence from the Mediterranean and in the summer the weather can be similar.

Language
Bulgarian uses the Cyrillic alphabet.

Russian was at one time compulsory for everyone at school (English was not widely taught in Communist times). Some of the older people speak German and French but now the younger generation tend to prefer English; in the seaside tourist resorts English is common.

Money
Currency lev (plural: leva) 1 lev = 100 stotinki.

The bank notes are 1, 2, 5, 10, 20, 50 and 100 leva. Coins are 1, 2, 5, 10, 20 and 50 stotink and 1 leva.

Currency exchange The lev is a freely convertible currency and can be changed back to a currency of your choice at any time. Most places will not accept notes which are dirty, worn, torn or have writing on them. Some do not accept notes with very old dates on them. Traveller's cheques are difficult to cash and many banks do not accept them; kiosks also don't accept them.

There are many dedicated small exchange offices and others located in shops and hotel reception areas. Although most are honest, some may have a large notice in the street advising of the National Bank Fixing Rates, but inside the kiosk is a smaller notice giving a lower rate. In 2005 new laws were introduced to try to reduce fraud and now displays should only show 2 digits after the decimal point. The bureaux will not be able to differ their exchange rates from the National Bank rate by more than 20%, so it is still worth shopping around. The bureaux should be registered with the financial intelligence agency with the finance ministry. They are obliged to display both the buy and sell rates and give the information in Bulgarian, English, German, French and Russian. If any of the above is violated the closed exchange deal is regarded as invalid and you would have justifiable grounds for complaint.

Do not change money with anyone in the street. You will get notes which are folded and counted twice, old notes, or from another currency such as Romanian lei, or counterfeit.

ATMs will be found in all but the smallest towns. All the major cards such as Mastercard, Visa, American Express and Maestro are accepted at ATMs, but are not in popular use for other goods and services.

Prices Bulgarian wages can be as low as €75 per month and the average monthly wage is €100 per month. Tips for services are therefore greatly appreciated with 10% or rounding up being typical.

Prices in the tourist resorts used by foreigners can be two to four times those in other parts of the country, but even then they are relatively cheap. Bulgarians now tend to avoid the tourist resorts catering for western clients and go to the smaller less popular resorts because of the prices.

Students and pensioners sometimes get reduced prices for entry to historic sights and museums, and proof must be produced.

Shops and kiosks work on low profit margins and bantering for lower prices is not customary, although if you buy a lot of something the shopkeeper may offer you a special discount.

Imported goods obviously have to reflect the price from their country of origin.

Medical

No vaccinations are required for a visit to Bulgaria. It may be wise to have a vaccination for diphtheria, tetanus, typhoid and hepatitis A. Situations change, and for piece of mind this can be verified before travel. Emergency treatment is free at polyclinics and hospitals, but poorly paid doctors and staff appreciate any tip you feel they deserve. Medicines are paid for and are available at the *apteka* (chemist). Remember to bring suntan lotion.

Hotels

Hotels and B & B's generally have highly inflated prices for foreigners but the owners quickly back down if you refuse the initial price. In one instance the price of 70 leva per person per night was reduced to 20 leva. Major hotels display their prices and they are fixed.

Electricity

220V 50Hz, round 2-pin schuko plug.

Taxis

All taxis are yellow and must display the price on a card on the window. This gives the day and night price, starting price and price per kilometre. It is compulsory for them to be fitted with meters. Ask for the meter to be switched on. (One of the major cons is for the driver to fiddle with the meter and at the destination you find the meter was not on. They claim it is broken and they charge a highly inflated price, so make sure the meter is switched on and working.) If going a long distance negotiate a price before getting into the taxi. The prices at tourist resorts can be up to 15 times higher than other towns in Bulgaria.

Toilets

There is a huge variation in the quality of toilets, from a hole in the ground in a shed at the bottom of the garden to spotlessly clean tiled establishments. A few may not provide toilet paper so it is always wise to carry some with you. Some still charge between 20 and 50 stotinki to use them. Some places provide a bucket for the paper and this should be used, since if paper is put down the pan the system could get clogged up.

Security

The newspapers report a mafia murder almost every week, but this does not affect the general population or tourists. A 2004 survey advised that for most categories of crime, the risk of a person becoming a victim is lower in Bulgaria than in the US, Denmark, Poland or Australia. Although crime levels are comparable with most European Union countries one must still be vigilant against petty crime such as pickpockets.

FORMALITIES

Visas

The passport must be valid for at least 3 months after the end of the intended stay. A visa is not required for passport holders from the following countries, and permission to stay will be given for 90 days within each 6-month period: all European Union countries, Argentine, Australia, Brazil, Canada, Chile, Malaysia, Mexico, New Zealand, Costa Rica, Croatia, El Salvador, Guatemala, Honduras, Iceland, Japan, Nicaragua, Norway, Panama, Korea, Switzerland, USA, Uruguay, Vatican, Venezuela, China.

Holders of valid ordinary passports do not need a visa if they come from Croatia, Czech Republic, Hungary, Lithuania, Macedonia, Malta, Republic of Korea, Poland, Romania, San Marino, Serbia and Montenegro, Slovak Republic, Slovenia, Tunisia.

Children will need their own passport unless their photograph is in their parents' passport.

All other countries require a visa, which will take about 10 days to process.

Ports of entry

Balchik
Varna
Burgas

Nessebar has applied to become a port of entry but in 2006 this had not yet been granted.

Although there is supposed to be one law covering the country, each port will interpret the law differently. The law is based on that for ocean-going cargo ships, and the documents that they require are the same ones that will be requested by a pleasure boat. At one port we spent days collecting many papers and 28 rubber stamps, with visits to several offices before we were allowed to proceed. The exception was Burgas where they are more in touch with the needs of the recreational boater. How did we manage to visit so many ports in Bulgaria? Firstly, we had a temporary registration from Burgas with permission to navigate all Black Sea ports. Secondly, we rented a Bulgarian boat with a Bulgarian crew whose local knowledge was invaluable.

The location of border police is as follows:

On the River Danube
Vidin, Lom, Oriahovo, Somovit-Nikopol, Svishtov, Russe, Silistra.

On the Black Sea
Bourgas, Varna, Balchik.

The border police also have fast launches that may intercept unfamiliar boats. They will contact you on Ch 16 then give you a working channel. Give them details of the temporary registration number and the port where it was issued. They will then radio the port

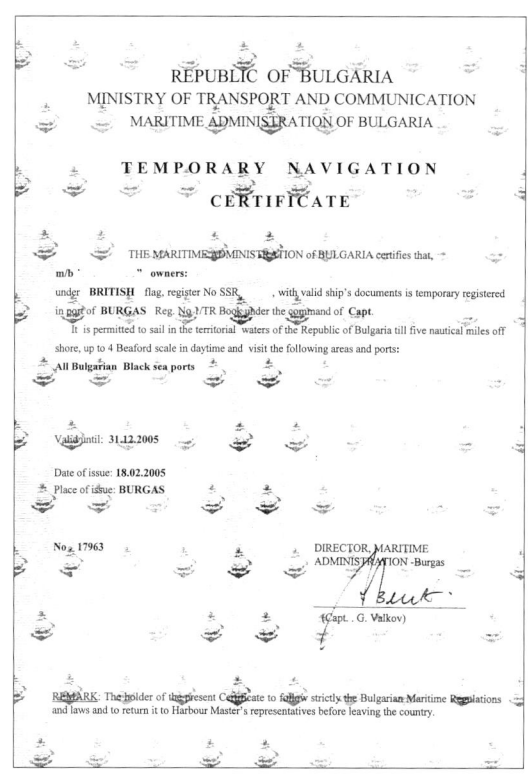

Left: Permission to sail

Right: Temporary Navigation Certificate

and if satisfied will allow you to continue. They may also send a boarding party to check your boat.

The Black Sea now forms the border and it will be the border police's task here to keep out illegal immigrants. Intercepting tourist boats forms part of their training. Although it is inconvenient, they are only doing their job and we have always found them to be polite, courteous and efficient.

The law requires all visitors to Bulgaria to register with the police within 48 hours of arrival. The normal procedure for landlubber tourists is to be registered by the hotel, or directly with the local police station that provides a stamped registration slip. This is surrendered to passport control when leaving the country. The border police and passport control visit the boat on arrival and stamp the crew list but do not issue a registration slip. This is also checked at the final port of departure. (The complication is if you arrive by boat and then wish to leave by road or air, you do not have a registration form.)

Foreigners can import or export Bulgarian banknotes and coins in circulation up to 10,000 leva. Sums in excess of this can only be handled with a permit from the Bulgarian National Bank. When entering or leaving the country with foreign currency in excess of 8,000 Leva (about €4,000), or equivalent in another currency, it should be declared to customs.

Documents (some or all may be required)

Ship's documents
- Ship's registration papers
- Certificate of insurance
- Ship's stamp (very useful but not essential)

Crew documents
- Passport (with a visa if required)
- Captain's certificate or International Certificate of Competence or similar national qualification
- Crew list (varies from 1 to 7 copies)
- Declaration that there are no firearms, narcotics or other dangerous substances and no stowaways on board
- Declaration of all provisions, spirits and cigarettes on board. We prepared a standard declaration stating 'Provisions, spirits, and cigarettes are typical for personal use for one week'

Pets
Dogs, cats, and other pets may only be brought into Bulgaria with a valid veterinary certificate issued within a week of arrival in Bulgaria, and a certificate that the pet has had a rabies shot within the last 6 months.

Transit log
On the River Danube at Vidin they can issue a 'permission to sail' certificate which specifies the places you are permitted to moor on the river. This has to be surrendered at your last stop on the River Danube. The cost is $20 US and must be paid with a $20 note. If you don't have one the harbour authorities (border police) direct you to a bank and as soon as you ask the teller for a $20 note, the teller immediately knows what it is required for; she said the same note circulates between the bank and the harbour.

Theoretically, the same procedure should apply at Silistra, although to date we have never heard of anyone managing to achieve this.

On the Black Sea the ports of entry should be able to provide a Temporary Navigation Certificate giving permission to sail the Black Sea. This cost €20 but can be paid in the local currency. The only port where this is working well is Burgas. The disadvantages of this, is that the certificate is in English and although you can understand it, the border police in other harbours cannot. Secondly, when this temporary navigation certificate is issued, your boat papers are taken away, and before leaving the country you have to return to the port which issued it to hand back the certificate and get your own papers back, although this is now being relaxed.

If you are only in transit then stop only at the ports of entry. You will be moved on from other moorings if you do not have the temporary navigation certificate.

Before we had the temporary navigation certificate, one night we were allowed to moor near the harbour mouth and not come any closer than 50m to the shore. On another occasion when the boat was single-handed and it was dark I complained that, not being familiar with the area, it was not safe to move. Two border police were put on board and we did a night sail to the nearest port of entry.

A retired couple we met were not so lucky. When a storm started, they made for the nearest harbour that was not a port of entry. Despite the weather conditions the border police forced them to leave the harbour and they had to moor in exposed conditions for 4 days.

It is hoped that things will change in the future.

TRADITIONS AND CUSTOMS

Religion
85% of Bulgarians belong to the Orthodox Church and 13% are Muslims.

Public holidays and festivals

New Year's Day	1 January
Orthodox New Years Day	8 January
Liberation Day(1878)	3 March
Orthodox Easter	Variable
Labour Day	1 May
Bulgarian Army Day, St George's Day	6 May
Alphabet, Education & Culture Day	24 May
Union Day	6 September
Independence Day(1885)	22 September
Day of the Leaders of the National Revival	1 November
Christmas Eve	24 December
Christmas	25–26 December

Hand-made lace sellers

Customs
The most confusing custom in Bulgaria is that shaking the head means 'yes' and nodding means 'no'. Some Bulgarians nod and shake their head in the conventional manner, thus adding to the confusion.

Putting a holdall or bag on the floor is frowned on, since Bulgarians believe this will bring you bad luck and you will lose your money. In a restaurant if there is no convenient place to hang the bag it will be placed on a seat.

When visiting someone's house never go empty-handed. Flowers given as a present should always be given in odd numbers, with 5 being a favourite. (An even number of flowers is given at funerals.) The colour is also significant: red for love, yellow for hate, white for respect and freedom, pink for good friends.

Martinetsa is a red and white woollen ribbon, tassle, or woven into other shapes. On the 1 March they are given to friends and lovers as good luck symbols, and the receiver wears them until they see a stork. In each area there is a dedicated *martinetsa* tree, and after seeing the stork they are hung on the tree to welcome the spring.

Name days, which are the day of the saint you are named after, are celebrated more than birthdays.

Although homosexuality is officially frowned on, gays have their own day on 2 February, magazines, dating agencies, bars and clubs. The age of consent for homosexual activity is 18, and the Bulgarian penal code prohibits homosexuality in public and activities which may 'lead to perversion'.

FOOD AND DRINK

Food
Bulgaria has rich fertile soil and a warm climate allowing many fruits and vegetables to flourish. These include aubergines, cucumbers, courgettes, garlic, melons, olives, onions, paprika, peppers, parsley, pumpkins, potatoes, sweet corn, tomatoes, lettuce and fruits like apples, apricots, cherries, figs, grapes, peaches, plums and strawberries. Sunflowers, nuts and tobacco also grow in abundance.

The River Danube supplies bream, carp, crayfish, catfish (sheatfish), eels, perch, pike, sturgeon, sterlet and trout. The Black Sea provides crabs, mackerel, sardines and tuna.

Tarator is a favourite soup made from yoghurt, cucumbers and ground nuts and it is served cold. Every restaurant will have a long list of salads with the most popular being *shopska*, local vegetables topped with sheep's cheese.

While enjoying a wine, beer or something stronger it is normal to have *meze*. This is a variety of small dishes which are shared with everyone at the table. This could be anything from meats, salamis, spicy sausages (*pasterma*), small fried fishes (*tsatsa*), nuts, cheese, chips, olives and salads.

The preparation of main dishes is simple and there is an absence of sauces, allowing flavours to predominate. Charcoal grills where pork, chicken, lamb and veal can be grilled feature in many restaurants. It is sometimes necessary to order the vegetables or salad separately, since only a small garnish may be included. The same grill is used to prepare kebab skewers or spits which, in addition to the meat or fish, include tomatoes, peppers and onions.

Gyuvech and *kaverma* are types of stew, which are prepared in earthenware pots, come in various varieties and can be meat or fish-based with a number of vegetables. Minced meat can be served as *kebabche*, *kufte* and *chevapchichi*.

Kashkaval pane is cheese fried in batter and *banitsa* is pastry with a savoury filling such as cheese or meat with herbs. *Musaka* is a pastry with meat and vegetables topped with yoghurt.

Sarmi is stuffed cabbage or vine leaves, but the Bulgarians also like to stuff aubergines, tomatoes and peppers. Yoghurt (*kiselo mleko*) is popular on its own or made into a drink, *airan*.

Pancakes (*palatshinka*), *baklava* (a sticky pastry with syrup and nuts), fruits, a choice of cakes and ice creams are the desserts. Breakfast could be coffee with *banitsa* (a cheesy pastry), toast, bread and yogurt.

There is a good choice of food for vegetarians in Bulgaria.

Today there are many fast food outlets serving pizza or doner kebab. The international fast food chains have set up shop here, but there is also a local one called Happy which originated in Varna.

Wine

The first recorded evidence of wine dates back to the Thracians who lived in what is now Bulgaria and European Turkey. This was as early as the 6th century BC, making it the oldest wine-producing country in the world. The Thracian rulers held symposia and drinking parties where, during the wine drinking sessions, they could discuss the daily life and battles won and those still to be fought. Dionysus was their god of the vines, vegetation and fertility. In the ancient world there were two temples to Dionysus and Apollo where the future was prophesied and the temple of Dionysus was more important than the temple of Apollo at Delphi. In the temple of Dionysus in the city of Perpericon, which was the capital of the ruler of the Rhodopi Mountains, there is evidence of the ritual with wines. It was located on the strategic road to Philippopolis (now Plovdiv) and it was here that the future of Alexander the Great was foretold. Amphorae and rhytons for ritual wine drinking sessions have been found in Thracian tombs around the town of Kazanluk, where the frescoes clearly depict a cupbearer with a jug and phiale (a Thracian wine bowl). The Greeks learned the art of wine-making from them. The Romans developed the wine industry by introducing new production methods and planting vines in new areas. In the Middle Ages the monks were the great wine makers. The Ottomans introduced dessert grapes to produce sweet wines, but apart from that the wine industry was held back by five centuries of Muslim rule. There was heavy investment during the Communist era and Bulgaria has now become the fourth largest wine exporter in Europe, with its wine being available in shops and supermarkets throughout the world. Sir Winston Churchill was a good customer for wine from the broad-leafed vine of Melnik, ordering 500 litres every year even during the second world war.

Vines grow all over the country, but we give details only of those wines that come from near the Black Sea or near the Danube River.

From the Black Sea area cabernet sauvignon, muskat and merlot are very reliable and highly impressive. The driest white is chardonnay, followed by sauvignon. Pamid is a dry red wine with a soft harmonious flavour and a pleasant aroma. Via Pontica is an amber golden-coloured wine produced from rkatsiteli grapes, then matured in oak casks for a minimum of 10 years. The specific weather conditions and closeness to the sea can give some wines a unique aroma and taste.

From the River Danube area come classic red wines like merlot, cabernet sauvignon, and gamza. Muscat, chardonnay and sauvignon blanc are fresh white wines with intensive rich fruit flavours.

Two fun drinks are Rousse pearl mango and spearmint, which are slightly fizzy with 6% vol. alcohol content. When the beverage is at the correct temperature to drink, the bikini on the lady on the label disappears.

Bulgarian champagne-type wine is a dry sparkling chardonnay marked as *iskra*.

Spirits

Mastika is a spirit similar to *ouzo*, with aniseed that turns cloudy when served (as is customary) with water. *Mastika* is actually the resin through which the spirit is distilled and which gives the spirit its distinctive taste.

Rakia is a type of brandy: when made from plums it is *slivova*, apricots *kaisieva*, quince *dyoleva*, apple *yabulkova*, and grapes, the most popular one, *grozdova*. The habit is to have a soft drink in a separate glass, and to take it with a salad. A wide variety of excellent Bulgarian vodka and brandy is available. In restaurants the typical smallest quantity for spirits being served is 50ml.

Beware of fake spirits in original labelled bottles; purchase bottles only from reputable-looking shops and be careful when buying from kiosks.

Beer

There is a wide selection of good locally brewed beers and internationally known brands. The most popular are the lager types.

Mineral waters and spas

Mineral water has been popular since Thracian times. The habit of drinking water went into abeyance under the Turks, but now bottled water is sold all over the country.

Bulgaria has a great wealth and variety of mineral waters with various physical and chemical compositions. Many of these are on the Black Sea coast, but not all are fully developed. Records show that some settlements based on thermal springs date back to Thracian and Roman times.

In the Black Sea coastal region there are mainly mineralised waters containing calcium and magnesium, as well as curative firth mud and healing lye. These are used in recreational, curative-prophylactic and rehabilitative programmes. Developed resorts are:

Bourgaski Mineralni Bani which has been operational since antiquity. The resort specialises in spa treatment of diseases of the locomotory, nervous, and reproductive systems. There are several hospitals and polyclinics which function in the resort.

Martinetsa seller

Pomorie is the most famous maritime mud-curing resort. It is profiled in medical treatment of the locomotory and nervous systems, gynaecological illnesses, sterility as well as some skin diseases. Mineral water in the resort is of a rare and valuable type, because though comparatively low in mineralisation the water has huge quantities of magnesium. There are several prophylactic and recreational centres.

In **Varna** and surrounding area there are 12 mineral water fields with low mineralisation, large temperature amplitude and a high total flow capacity. Only two of them contain higher mineralisation. Varna Firth Lake yields the mineral healing prophylactic factor firth mud. There is a polyclinic in the city that utilises these materials.

St Konstantin and Elena This is one of the best appointed places for spa treatment, with many hotels with spa medical facilities.

Zlatni Pyasatsi (Golden Sands) Spa treatment facilities are provided in several hotels and are due to be expanded to others.

Riviera This has slightly mineralised hyper-thermal, mineral water with alkaline reaction. The spa treatment base is equipped with modern spa, physio therapeutic and other theraputic facilities.

Albena The mineral water here is slightly mineralised. The hotel here is a spa-physio-medical base equipped with modern spa healing, physio-therapeutic and other therapeutic facilities.

Balchik Here the mineral water contains calcium, magnesium, and radon. With the neighbouring resort of Balchishka Tuzla, it can offer mud-healing facilities. Unfortunately, the hospital and spa healing facilities could do with some renovation.

HISTORY

Very recent discoveries at Kozarnika Cave in northwest Bulgaria by French and Bulgarian researchers reveals evidence of occupation between 1.2 and 1.5 million years ago. This makes Bulgaria one of the places of earliest civilisation in Europe. Since then many nations have left their mark and in ancient times it was the home of Spartacus and Orpheus. It was part of the Kingdom of Macedonia, having been occupied in places by Celts, Thracians and, by AD46, the Romans. In the late 600s the Bulgars migrated from Central Asia and their first empire, from 681 to 1018, was based around Pliska. Tsar Simeon (893 to 927) moved the capital to Preslav and led it to its golden era when the empire touched the three seas (Aegean, Adriatic and Black Sea). In this era two monks, Cyril and Methodius devised the Cyrillic alphabet.

Preslav was overrun by the Byzantines after Simeon tried to take the Byzantine crown for himself and there were internal conflicts in the country. The capital was moved to Ohrid. Military fortunes were reversed in 1185 when the Byzantines were defeated, and the second Bulgarian empire survived from 1185 to 1396, based around Veliko Turnovo. Tsar Asen II (1218–41) was a powerful king of the Bulgarians and Greeks. Again there was internal strife and after his death Tartars and Arabs occupied part of the area.

The Ottomans controlled the area for about 500 years, but while they were in decline a new capitalist class was emerging in Bulgaria and people were rediscovering their identity. Guerilla fighters such as George Rakovski, Hristo Botev and Vasil Levski were preparing for the uprising to make Bulgaria politically independent, but the Turks massacred thousands of Bulgarians and destroyed 58 villages. With the intervention of Russia, Turkey lost 60% of the Balkan peninsula. The western powers were not happy about this and at the Congress of Berlin returned part of the land to Turkey. Every country felt they were treated unfairly by this, and it may have been one cause of the recent conflicts in the Balkans.

In Veliko Turnovo, the first national assembly was set up in 1879 and again there was an era of economic development, with Bulgaria becoming fully independent from Turkey in 1908. Not content with this, in 1912 the first Balkan war started, with Bulgaria, Serbia and Greece declaring war against Turkey, and after their victory the internal fights started and this led to the second Balkan war, which this time Bulgaria lost. In the two world wars, Bulgaria sided with Germany and lost again, but between the wars there was political turmoil resulting in nearly 1,000 political murders. Near the end of the second world war the resistance groups and Communists formed a government and the peoples' courts handed out death sentences or imprisonment to thousands of 'monarcho-fascists'. The Communists pushed the coalition partners aside, took control in 1945 and declared a people's republic with Georgi Dimitrov as its first leader.

Until 1989 there was a centralised economy and a large programme of industrialisation was implemented. During the 1990s there was a series of ineffective governments, with various groups deliberately trying to undermine political efforts and encourage general dissent in the population. Bulgaria, which was one of the more prosperous countries in the Communist era, has been more backward in converting to a free market economy. There is now a network of organised criminals, and the grip they have on the economy does not benefit the general population. However, hyperinflation has been stopped and the currency was pegged to the Deutschmark, and subsequently the Euro. In 2004 Bulgaria joined NATO and in 2007 the European Union.

INTRODUCTION

ROMANIA

GENERAL INFORMATION

Time
GMT +0200

Communications
Telephone Telephone code from abroad +40
Telephone code to the UK +44
Emergency hospital 962
Ambulance 961
Police 955
Fire 981
International emergency calls 971
Taxis 953
Domestic trunk calls 991
Information 951
Directory enquires (business) 930
Directory enquiries (individual A–L) 931
Directory enquiries (individual M–Z) 932

A telephone fibre optic network is being installed throught the country, but in some areas the system is still very primitive.

Internet country code .ro

Post offices are open daily including Saturday morning.

Charts
For the Black Sea
Admiralty charts
2213   Gura Sfîntu Gheorghe to Dnistrovs'kyy Lyman
2230   Constanţa to Kefken Adasi
2232   Constanţa to Yalta
2282   Plans in Romania
2284   Portul Constanţa and approaches
Turkish charts
10A   West Black Sea
17   Mis Kinbun to Nos Kaliakra
1722   Danube Delta
1822A   Sulina

For the River Danube
Donau volumes 6, 7, 8, 9 (official charts from the Danube Commission). These are very expensive and detailed, approximately 3 centimetres: 1 kilometre.

We found a good series of maps from Publirom a Romanian company, and these are available in bookshops and newspaper kiosks. The map *Constanţa, Litoralul ş Delta Dunării* was useful in the Danube Delta, as was *Danube Delta Biosphere Reserve* by Gradi of Tg Mures.

Weather
Continental temperate: hot summers, cold winters, distinct seasons. Winters can be extremely harsh. The summers are pleasant and from June to September the Black Sea resorts are busy with tourists. The south Black Sea area is warmer than the Danube Area.

Language
The Romanian language is based on classical Latin and was introduced when the Romans occupied the territory. An Italian speaker could be understood by a Romanian and vice versa, and Spanish and French speakers will understand many of the words. Other words from Thracian, Greek, Turkish, Hungarian, French, German, English and Slavonic have crept into the language, and English and German are widely understood. Knowledge of foreign languages is not so widespread in the towns and villages along the Danube, but tourism is popular on the Black Sea Coast and language here is not a problem.

Money
Currency: leu (plural lei) 100 bani = 1 leu.
The banknotes are 1, 5, 10, 50, 100, 500 leu.
Coins are 1, 5, 10, 50 bani.

The currency had four zeros removed in 2005. Prices were quoted in old and new lei until 31 December 2006 and the old notes accepted until 3 December 2009.

Currency exchange Banks, money exchange kiosks, hotel receptions in all main towns can change money. Banks and many exchange kiosks are shut at the weekend, and those that are open give poor exchange rates. Since there are only small villages in the Danube Delta area they are not so frequent, and in many places are non-existent.

Traveller's cheques are difficult and sometimes impossible to cash.

ATMs are becoming popular in all but the smallest towns. Exchange rates vary in different offices so it pays to shop around.

Do not change money with individuals. Apart from it being illegal, you will probably be cheated.

Credit cards are accepted in some major establishments but are still not universally accepted.

All payments are made in Romanian lei but some harbour charges may be in US dollars. It is advisable to keep a small supply of small denomination dollars or Euro. Defaced or torn notes will not be accepted. Sometimes large denomination notes are not accepted.

Prices Money will go a long way in Romania since it is relatively cheap for foreigners. The average wage is less than €100 per month. Romanians will get embarrassed about this and it is advisable to keep off this subject unless they bring it up first.

The area on the Black Sea that is familiar with tourists reflects this in its higher prices. The cheaper establishments are the ones that the locals patronise rather than the ones operated for foreign tourists.

Ihneada. Meal with the locals

Tipping is expected in tourist resorts, but is not a common habit by Romanians in the smaller towns, although we never had a tip refused.

Medical
No vaccinations were required at the time of writing, but situations can change and this should be verified before visiting the country. It may be wise to get a vaccination for hepatitis A, polio and a typhoid booster. Visitors from some countries may be required to produce a 'sanitary certificate'.

Medical treatment is available in state and private health establishments. Costs at state hospitals will depend on any reciprocal agreements Romania has with the patient's country.

Electricity
220V 50Hz round 2-pin schuko plug.

Taxis
Official taxis have the roof painted yellow, must operate a taximeter, and display the charges on the door. Make sure the taximeter is switched on and working.

Clothing
If you have forgotten something, Romania is a good place to buy clothes. Many international companies get their clothes produced here, and sometimes it is possible to find their labels in the shops here. These clothes could be production overruns, wrong colours, or slight defects, but always a fraction of the price you would pay at home. (There is also fake clothing of poor quality on sale.)

Beachwear should not be worn away from the beach or the pool.

Toilets
Many leave much to be desired outside the main tourist areas, but the new restaurants and hotels have improved the standard. It is advisable to carry toilet paper with you as there may be none.

Photography
Photographs should not be taken of military installations. At some tourist attractions there is a fee for taking photographs.

Boating
Recreational boating was not encouraged during Communist times. There are about 10,000 boats registered in Romania, but those are mostly small fishing boats. To have a private boat in Romania you must join a boat club and get official training for about 3 months then take a test. (This substantiates the RYA claim that compulsory testing will not improve seamanship.) Be aware for your own safety that seamanship can be of very poor quality, particularly on the River Danube near developed tourist complexes.

In 1990 the Romanian Sailing Federation was founded. Their main activity is arranging competitions every weekend at Lake Herastrau in Bucharest and Lake Siutghiol near Constanţa.

Romanian Sailing Federation
Str. Vasile Conta 16, Sector 2, Bucharest, Romania
☎ +40 21 2102546 *Email* neaica@totalnet.ro

FORMALITIES

Visas
Romania is visa-free for persons with valid passports from over 100 countries. Check on the Romanian Ministry of Foreign Affairs website www.mae.ro/index.php. The time you can stay in the country varies from 30 to 90 days depending on your country. For others a visa must be obtained in advance, and could take up to to 30 days to be processed. Entry requirements may change and you should check with the relevant Romanian embassy or consulate before commencing the journey. A passport must have 6 months' validity after the date of entry into Romania. For those who need a visa the cost for single entry is £25 and multi-entry £60.

Romanian law regulating foreigners states that 'in the case of a continuous stay exceeding 10 days, the alien ... shall be bound to inform the territorial competent police authority of his stay within this term.' However, many local police maintain registration is not necessary. (There is a good chance they will come to the boat anyway.)

Ports of entry
From Serbia: Moldova Veche
From Bulgarian side of the Danube: Cernavoda
From Ukraine using Chila arm of the river Danube: Tulcea
On the Black Sea: Mangalia, Port Tomis, Sulina.
Romanian border police are present at the following water border crossing points:
Romania-Serbia border
Moldova Veche, Orsova, Portile de Fier 1, Drobeta Turnu Severn, Portile de Fier 2
Romania-Bulgaria border
Calafat, Bechet, Corabia, Turnu Magurele, Zimnicea, Giurgiu, Ostrovul Mocanasu, Oltenita, Calarasi (Chiciu) (not operational in 20040, Ostrov, Negru Voda, Vama Veche.
Romania-Moldova
For Moldova (River Prut) check out at Galati
Romania-Ukraine
Siret, Vicsani, Campulung la Tisa, Halmeu
Inland
Braila, Cernavoda, Tulcea
Black Sea
Sulina, Constanţa (Port Tomis), Constanţa (Agigea), Mangalia.

At these locations you may get a visit from the border police to check documents, but it will be as much out of curiosity to see a foreign boat as anything else.

The staff were always smart, fast, and efficient and completed their duties in a competent manner, except in Tulcea. Our experience with each place is detailed where appropriate. Stay by the boat until the authorities arrive. Contact them by radio or find a local to telephone them to advise them of your arrival.

Romania is a signatory to the international regulations of the convention for customs facilities for touristic travel. On entry valuable goods such as jewellery, art, electrical items and foreign currency should be declared. The endorsed declaration must be kept for production when leaving the country. The import of the usual things such as weapons,

INTRODUCTION

ammunition, explosives, narcotics, and pornography is forbidden unless a licence has been obtained in advance. It is forbidden to take out of the country items of historic, cultural, or artistic value and currency unless previously declared.

Transit log
Not used.

Pets
Dogs and cats require an anti-rabies certificate. There are many stray dogs, some of which may have rabies.

TRADITIONS AND CUSTOMS

Religion
The main religion is Romanian Orthodox Christian.

Public holidays and festivals

New Year	1 and 2 January
Epiphany	6 January
Orthodox New Year	14 January
Orthodox Good Friday and Easter Monday	Variable
Labour Day	1 May
National anthem day	29 July
National Unity Day	1 December
Constitution day	8 December
Christmas	25 and 26 December
Festival days	
Mărţişor	1 March
Women's day	8 March

Customs
When Romanians meet each other the greeting can be emotional, with men and women kissing each other, or two men can give a vigorous handshake or a slap on the back. It is customary for men to kiss a woman's hand when being introduced.

Leaving a drink unfinished is believed to bring your host bad luck (the more you leave the more bad luck for the host). This is never a problem for our crew.

When invited to a private house it is customary to take flowers or some other small gift and it is customary to take off your shoes in the house.

Mărţişor is the custom when girls and ladies are given a red and white ribbon or small badge on the 1 March. It is worn until she sees the first flowering tree, which she then hangs it on. This symbolises love and the happiness that spring is coming.

Homosexual relations have been decriminalised in private, but in public it is still a criminal offence. If a crew decide to have a night in a hotel and decide to share a room to save money care should be taken to make sure the hotel staff do not misunderstand the motives.

The church encourages a close relationship between the living and the dead and at a funeral the body is in an uncovered coffin. After the initial burial there is a blessing and a feast, and after 7 years the bones are exhumed and blessed before they get a final burial. Icons are popular in Romania as a type of 'mobile shrine'.

FOOD AND DRINK

Food
It is difficult to identify what is traditional Romanian cuisine. Due to the fertile soil and warm weather good fruit and vegetables are produced. The River Danube, particularly at the delta and the Black Sea, supplies plentiful quantities of different fresh fish. Most restaurants have an extensive menu of salads, and fish prepared as a soup, or on a spit, or as a ghiveci (fish stew). Ghiveci (meaning earthenware bowl) can also be made with meat and a selection of vegetables. Every chef appears to have his own recipe, or they just use the vegetables available that day, but it never tastes the same in different establishments. Tocana is similar, but predominately with onions.

A lamb *ciorba* is halfway between a soup and a stew with lamb and vegetables. Other soups are *ciorba de perişoarf* (meatballs, vegetables and spices) *ciorba de legumă* (broth made with meat stock). *Muşchi* (cutlet) is made from *vacă* (beef), *porc* (pork) or *miel* (lamb).

Romania has been influenced by many nationalities and you can see this reflected in the food. The Turks introduced *meze* (small dishes taken with a drink or as a starter; these can be salads, vegetables, meats, cheese or fish). The Greek and Russian influence gives *samarale* (stuffed cabbage leaves of minced meat with herbs, spices and rice. The minced meat could include the same ingredients as *mititei* and could be considered as upmarket hamburgers, (better than supplied in international fast food chains). The Central European influence is dumplings, while the Hungarian one is goulash. The Italian influence of polenta (known here as *mămăliga* and produced from cornmeal (maize)) was the traditional food for the peasant class but was also enjoyed by the middle classes.

The German influence is shown by cooking in beer, the Armenian in the use of cabbage and, the Middle East in pastries, grilled beef (*carne de vacă*), and lamb (*miel*). Greek recipes include chicken with wine and olives or chicken with egg and lemon sauce, while a meal could be completed with *satou* (in French *chaudeau*), a type of custard, or *plăcintă* (turnover tarts) or *clătite* (pancakes).

The Danube Delta area is famous for the wide variety of fish dishes that are served.

Wine
Grapes have been cultivated and wine produced in the Romania area since Roman times. Romanian wines are excellent. A tour can be taken from Port Tomis (Constanţa) to the Murfatler Wine Factory 19 kilometres to the west. Here you can sample the dry fragrant white Murfatler wine. A tributary of the Danube is the River Olt, and in the valley of this poor but picturesque region is the village of Dragaşani near Slatina, famous for its sweet white wine. Rekas near Timisoara area gives us a full-bodied high quality Banat Riesling. A full-bodied red Merlot is the speciality from the Carpathian foothills. Other fertile regions produce chardonnay, riesling, pinot and muscat grapes. Romania also produces a dry white champagne-style sparkling wine. A local vermouth is called Pelin.

Spirits

Țuică is the local spirit which is dry, colourless plum brandy, famous for its after-smell and powerful kick. It is often served as an aperitif. On a cold winter's day a friend took me to visit some of his relations and in each house we were served hot *tuică* in small cups. The after-effect was disastrous! Also made from plums are *palincă* and *horincă*, which produce the same results as *tuică*.

Beer

There is a good selection of local and internationally known brands of beers. *Braga* is a Romanian bread beer made from fermented bran.

HISTORY

There is evidence of Romania being inhabited since the Palaeolithic and Neolithic ages, up to 10,000BC. By 3,000BC the inhabitants were the Thracian tribes known as Getae by the Greeks and Dacians by the Romans. Greek trading colonies from as early as the 7th century BC were established at Callatia (Mangalia), Tomis (Constanța), Histria and other places. In the 1st century BC the Dacian state was formed but this became the Roman province of Dacia under Emperor Trajan (who reigned from AD98–117) In 271 Emperor Aurelian withdrew to the south of the Danube but the Romanised Vlach peasants remained in Dacia. Until the 10th century the migratory peoples included Goths, Huns, Avars, Slavs, Bulgars, and Magyars. By the 13th century Transylvania was a principality under the Hungarian crown. King Bela IV of Hungary offered the German Saxons free land here to defend his southeast flank from Tartar raids.

In the 14th and 15th centuries the principalities of Wallachia and Moldovia fought to stop Ottoman occupation, with Vlad Tepeș ('the Impaler') becoming a hero in this fight. The 'Impaler' got his name from the punishment he gave to his Turkish enemies by having a wooden stake driven through the victim's backbone without touching a vital nerve so that they had a lingering death.

Vlad's father was Vlad Dracul, who was a knight of the Order of Dragons. These characters inspired Bram Stoker to create his fictitious character Count Dracula, for which the Romanian Tourist Board should be forever grateful.

In the 16th century when the Ottoman Turks conquered Hungary, Transylvania, Wallachia and Moldovia became Vassals of the Ottoman Empire but retained autonomy by paying tribute to the Sultan. These three states became united under Mihai Viteazul in 1600. After the Turks were defeated at the gates of Vienna in 1683 Transylvania came under Hapsburg rule, but the other two territories remained under Turkish domination, combining in 1862 to create Rumania. They became independent from the Ottomans in 1878 when Dobruja also became part of Rumania and this was recognized both in the Treaty of San Stefano and the Treaty of Berlin.

After the second Balkan war (1913), the first and second world wars there were boundary changes in Dobruja, Bukovina, Bessarabia and North Transylvania before the present boundary was determined by the peace treaty signed with the allies in 1947.

From 1881–1947 the country was a monarchy ruled by a branch of the Hohenzollern family.

In 1947 the Communist Party had secured a dominating position and King Mihai was forced to abdicate. The country was proclaimed a republic and the named changed to Romania.

In the 1950s after Stalin's death, Romania began to distance itself from Moscow. Nicolae Ceaucescu took power in 1965 and in 1974 was given the post of president. He placed his family in important political positions and embarked on many grandiose schemes. Some were successes but others were expensive failures. To finance these follies food was exported, leaving the country with food shortages. This triggered the revolution in 1989 and after ten days of people taking to the streets where 7,000 lost their lives, Ceaucescu and his wife were condemned to death by firing squad by an anonymous court on Christmas Day.

The reform process is still in turmoil; there is high unemployment, extreme poverty and high inflation, but life goes on and Romania joined NATO in 2004 and in 2007, the EU.

II. THE BLACK SEA

The western side of the Black Sea has 378km (230 miles) of coastline in Bulgaria and 245km (152 miles) in Romania. In antiquity the Black Sea was known as Pontus Axeinus and many of the ports that can be visited have a history going back thousands of years.

SEA AND WEATHER

Currents

Currents in the Black Sea are generally weak and inconsistent. The main feature of the current is the anti-clockwise flow since there is almost a regular flow of water into the Bosporus. The Black Sea is generally estimated to be about 0.4m (17 inches) above that of Marmara Denizi (the Marmara Sea), but this is not constant throughout the year, and can change from year to year. This in turn causes Marmara Denizi to be higher than the level of the Mediterranean.

The north and west corner of the Black Sea, in particular, is supplied by fresh water from the great rivers such as The Danube, Dniester, Dnieper, and Don. The Danube alone contributes about 300 thousand million cubic tonnes in an average year. If evaporation and flow through the Bosporus did not exist, this could raise the water level by about 0.3m (1ft) every year. In the eastern side of the Black Sea there is a relatively high rainfall which also adds to the water level. With a high proportion of fresh water flowing into the Black Sea this gives a different specific gravity from the saltier Marmara Sea, aiding the current flow through the Bosporus. The inflow of water from the rivers and rainfall is balanced by evaporation and outflow through the Bosporus. The current is also influenced by the prevailing north and northeasterly winds. The current can be reduced, or occasionally reversed, in a prolonged strong southerly wind. The current flow is also greatest when the rivers are in spate, and more so when this coincides with a northerly wind.

Offshore the current north of the Danube is 0.5 to 0.75kn. With the addition of the water from the Danube it sets south-southwest but becomes wider and weaker. At Constanţa the current is less than half a knot. Near Varna the flow is joined by a weak current from the east which flows from the south coast of Crimea. The combined current sets southerly towards the eastern end of the Bosporus.

Inshore there are eddy currents which are obviously dependent on the main current, and are affected by the reasons given above, and can vary in strength and direction. Inshore between Nos Kaliakra and just north of the Bosporus the main influence is the eddy current flowing northwards. This flows up to 0.5kn from southern Bulgaria and rejoins the main current offshore from Nos Kaliakra. There is also a small counter-current just south of Constanţa. The discharge of water from rivers can produce local current systems and may produce an eddy setting towards the mouth.

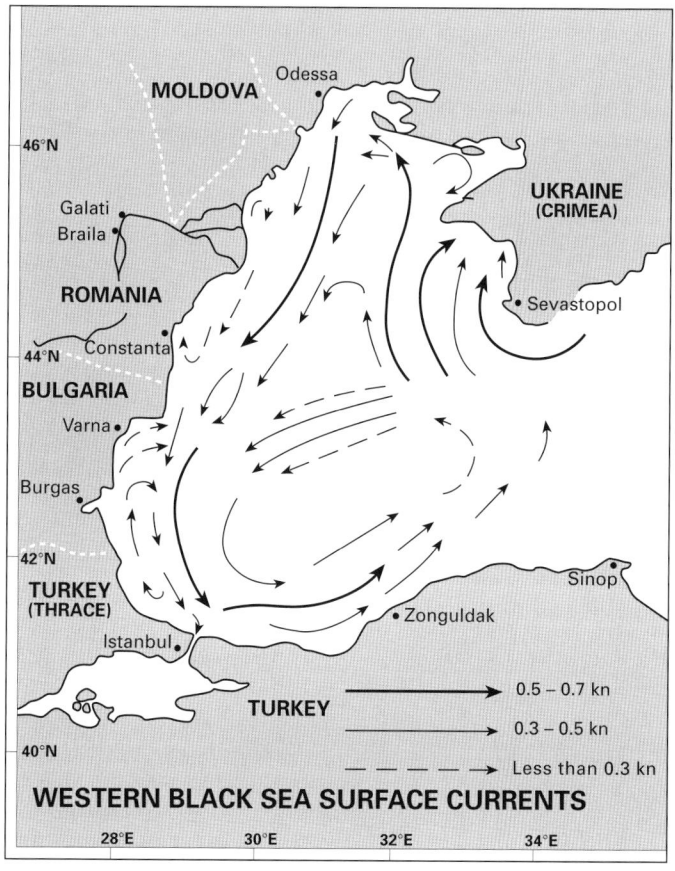

The water

At the mouth of the River Danube the shelf goes miles out to sea; the sun can reach the bottom and the water is highly oxygenated and it therefore attracts many fish. The catch can be four times greater than in the Mediterranean, with species such as grey mullet, shad, scad, sturgeon, shrimps, salmon, crabs, and crayfish. In contrast, other areas of the Black Sea can be up to 2,200m deep. The rivers bring too much organic matter into the Black Sea and the bacteria is unable to decompose all of it. The oxygen in the sea is used up and the chemical process produces hydrogen sulphide. This introduces a sterile area that varies between 150 and 200m below the surface. In the deeps of the Black Sea is the world's largest body of water where there is no life.

Lights

Many lights (particularly in Bulgaria) often do not work, are switched on long after sunset, or are switched off when it is still dark.

Fixed nets

This is a major problem on the Black Sea coast of Bulgaria and Romania. Bulgaria tends to have long poles with the nets strung between them. In Romania there is more use of small plastic bottles that sometimes are almost impossible to see.

Fishing boats far out to sea
Groups of small fishing boats were seen many miles offshore. These were small inshore boats only powered by oars. We thought the men must have been extremely strong to have rowed such a distance, but then we discovered the secret: one powerboat takes 6 to 10 boats in tow to the fishing ground, then after the day's fishing is done, tows them all back into the harbour again.

Sea level

The average spring range in the western part of the Black Sea is 0.08m. There are more considerable changes in the sea level due to the amount of water discharged from the rivers or changes in atmospheric pressure and the wind. The mean annual change in the level is about 0.05m, but exceptionally a rise of 0.15m and a fall of 0.18m have been recorded. The discharge from the rivers is highest in late spring and early summer; the lowest levels are recorded in the autumn, and then gradually rise until the late spring. An onshore wind could raise the water level and an offshore wind lower the level. The effect is therefore more noticeable near the shore, particularly in bays and gulfs, and will therefore be localised. At Constanţa a strong northerly wind can reduce the level by 0.6m.

For all practical purposes the tide need not be taken into consideration.

Wind

In summer the prevailing wind is north to northeasterly and can be considered as part of the general monsoon flow which affects the Aegean and eastern Mediterranean. In Greece this wind is known as *Etesian* and the Turks call it *meltemi*. In winter the wind is predominantly westerly, but varies considerably with the passage of the depressions. The average wind is lighter in summer than in winter.

Within 20 miles of the coast on sunny days with clear skies the land heats up more rapidly than the sea. The specific heat of the land is less than half that of the water and the sun's rays penetrate deep into the water, giving it a larger volume to heat. The air over the land rises, leaving a gap which is replaced by air flowing in from the sea. The typical time for this to take effect at the Romanian and Bulgarian Black Sea coast is at about 1300. On extremely hot days the wind can whip up the waves to over a metre in height. (No waves are produced on the cloudy overcast days.) The anabatic onshore wind can increase the gradient of an easterly wind and further increase the wave height. In the evening the reverse is true. The heat radiates from the land and it cools, also cooling the air above it. The cooler denser air flows down the slope forming a katabatic wind blowing out to sea. The higher the hills near the coast the more noticeable the effect.

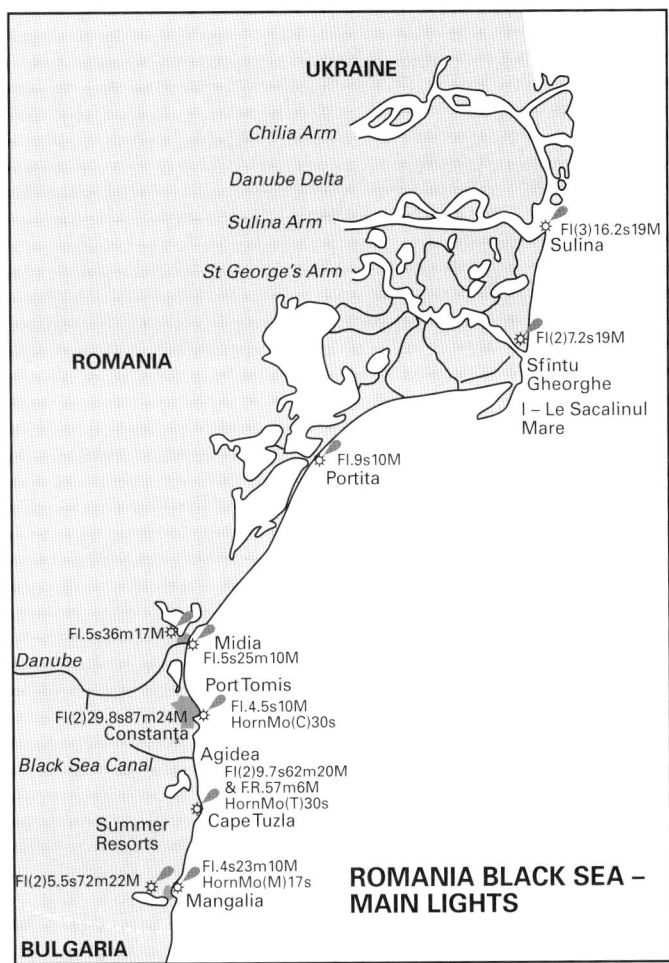

ROMANIA BLACK SEA – MAIN LIGHTS

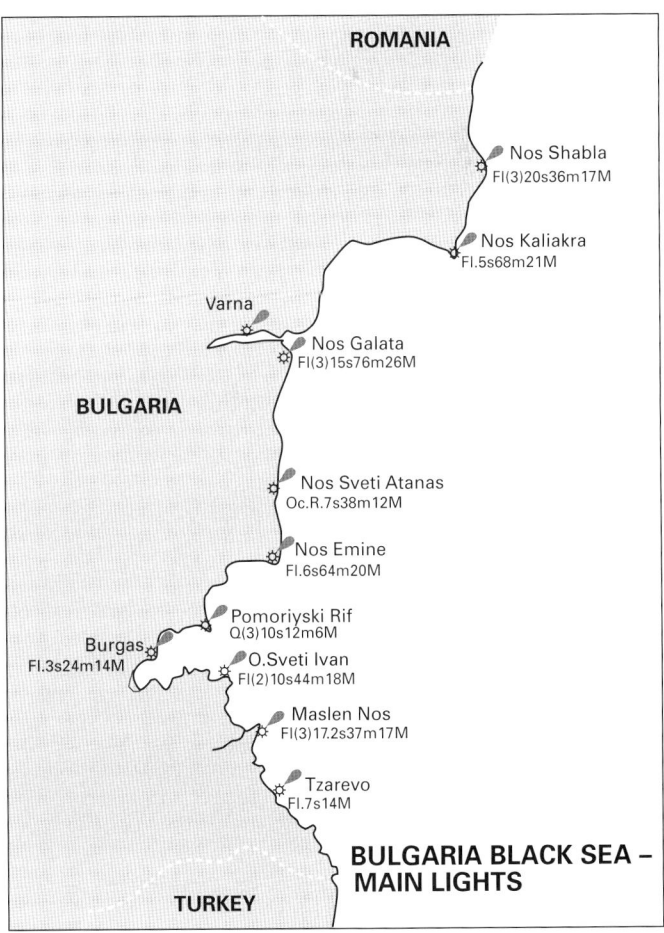

BULGARIA BLACK SEA – MAIN LIGHTS

Climatic conditions

Cloud In the summer months it is generally fine and clear and the winter can be moderately cloudy. The cloudiest month is December and the least cloudy is August.

Fog Fog is not a problem in the summer months, but from October to March an average of 3–5 days of fog per month could be recorded.

Ice The Black Sea has half the saline content of the Atlantic because of the high proportion of fresh water that flows into it. It therefore freezes more easily than most salt seas.

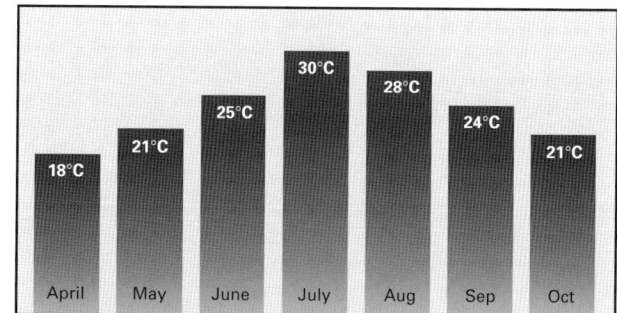

AVERAGE DAILY TEMPERATURE BULGARIA SEASIDE

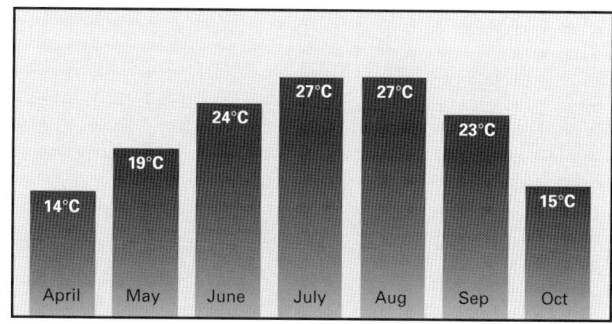

AVERAGE DAILY TEMPERATURE ROMANIA SEASIDE

Mangalia beach and harbour

TURKEY (THRACE)

The Bosporus to the Bulgarian border

Charts
Admiralty
2230   Constanţa to Kefken Adasi
1272   Iğneada
1158   Northern Bosporus
3930   Northern Approaches to the Bosporus
Turkish
10A   Western Black Sea
18   Nos Kaliyrakra to Istanbul Boğazi
181   Iğneada to Istanbul Boğazi

PASSAGE NOTES

At the northern end of the Bosporus is the busy fishing harbour of Rumelifeneri, with the rocks forming part of the harbour wall. Perched on top is the Turkelifeneri lighthouse Fl(2)12s58m18M Horn(1)20s. Passing round the Clashing Rocks, which were mentioned by Jason and the Argonauts, the castle is seen located near the lighthouse. North of the castle the rocks extend well out to sea. Pass close to them at 41°14´.70N 29°06´.32E. The headlands are rugged with trees on top, but intersected by three small sandy bays with tourist facilities. At Dalyan Burnu, on top of the white metal framework tower, the light displayed is specified on the *List of Lights* as Fl(3)15s14m10M (on Admiralty and Turkish charts Fl(3)10s13m10M). Well offshore north from the lighthouse is a rock just under the surface and the sea breaks over it in certain conditions. We made one passage between the rock and the cliff with a minimum depth of 11.5m, but if you are not familiar with this headland it is better to give it a wide berth so that you do not finish up like the conspicuous wreck at the foot of the cliff (see below).

Looking southwards you see the large sandy bay of Kumköy (Kilyos), with rolling wooded hills in the background. This would offer a sheltered mooring from southerly winds. At 41°17´.13N 52°52´.59E is an exposed rock which is not on the charts. Going north for the next 6.5 miles, up to 5 cables offshore are some shallow areas. It would be wise to stay outside the 20m contour. On shore the hills give way to a barren plateau that has trees further north and cliffs coming down into the sea. This then gives way to a lot of tipping into the sea from open-cast mining between 41°18´.5N 28°47´.3E and 41°19´.6N 28°45´.2E, before opening out into the sandy bay surrounded by

Dalyan Burnu

Clashing Rocks

low-lying grassy ground before Karaburun. On the cape at Karaburun (41°21´.0N 28°41´.0E) is a lighthouse, Fl.5s54m15M On rounding the cape with the town on top, the terrain gives way to low-lying white cliffs with scrub and trees on top and narrow sandy beaches or small sandy bays. In the area from 41°23´N to 41°31´N we had many soundings less than 20m inside the 20m contour. We also noted exposed rocks that are not on the charts. The Turkish chart 181 does not complete the 20m contour in this area and at 41°25´.5N 28°28´.3E notes a depth of 3.6m PA (position approximate). In this area we suspect the 20m contour should be further east. One of the victims of this poorly charted area is the wreck of a cargo ship lying at the foot of the cliff at 41°23´.3N 28°34´.0E.

At 41°28´.49N 20°19´.93E there is a metal jetty just south of the village of Yaliköy. The village fills the break in the cliffs, and a few fishing boats rest on the beach, but there is no harbour. Inland there are three prominent masts. The chalky yellowish cliffs continue northwards until Çilingos Koyu and stay similar to Kasatura Koyu with trees and scrub on top of the cliffs.

Just south of Kiliköy there has been soil erosion, exposing light brown scars. At Kiliköy the red and green lights at the breakwater heads are on 7m high concrete towers and flash every 5 seconds. The town is on the hill above the harbour and on this headland, there is a light, Fl.10s32m12M according to Admiralty and Turkish charts, but the *List of Lights* specifies the height as 37m. Between the town and Servı Br (Kayali Br) headland that shoals out for a considerable distance, there is a sandy bay that the charts indicate as an anchorage. From here to Sandal Br the steep grey cliffs continue northwards, gradually becoming lower as the hills in the background become higher. The only break in the cliffs is at Sandal Br (41°44´.2N 28°02´.3E) where there is a long sandy bay.

Iğneada is located in the corner of the next long sandy bay. The high ground returns to give the Koru Burnu headland, which can be passed close inshore, and the town of Limanköy and the lighthouse are conspicuous on the top. The white stone lighthouse at 41°53´.2N 28°03´.4E gives the signal Fl(2)15s 44m20M (according to the *List of Lights*, but the Admiralty and Turkish charts specify 5s not 15s). North of the cape the cliffs have fields on top of them, but there are three sandy coves that could be used for short stopovers. These are at 41°54´.4N, 41°54´.5N, 41°54´.7N but they do not offer much protection.

At 41°55´.8N there is the start of the next series of bays which have steep cliffs with trees on top and shingle beaches.

THE BLACK SEA

Karaburun Cape lighthouse

The penultimate mooring in Turkey is at Begendik Br (41°57'.6N 28°02'.60E).

The River Rezovska that flows into the corner of the next sandy bay forms the international border with Bulgaria, and this is marked with large signs on either side with both sides having their watchtowers. On some charts this bay is marked as a mooring, and although it may be a good mooring it would be unwise to moor here, as the border police on both sides may be rather sensitive.

HARBOURS AND MOORINGS

Karaburun 41°20'.68N 28°41'.23E at the entrance

It is very silted with sand at the entrance, and since the sand is so good one hazard is swimmers. They assume they have the right of way and they don't move for boats. On the opposite side there are rocks at the edge of the breakwater, not leaving much room to negotiate the narrow entrance. On the first three visits here we thought the mole to the north was a bit redundant, but on the fourth visit when there was a strong northerly this mole was very effective in calming the sea and allowing us to negotiate the narrow entrance. The 3 lighthouses have been vandalised, are not operational and the locals know of no plans to get them working. We were advised that there were plans to dredge the harbour entrance, but nobody knew when.

There is water on the harbour and electric, at the fishermen's huts, but it is a long distance away from the good moorings. The locals tap into the electricity at the lampposts, in a very unsafe manner. Showers and toilets are on the beach beside the restaurants.

The restaurants are at the head of the harbour and, although not the best-looking, are very friendly. The main food served is fish. After we had made our selection, one of the restaurant staff was sent off to

Karaburun

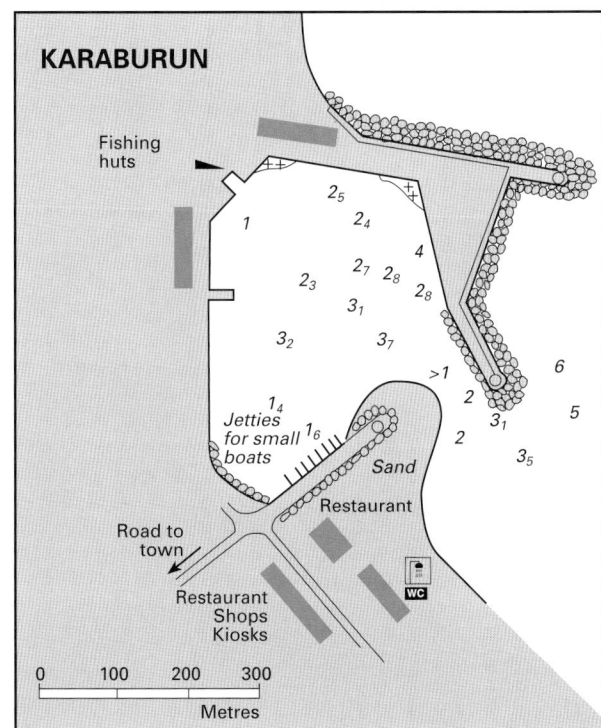

find and introduce us to the actual fisherman who caught our selected fish: you don't get that service even in a 5-star restaurant.

There is no fuel nearby. Mooring is free. This is a quiet place and nobody troubles you. It is a base for Kiyi Emniyeti (Coastal Safety) who are equipped with a powerful RIB with two 150hp outboard engines. This is manned full time with the staff alternating between the RIB, the lighthouse and observation station.

Yaliköy 41°28'.49N 28°19'.03E

Located at a break in the cliffs, this is only a commercial jetty where large boats tie onto the end. It may be useful to tie onto the side in an emergency. Use the north side since there is a pipe that discharges water on the south side, and you may get flooded. There are no services and it is not a picturesque place as it services a cement works.

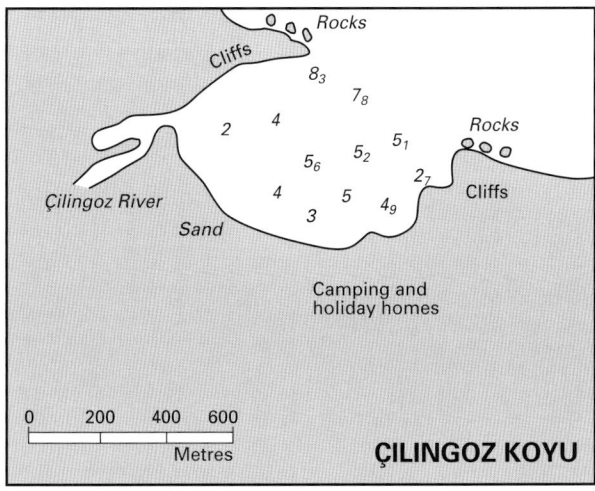

Çilingoz Koyu 41°31'.6N 28°13'.3E

The sandy bay makes it a popular place with the locals, but it offers no shelter from an easterly wind.

BOSPHORUS TO THE BULGARIAN BORDER

Çilingoz Koyu

Kiyiköy Harbour

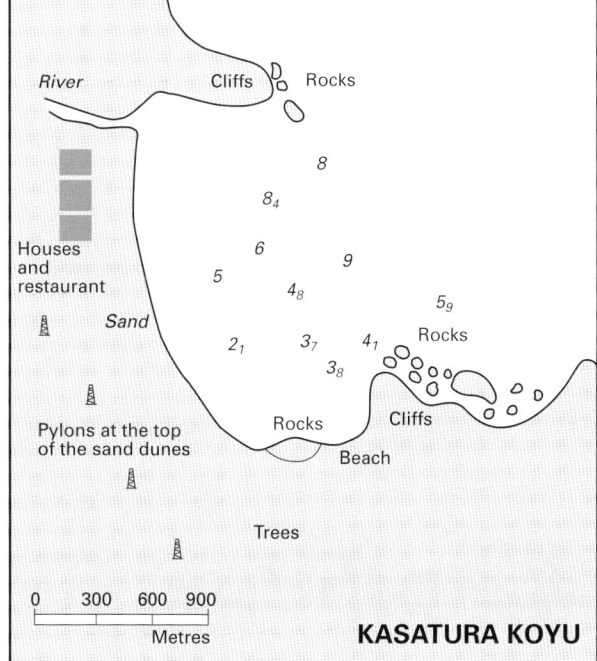

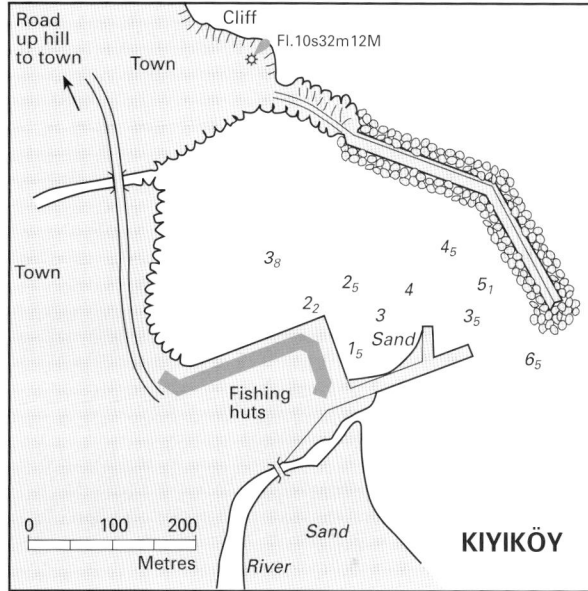

Kasatura Koyu 41°35´.3N 28°08´.9E

There are many rocks at both ends of the bay. Two rivers run into the bay, and there are cafés and a restaurant. Swimming is not recommended here due to undercurrents.

Kasatura Koyu

Kiyiköy (Midye) 41°37´.89N 28°05´.96E at the jetty

There are moorings alongside on the southern pier or stern-to on the west pier, and they are free of charge. Fuel is carried from the garage since the pump at the harbour is broken and the locals don't know of any plans to repair it. There is water on the harbour, and it may be possible to negotiate electricity from one of the fishermen's huts. The main town with the old houses, remains of fortifications and restaurants is on top of the cliff. In the restaurants there is still segregation, with men in one area, families in another and no place for women alone. It is a friendly place, and a local insisted on showing us the town.

The town was known as Salmidisos when it was built in antiquity. Goths invaded it in the second century, but it was rebuilt in Byzantine times with strong fortifications, some of which – along with some houses survives – today. Pirates used many of the caves in the area; one cave on the road to Papug now houses the Hagia Nicola Church. The upper floor housed the monks, and the lower floor was the church with a spring underneath that. The town now depends on fishing, tourism and forestry for employment.

On one visit the locals were very happy since a fishing boat had been washed into the harbour. It was undamaged, had no registration number, and no owner could be found. They said 'it was their gift from the sea'.

THE BLACK SEA

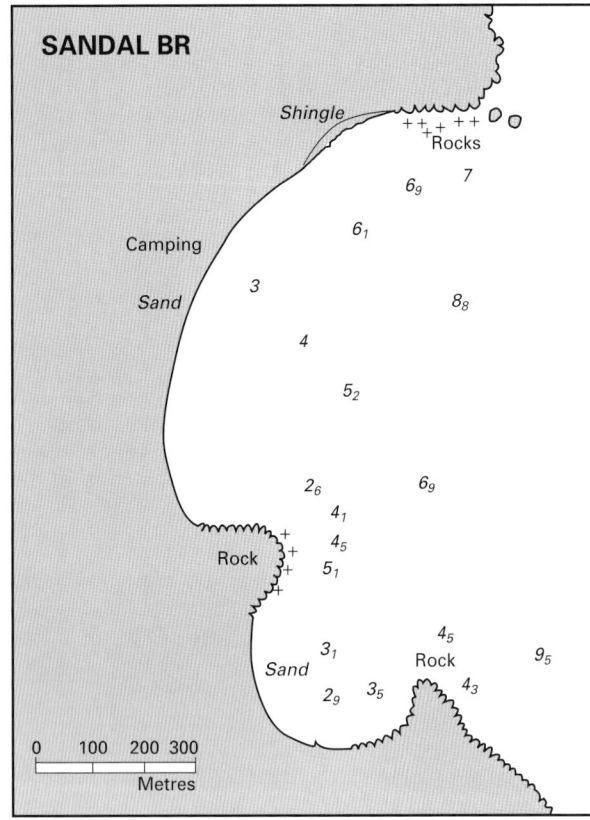

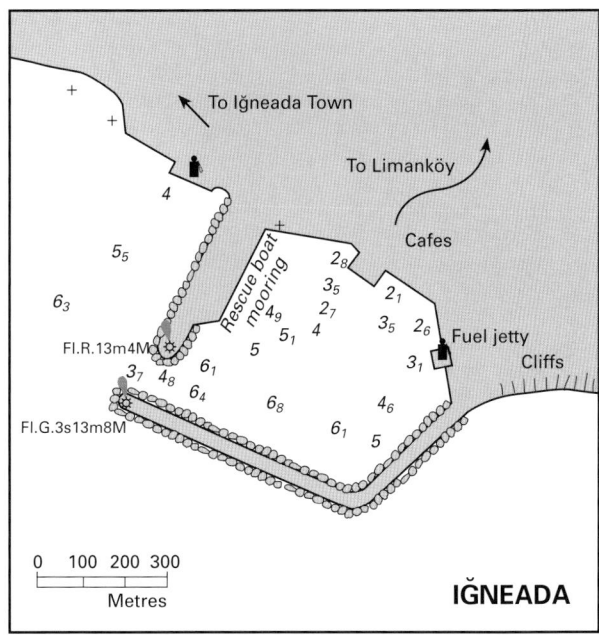

Sandal Br

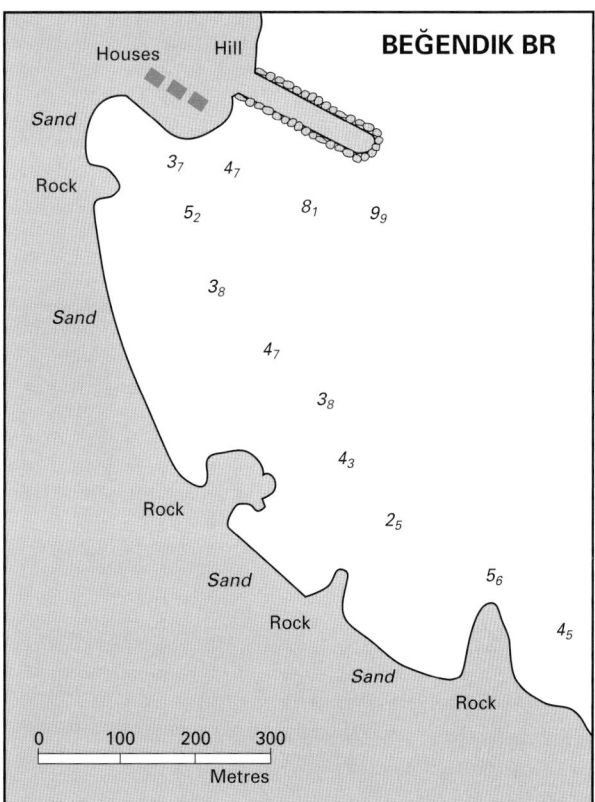

Sandal Br 41°44´.2N 28°02´.5E
A small bay suitable for a day stop, but not offering much shelter.

Iğneada 41°53´.3N 28°01´.4E at the entrance
The harbour is about 4km from Iğneada in the west and 2.5km from Limanköy in the east on top of the cliffs. Behind the harbour are the Yidiz Mountains. The entrance is marked at the end of the main breakwater on a white concrete tower Fl.G.3s13m8M. The northern breakwater has Fl.R.13m4M (the Turkish chart has the heights as 16m and 17m respectively). There are two hazards, one is marked with a yellow buoy Fl.Y.5s6M at 41°52´.50N 27°59´.55E, and the other is a wreck with masts above the water at 41°52´.0N 28°01´.0E

Iğneada can be a port of entry when prior permission is obtained. It is a good refuelling stop, with a garage within the harbour and a dedicated refuelling jetty just outside the north pier. It has a deep draught and takes credit cards. Water is available at the fuel station and on the jetty. Electricity is installed at some parts of the harbour, or from kiosks, but a long cable is required.

There is no cost for mooring. The mooring was rafting off local fishing boats, and their owners insisted on preparing us a fish meal from the day's catch. We therefore never experienced the restaurants at the harbour, or walked the 4km into town where there are restaurants and shops.

Between Koru Br headland and Beğendik Br, there are three bays that could be used for day stops.

Beğendik Br 41°57´.5N 28°02´.6E
The penultimate stopping place in Turkey. It is a long bay with alternating sand and rocks. The mole in the north corner can give some protection from northerly winds. The holding is variable depending on where you are mooring.

BULGARIA

The Turkish border to Burgas Bay

Charts
Admiralty
2230   Constanța to Kefken Adasi
2283   Maslen Nos to Nos Kaliakra
Turkish
10A   Western Black Sea
18   Nos Kaliakra to Istanbul Boğazi

PASSAGE NOTES
Rezovo to Sozopol

The River Rezovska flowing into the head of the bay at 41°58′N 28°02′E forms the international boundary between Turkey and Bulgaria. From here to Sinemorets is dense wooded countryside or fields with large sandy bays in between the cliffs. In the background the hills start to rise when coming towards Ahtopol. Stay well offshore at the cape just south of Ahtopol, as there are many visible rocks. Likewise, there are also rocks at the north side of Ahtopol Bay and they extend beyond the yellow and black cone-shaped lighthouse. On Nos Akhtopol the light displays Q(6)+LFl.15s15m5M.

Between here and Tzarevo the hills rise in the background with the triangular Mount Papiya (502m) being the most prominent. At 42°08′.68N 27°53′.8E there are uncharted rocks. In the bay at 42°09′.05N 27°53′.47E (offshore GPS reading), there is a large

Turkey-Bulgaria border

white factory where fibreglass boats were produced. It has a slip and presumably fibreglass repairs can be carried out here. On the seaward side of this bay are many rocks. After a rocky shoreline with grass and trees on top, Tzarevo also has rocks at both sides of the bay, with lighthouses being located on either side of the entrance. The main light is Fl.7s41m9M, but the chart specifies 7s14M. At 42°11′.6N there is a mussel farm at the head of the bay, that is marked with many white buoys. At 42°11′.63N is a camping area at the head of a bay, with a lot of nets offshore and tourists in small fishing boats. At 42°11′.7N 27°50′.6E there are rocks projecting out to sea from the headland.

On the approach to Kiten there is a sunken reef 1 mile southeast of the town. There are fish traps to the east and southeast of the jetty. (At this section of the coast it is advisable to stay further offshore to avoid all these hazards.) Kiten has two high-rise apartment blocks projecting out of the woods, which are a good landmark. After Nos Urdoviza is the long sandy bay which is divided with a rock outcrop where Pomorski is located on top of Nos Kyupriya, which has a reef extending 1.5 cables SSE. At the end of the pier is exhibited a light LFl.5s8m6M, with the chart indicating every 6 seconds. Maslen Nos displays a light from a white circular stone tower, with a lookout tower, Fl(3)17.2s37m17M, and should be given a wide berth of about half a mile due to sunken rocks. The cliffs up to Korakya have woods on the top, and Nos Korakya can be passed close inshore. After this there is a long sandy bay with Ropotamo tucked into the southern corner. Nos Kolokita has some visible rocks on the south side of it but appears to be clear on the north side.

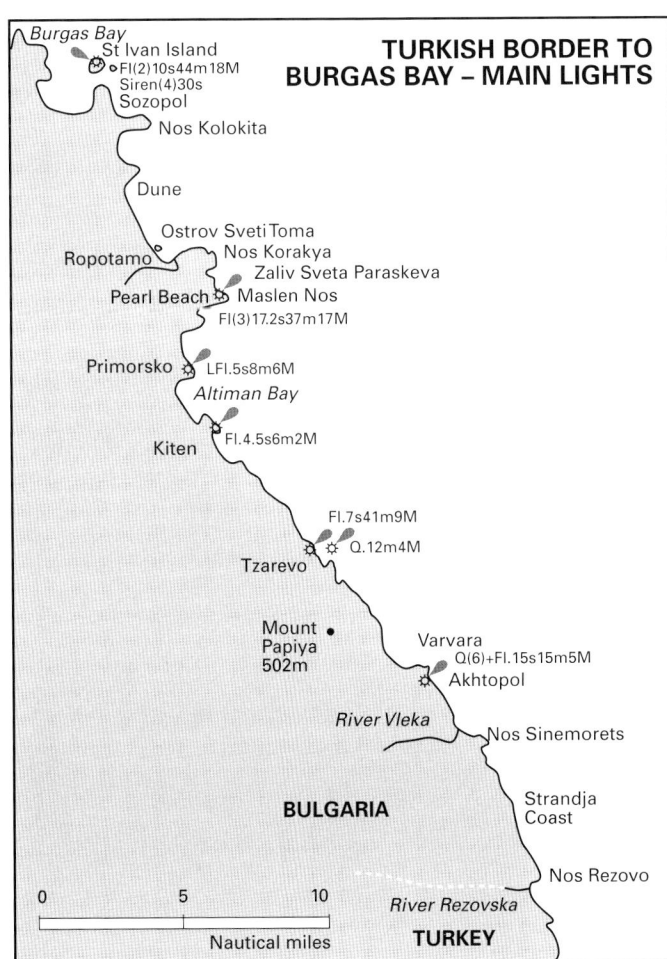

HARBOURS AND MOORINGS

THE STRANDJA COAST

This is the first area you come to after crossing the border from Turkey and it takes its name from the Strandja Mountain. During Communist times this area was out of bounds, being near the border. It is therefore one of the least spoilt in the country, and a nature park covering 1,116km² was established in 1999.

The tourists have not yet discovered some of the bays at the south since there are almost no roads to the coast. You can have a bay with beautiful sand and good holding for mooring, almost for yourself. The

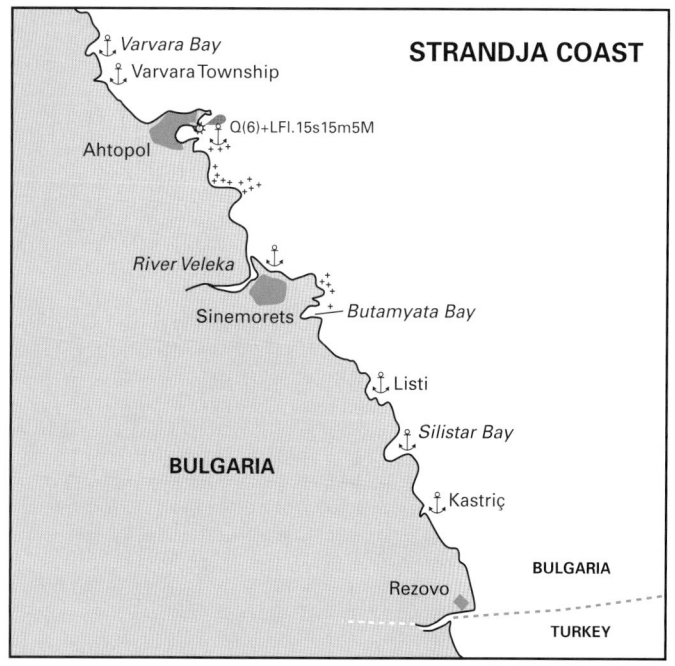
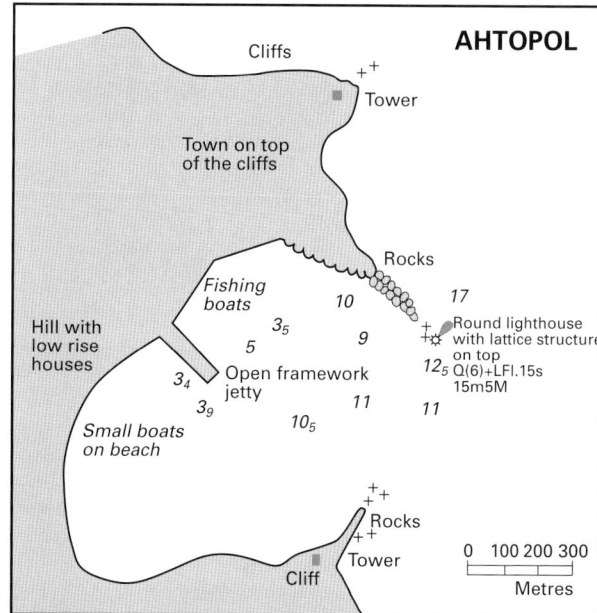

Ahtopol

nearer you get to Sinemorets the more popular the bays become, with Butamyata Bay just to the south of Sinemorets having all the tourist trappings.

Kastrič (Castrich) 42°00′.5N
This is still within the guarded border zone.

Silistar 42°01′.5N
Silistar is identified with a navigation sign that is a steel rectangle with horizontal black and white strips, 33m above sea level The beach here is superb.

Listi 42°02′.2N
Fishermen come here to catch a special type of large crab.

Not only does the area have beautiful land and seascapes, but it also has a culture going back to Thracian times, and today you can visit beehive cells, dolmens and sacrificial altars. A tradition (from Thracian times) of walking and dancing on hot coals still takes place on 3 June, St Konstantin and St Elena Day, in the village of Balgari. The Strandja occupies an important place for biodiversity, with the forests being of broadleaved, temperate deciduous trees, with heavy undergrowth. This forest is home to the booted eagle, semi-collared flycatcher, olive tree warblers and masked shrike among others.

Sinemorets 42°04′.22N 27°58′.36E in the bay
The sandy bay to the north near the mouth of the River Veleka, which runs from the heart of the Strandja Mountains, could be suitable for a short stop. Sinemorets is a windswept hilltop settlement that was out of bounds to outsiders until 1989 due to its proximity to the Turkish border. Now it attracts the younger set, and nude bathing would not raise an eyebrow.

Ahtopol 42°05′.98N 27°56′.71E
The border police arrived before we finished mooring. They can be contacted on Ch 8. Access is clear with taking a bearing of 270° at the centre of the bay.

There is no water or electricity on the pier. Fuel is by can and taxi. The metal lattice jetty does not give much shelter.

The Thracian tribe Tini in the 4th century BC called the place Avleotihos (The town of love). 200 years later the Greeks changed it to Agatopolis (City of Happiness). Then came the Romans who changed the name to Peronticus and they fortified it. Artefacts from all these periods are in the town museum. In the 16th century an earthquake destroyed the town and it was not fully rebuilt again until the 18th century when it became known as Ahtebol. Again in the 18th century the Greeks from the Crimea returned at the invitation of the Turks and were employed building a lot of ships for the Turkish navy. By the end of the 19th century this was the most beautiful and prosperous town on the south Bulgarian shore. After a big fire in 1918 only a few of the original buildings remain. At the head of the peninsula stands Hram Vasnesenie Gospodne (Chapel of the Ascension). Ancient coins have been found near the town from such diverse places as Mexico, Brazil, Argentina and most European Countries.

Varvara
There are two bays at Varvara, the southerly one at 42°07′.85N 27°54′.46E. We shall call this one Varvara Township; it has plenty of depth and is sheltered in all but easterlies. The small jetties at the head of the bay are only suitable for the small fishing boats. The holding is reasonable. At the head of the bay are the small houses of the fisherfolk. They will give you a warm welcome, but would be even happier if you purchased some of their catch or vegetables from the gardens.

TURKISH BORDER TO BURGAS BAY

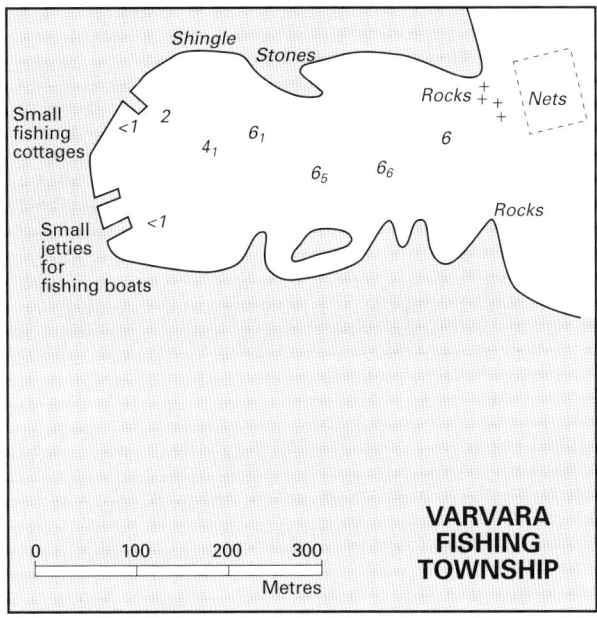

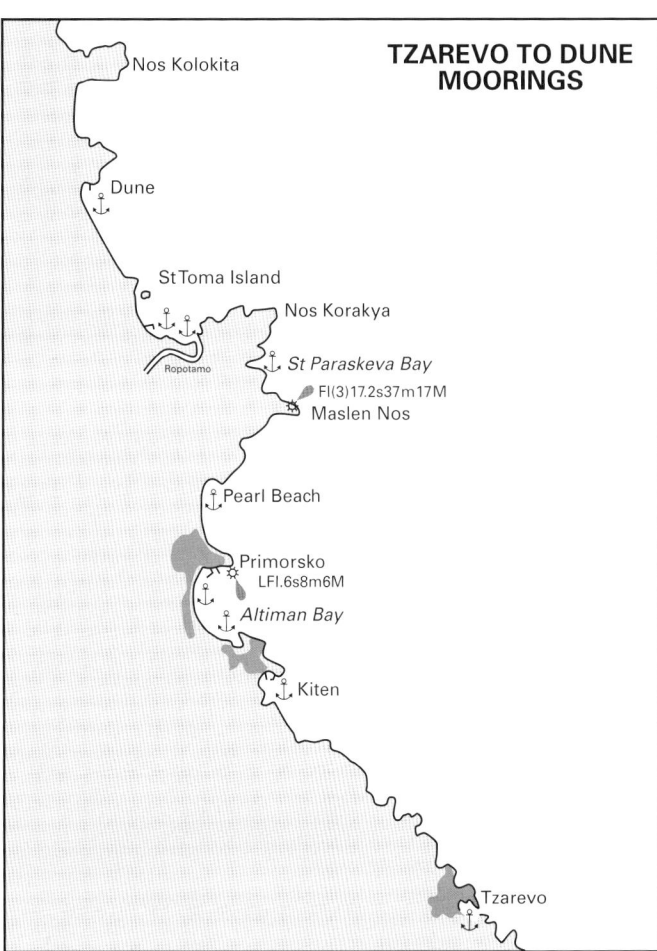

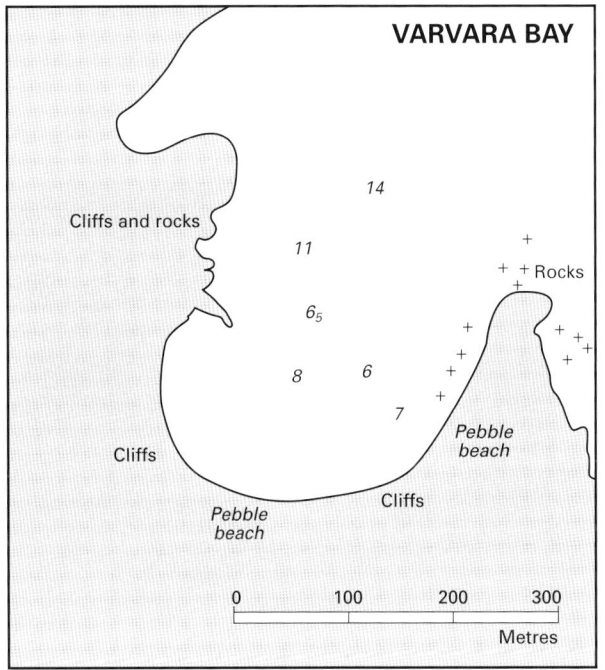

Varvara Bay 42°08'.18N 27°54'.28E
Varvara Bay is just to the north of the bay with the township. It is surrounded by cliffs and and is well sheltered to all except a northerly wind. (The main township is slightly inland between the two moorings.) This place has always been dependent on fishing and as such has been a late starter in the tourist boom. As a result there are not such well developed bars and restaurants, but this is also reflected in lower prices. It is a favourite place for divers and those who want a quiet holiday.

Tzarevo (Carevo) 42°10'.15N 27°54'.28E
This is the largest harbour south of Burgas. At the southern entrance to the bay rocks extend 3.5 cables offshore and near the end is a light on a pillar with a yellow round concrete base that displays Q.12s4M. The single-storey long red roof building (a church) on the cliff at the head of the bay is a good lead line into the bay. The way in is straightforward coming on a bearing of about 220° until just past the eastern breakwater, then go due north. The harbour gives good shelter. There is water and electricity on the jetty, but fuel is with a container and a taxi visit to the garage. This could also be a place to stop for fibreglass repairs since the boat factory is only about a mile away. Some general spares can be obtained from the local shops. The border police will visit on arrival. It is advertised that boats can be left all the year round here; they have a large hard standing area and cranes can be hired for lift-outs. In the town that is on top of the cliffs there are sufficient shops, cafés and restaurants.

This was the ancient Greek colony of Vassiliko, and a fishing settlement. In 1880 a big fire burnt down the town, now a high proportion of the population are

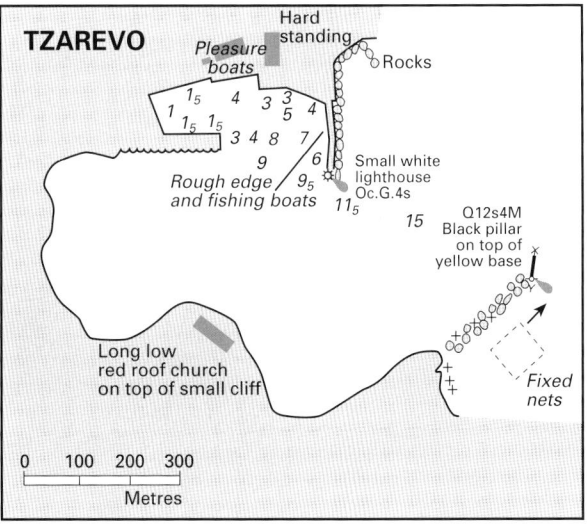

CRUISING BULGARIA AND ROMANIA 27

refugees from eastern Thrace in 1913. It came within the Bulgarian boundary in 1912. Tzarevo was the name given to the town in the 1930s, but in September 1944 the Communists renamed it Michurin after a Russian biologist. It retained this name until the fall of Communism when it reverted back to Tzarevo. (On some charts it is still called Michurin.)

Kiten 42°13´.80N 27°46´.87E

Kiten is easily spotted by its multi-storey flats protruding from the trees on top of the hill

On the approach to Kiten about 1 mile southeast there is a sunken reef that was not on the chart, but was well known to the locals. Many fish traps are fixed to the east and southeast of the jetty. It would be wise to stay 1 mile offshore. Another hazard are swimmers who go out as far as the harbour entrance.

There is a yacht club, bars, and restaurant on the harbour; also a slip and a boat-hoist.

Electricity and water are available on the harbour. The friendly boatclub staff give a good welcome in this sheltered harbour. They will advise where to moor.

Fugitives from Greece and immigrants from surrounding villages founded the village in 1931. After 1970 it was developed as an attractive resort. As well as the sandy beaches the town offers all the usual tourist facilities. After Nos Urdoviza on the north side of the peninsula there are two breakwaters. The one at 42°14´.7N 27°46´.6E has a jetty on it but is exposed to the north. Going west, Nos Konnik (Athanatos Point) has sunken reefs extending 1.5 cables northward. This then opens into Dyavolski Zaliv, which is known to the locals as Altiman Bay.

Altiman Bay 42°14´.58N 27°46´.25E

There is an old metal jetty but it is in a fairly derelict condition. This is a beautiful sheltered bay with all the tourist facilities and it is excellent for a day stop but beware of swimmers and people on airbeds. We moored at 42°14´.58N 27°46´.25E in 5m of water on a sandy bottom. To the east side of the bay is a smaller bay and it is worth going ashore in the tender to visit

Kiten Harbour

Altiman Bay

Zangadora

it. You will find the unique Zangadora bar that serves good food and drink during the day and has a lively disco in the evening. (Zangadora was named after a Greek hermit who stayed on the peninsula.)

Primorsko 45°15´.99N 27°46´.14E

The jetty is visible, with the white light tower at the end of the pier. There is no electricity and water is obtained from a well at the head of the pier. Fuel is from garages and other supplies are obtained from the town up the hill. The maritime administrator owns the café at the head of the pier; he is also the hoist driver

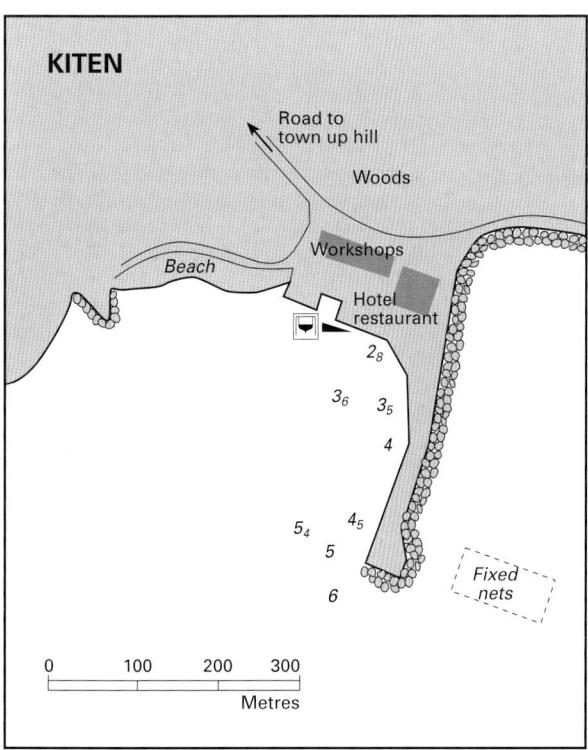

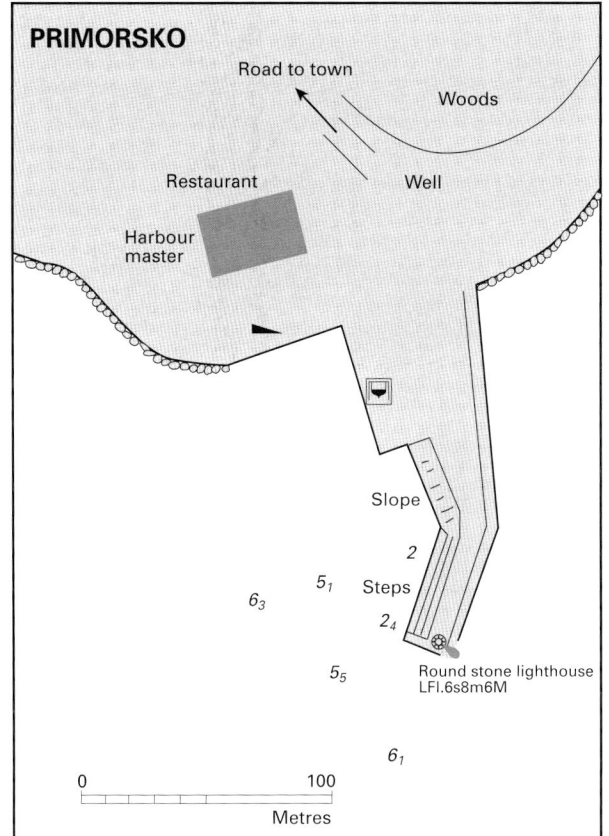

Primorsko

Primorsko

and speaks German. The boat-hoist is one of the best seen in Bulgaria and costs about €5 per lift. The area is famous for its 10km long beach, the largest and one of the prettiest in Bulgaria. Primorsko stands on a rock outcrop, Nos Kyupriya, in the centre of the sandy bays known as Stomopolo and Dyavolski (Devil's Bay). The reef extends 1.5 cables SSE from the cape. The town was previously called Chenger and the Turks changed the name to Kupria. It is a centre for international youth camps.

Pearl Beach 42°17'.3N 27°45'.6E

Entrance to the harbour is straightforward. When we arrived there were friendly boaters who showed us where to moor and helped us. We also received a good welcome on the sandy beach. In the woods there is a beach bar where, when having a beer after a near disaster with an armed security guard, we renamed the place Pearl Harbour. The key for the toilets is kept at the kiosk and there is a cold shower on the beach. Small amounts of water could be obtained from the kiosk, but there are no other services.

Zaliv Sveta Paraskeva (St Paraskeva Bay)
42°19'.25N 27°46'.37E at the mooring in the bay

This bay is surrounded by cliffs, has a rocky shingle beach at the head of it, and a dense forest on top of the cliffs. It has excellent shelter in all but easterly winds. In the northwest corner were the ruins of a chapel which was destroyed by the Communists. Evroastral, a foundation from Burgas, intend to restore it.

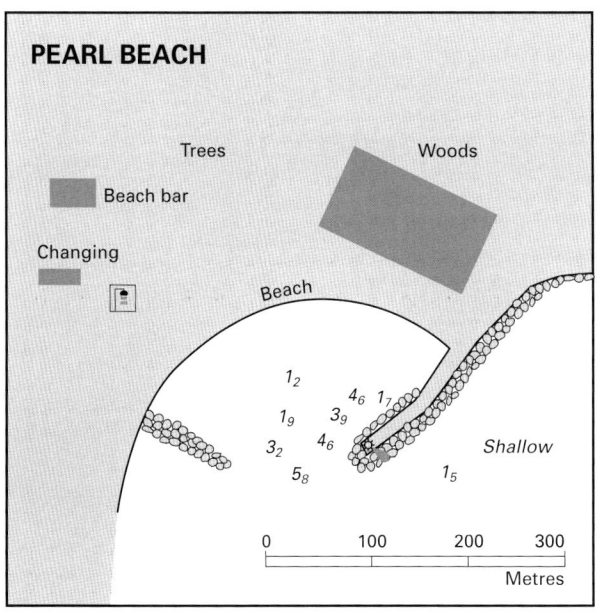

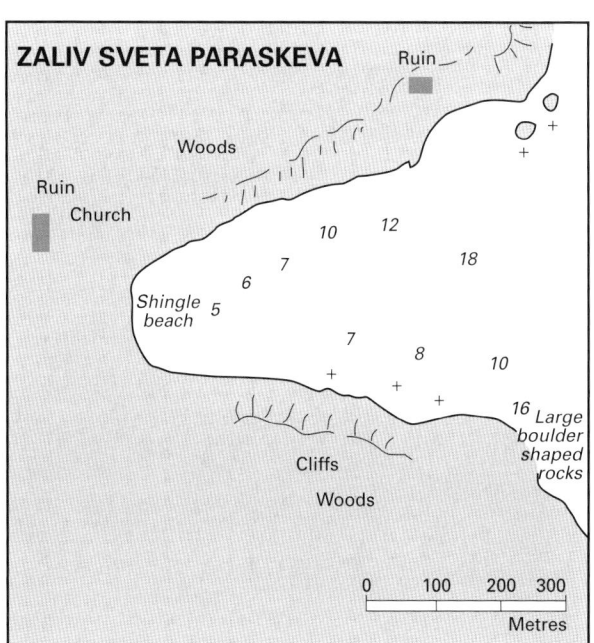

Ropotamo 42°19´.80N 27°45´.38E

The entrance to the bay is straightforward and there is good holding in sand in many parts of the bay.

This area is a partial reserve, natural monument, maintained reserve and protected area which was extended to 5500 hectares in 2002. It was named after the Greek Goddess Ro and *potamo* (river). Ro is reputed to have charmed the pirates with her song, who in turn agreed to leave the area in peace. The river starts 50km away in the Strandja Mountains and is a popular destination for nature lovers.

During the 1980s training walls and dams were constructed, which affected the natural flow of the river. This has led to silting at the mouth of the river so that there is only about 30 cms of water over the bar. After that the river becomes deep again. There is a small jetty, just inside on the east bank of the river, and it is possible to attract the tourist boatman's attention and take the trip upstream for a cost of about €5. The boats run about every half-hour in the summer. One thing to check is that it is not the last boat of the day and there will be another one back to the mouth of the river, otherwise you will be stranded upstream. This is the best way to see the natural environment of the area.

The low stemmed oak, yoke elms, flowering ash, dewberry and many other trees and plants, some with their roots in the water, give the impression of a jungle swampland. Grasses, reeds and ivy add to this effect. This gives favourable conditions for other mammals, animals, and insects to take shelter and find good food. Other marshy areas are famed for the floating waterlilies. The first 7km going upstream are home to over 100 different species that are listed in the Bulgarian red book of endangered species. Turtles, watersnakes and butterflies make their home in the riverbanks, while in the woods are wolves, foxes, jackals, deer, boar and other game species.

Overhead there could be the white-tailed eagle with its wingspan of 2m, or (since the migratory highway of the Via Pontica passes over the Ropotamo), wild duck, geese and woodcock. On this site there are 7 types of birds, 2 plant species, 8 invertebrate and 7 mammal species, all from globally threatened species.

Arkutino Bay 42°20´.3N 27°43´.9E

Between the entrance to the Ropotamo River and Ostrov Sveti Toma in front of the sand dunes is an unfinished hotel complex with a jetty which offers excellent shelter. You have to go very close to the rocks that protrude out at the end of the jetty to enter since the centre is silted up.

St Toma Island (Snake Island) is the breeding place for waterfowl and is the habitat of the Gunther vole and snakes.

Dune (Duni, Dyuni, Djuni, Dunes Holiday Village)
42°22´.26N 27°42´.76E

There are no complications in entering the harbour, which is deep and provides a good shelter. We got a good reception and help to moor, but when we got ashore it was explained that this was an all-inclusive resort and it was impossible to buy anything. We offered to leave but a staff member suggested we go to a beach bar outside the complex. He came with us and introduced us to the security guards and bar staff; in the end it was a pleasant afternoon and everyone was very helpful. This could possibly be a useful stopping place if you wanted some time ashore and the accommodation was prearranged. The resort has many facilities and can arrange car rental. It has an excellent location in a nature reserve.

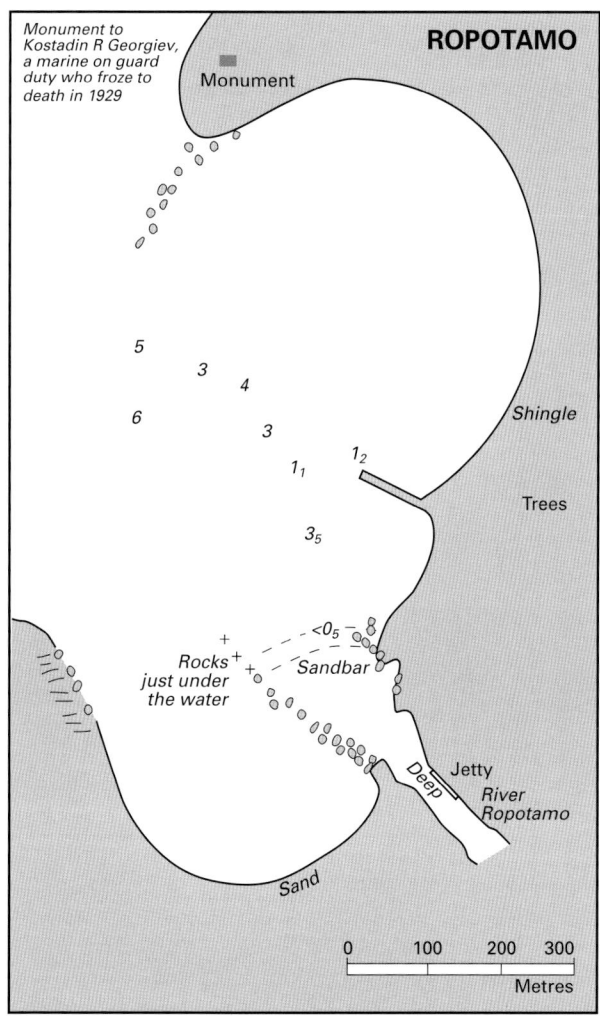

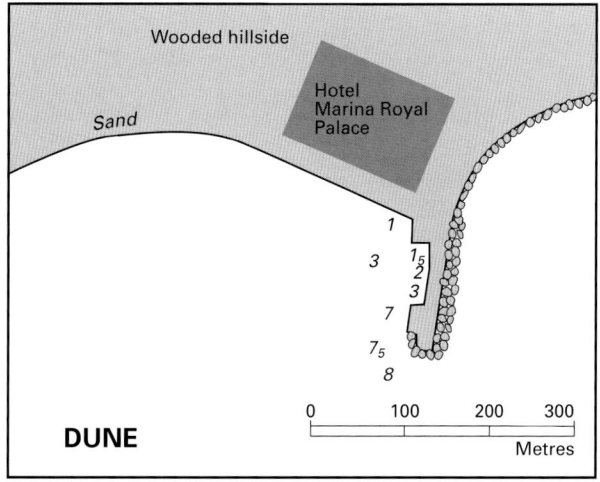

Dune

Burgas Bay
Sozopol to Nos Emenie

Charts
Admiralty
2399 Burgas and approaches
2283 Maslem Nos to Nos Kaliakra
2230 Constanța to Kefken Adazi
Turkish
10A Western Black Sea
18 Nos Kaliakra to Istanbul Boğazi
1821 Burgas Bay

Burgas Bay stretches 31km inland and at its widest point is 41km and the deepest point is 25m.

Sozopol 42°25′.14N 27°41′.42E at mooring

This is a large naval, commercial and fishing harbour. The easterly side is the town harbour, which is busy with fishing and tourist trip boats, although visiting boats are welcome. The harbourmaster will direct you where to moor. When the fishing boats are at sea their wharf is free. (They typically return at about 1700.) The tourist trip boats typically stop running about 1900, and after that time their quay is vacant.

A visit here may involve moving moorings. Mooring costs 5 leva (approx €2.5) per night. Water is the only facility near the jetty, but a visit from a fuel tanker truck and small repairs could be arranged. The southwest wall of the harbour is owned by the private fishing company Ribex. When space permits it is also possible to moor here; permission is given by the harbourmaster who has an office next to the gatehouse, to the west of the café. He will direct you to a mooring. These jetties have water and electricity. The cost is 10 leva per night (about €5).

It is compulsory to visit the border police. They may find you first since they regularly patrol the harbour area, either in a Land Rover or on a scooter. The border police here use radio Ch 8 and they can also be contacted this way.

On the road to the Ribex Harbour is a wholesale market, so it is a good place to stock up on provisions.

On the northwest side of the peninsula is the former island that is connected by a causeway, and this is home to the naval academy and naval base. Entry to this side of the harbour is forbidden. It is, however,

Sozopol

Sozopol

rumoured that the navy intend to leave here within the next few years and the harbour could then be developed for recreational craft.

Sozopol, (the 'town of salvation') was known as Apollonia by the Greeks who founded it in 610BC. Named after the God Apollo (the healer), there was in those days a Temple of Apollo with a 13-metre high statue which was created by the Athenian sculptor Calamis in the 5th century BC. The Greeks from the rich town of Milet transformed the old Thracian town into a rich Greek colony and independent city-state. Trade, culture and art flourished, and it minted its own coins. Its downfall was in 72BC when the Roman legions of Marcus Luculus destroyed the walls, Apollo's Temple and many other fine buildings. The Statue of Apollo was taken to Rome as booty.

With the growth of Constantinople it became more important again and the Romans carried out some construction work and named it Sozopolis. Barbarians invaded the town from the 3rd to the 7th century AD, but those attacks were successfully fended off. In 813 Khan Krum annexed it to Bulgarian territory. From 972 to 1366 it was regularly conquered by Byzantium, but in the 13th century it had regained importance as a harbour, trading post, commercial, and religious centre.

In the Middle Ages it belonged to Byzantium and Bulgaria, before the Turks conquered the Balkan Peninsula. It then declined again, becoming a small fishing village and vine-growing area.

After the liberation of Bulgaria in 1878 it began a quick development to become the important local centre it is today. In this era many houses and churches

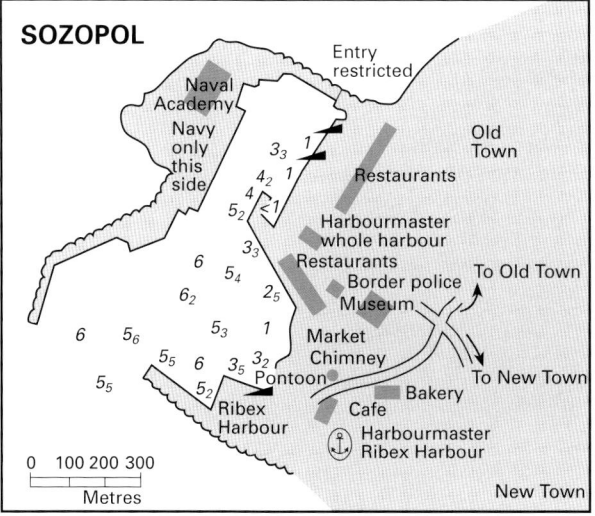

were built including St George, St Mary, St Cyril and Methodius. The houses are built in typical 'Black Sea' architectural style, with the lower floors in stone choke and the upper floors in wood. The gardens beside the houses are protected by stone walls, and many of these courtyards are now converted into cafés. The narrow cobbled streets are lined with tourist kiosks and lead to many cafés, bars and restaurants. In early September the Apollonia arts festival is held here.

The rocky peninsula with its two beaches has a charm that attracts artists and writers. For those interested in old boats there is a display of ancient ship models in the archaeological museum near the harbour. The original old town is on the peninsula near the harbour, and the art gallery, museums and churches are all located in this area. Up the hill is the new town that does not hold much interest for tourists. The east side of the peninsula has two good beaches.

Offshore from the harbour is the island of Sveti Ivan (Saint John), where until the end of the 19th century there was an Orthodox monastery, much of which is still preserved. Other remains are an antique lighthouse and a furnace for iron production.

The smaller island is Sveti Petăr (Saint Peter), which is a rocky outcrop that is a nesting place for birds. Legend has it that it was once a hiding place for pirates. Offshore from Sozopol under 18m of water is a fossilised wood.

> **Ice for the drinks**
> Around 1700 the large fishing boats return to Sozopol with the day's catch. A lorry with crateloads of ice is there waiting to meet them. As the crates of fish come up the ramp onto the lorry, the tops of the crates are filled with ice covering the fish. The workers are very obliging and can supply buckets of ice for the drinks. However, one word of warning. They advise that the quality of the water that the ice is made from may not be very good, so it is best to use it like a champagne bucket and stick the bottle in the ice in the bucket.

PASSAGE NOTES
South Burgas Bay (Sozopol to Burgas)

Sozopoloski Zaliv (Sozopol Bay)

To the north of Sozopol is the island of Sveti Ivan. Located on the island is a lighthouse Fl(2)10s44m18M Horn Mo(H)30s. To the west of the island is a large mussel farm stretching a good distance from the island and is very poorly marked; smaller one exists at the south of the island. Around most of the island is area 319, where fishing, anchoring, and underwater activities are prohibited for conservation reasons.

At the southern end of Sozopol Bay is a long, sandy beach with no shelter from the north. It is a good place for a short stop, and near the entrance to the campsite is the bus stop for Sozopol and Chernomorets. At the western end of the bay is a natural shelter and good mooring behind Nos Khrisosotira at 42°25´.85N 27°39´.05E which also has a metal jetty. Some locals keep boats moored here. There are no facilities, and it is about a mile to walk into Chernomorets. At the head of the bay are fixed nets, but scattered in many areas are other nets with almost non-existent marking.

Travelling westerly up Burgas Bay, Nos Talasakra can be passed after 1 cable from the shore. We passed at 42°27´.15N 27°39´.19E. Nos Atkin, the next cape, is entirely the opposite, with rocks extending a quarter of a mile offshore. They are called Skala Malatsite ('young buffalo rocks'). The closest we have passed them is 42°27´.695N 27°37´.969E.

To the west of Nos Atkin are fixed fishing nets, at the start of Vramos Bay (Zaliv Vramos). This bay, with its grassy slopes and low wooded hills behind, could provide a mooring with the side of the bay being chosen depending on the prevailing wind. There is no shelter from the north.

Before the next headland (Nos Atiya), on chart 2399 is an area marked as 'area 318 entry prohibited', but no explanation why. To clear the northerly point of

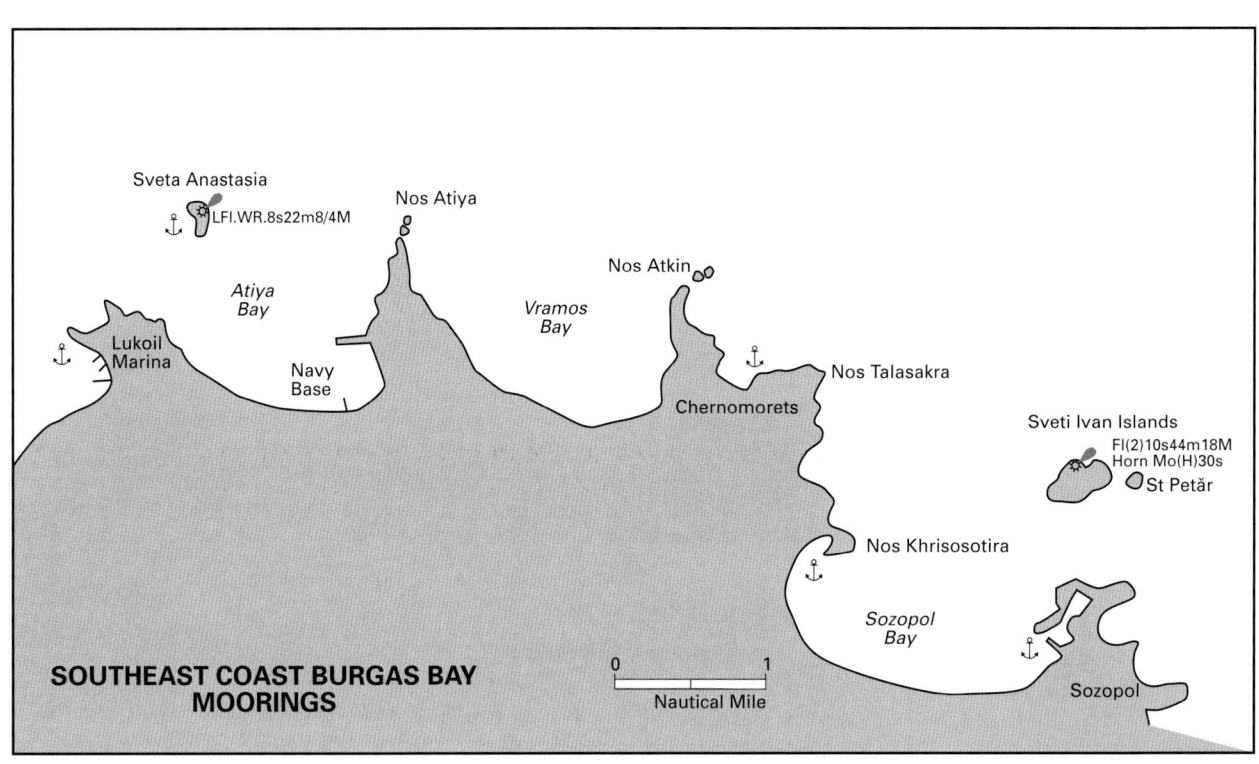

SOUTHEAST COAST BURGAS BAY MOORINGS

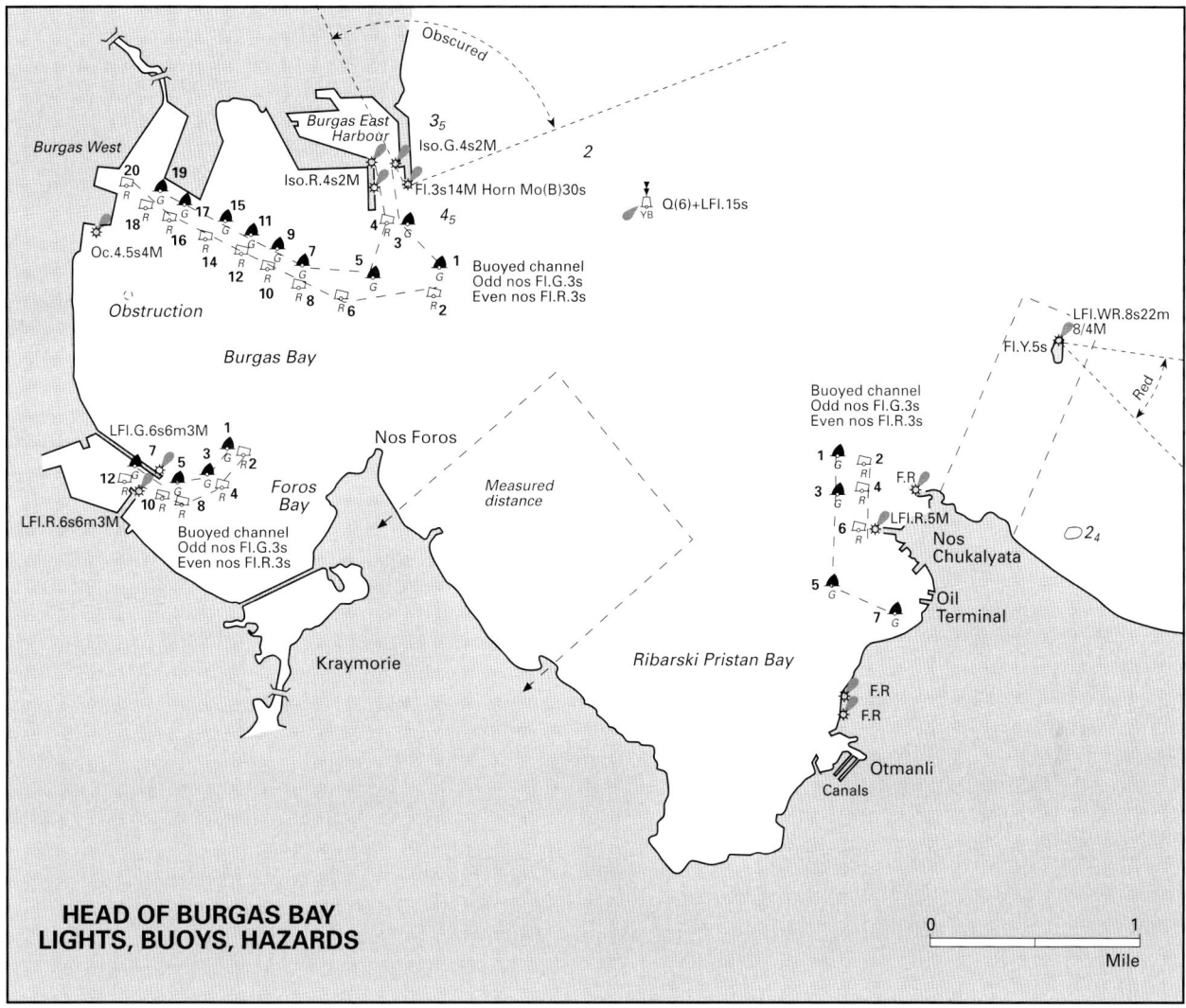

this you should be positioned north of 42°28´.2N. To the south of this area 3 cables offshore is a rock with less than one metre over it.

Nos Atiya, which can be identified by the lookout control tower near the point and a square grey-white building just further inland, also needs to be given a wide berth. There is an obvious rock close inshore, but an isolated one further offshore. The closest we have passed is 42°27´.96N 27°35´.11E. The rocks are covered by the red sector of the Sveti Anastasiya lighthouse.

On the west side of the headland are 2 sets of fixed nets and area 018, which has 'entry forbidden'. The harbour in the east corner of Atiya Bay is for the navy only, and must be avoided. At the head of the bay are two pillars which, when lined up, give a compass reading of 180°.

Seen on the next headland, Nos Chukalyata, are the large storage tanks of the Lukoil oil terminal (on the chart it is called by its old name Rossenetz oil terminal). To the north of these headlands is a traffic separation scheme for boats heading for Burgas harbour and Lukoil oil terminal.

Offshore from the western end of Zaliv Atiya is the island (*ostrov*) of Sveta Anastasia where there is the lighthouse LFl.WR.8s22m8/4M. Between the island and the cape is area 317 where anchoring, fishing and all seabed or submarine operations are prohibited; this is because the water and electricity services run out to the island. Just to the north of the island in the vicinity of 42°28´.1N 27°33´.2E is a local magnetic anomaly which can vary between –002° and +012°.

Nos Chukalyata has a light F.R and can be taken close inshore 42°27´.56N 27°32´.40E. After this is a buoyed channel with lights Fl.G.3s and Fl.R.3s. This is for entry into the oil terminal and should be avoided. A lead line for this channel is F.R lights on 2 black and white pillars located just north of Otmanli. Between the end of the oil terminal and Otmanli is an extensive set of fixed nets.

At the head of the bay, which is surrounded by low wooded hills, is a damaged metal jetty. Some local boats are there on moorings. It is a possible place to anchor, but is exposed to the north. There are fixed nets in the centre of this bay. The small headland in front of Kraymorie has sandy beaches on either side. From the headland projecting well out to sea and also on the west side of the headland are extensive fishing nets. This was cleared at 42°26´.85N 27°29´.9E. On the west side of Zaliv Ribarski Pristan is a measured distance of 1,851m (one nautical mile, almost). The shore marks at either end are black and white pillars, and the transit angle is 141°–321°.

Nos Foros has a tall thin pylon near the headland and some rocks just under the water. The nearest we passed to this was 42°27´76N 27°28´.81E. After Nos Foros is Foros Bay (Zaliv Foros) where at the head of the bay is Korabostroitelnitzy, a commercial port. On

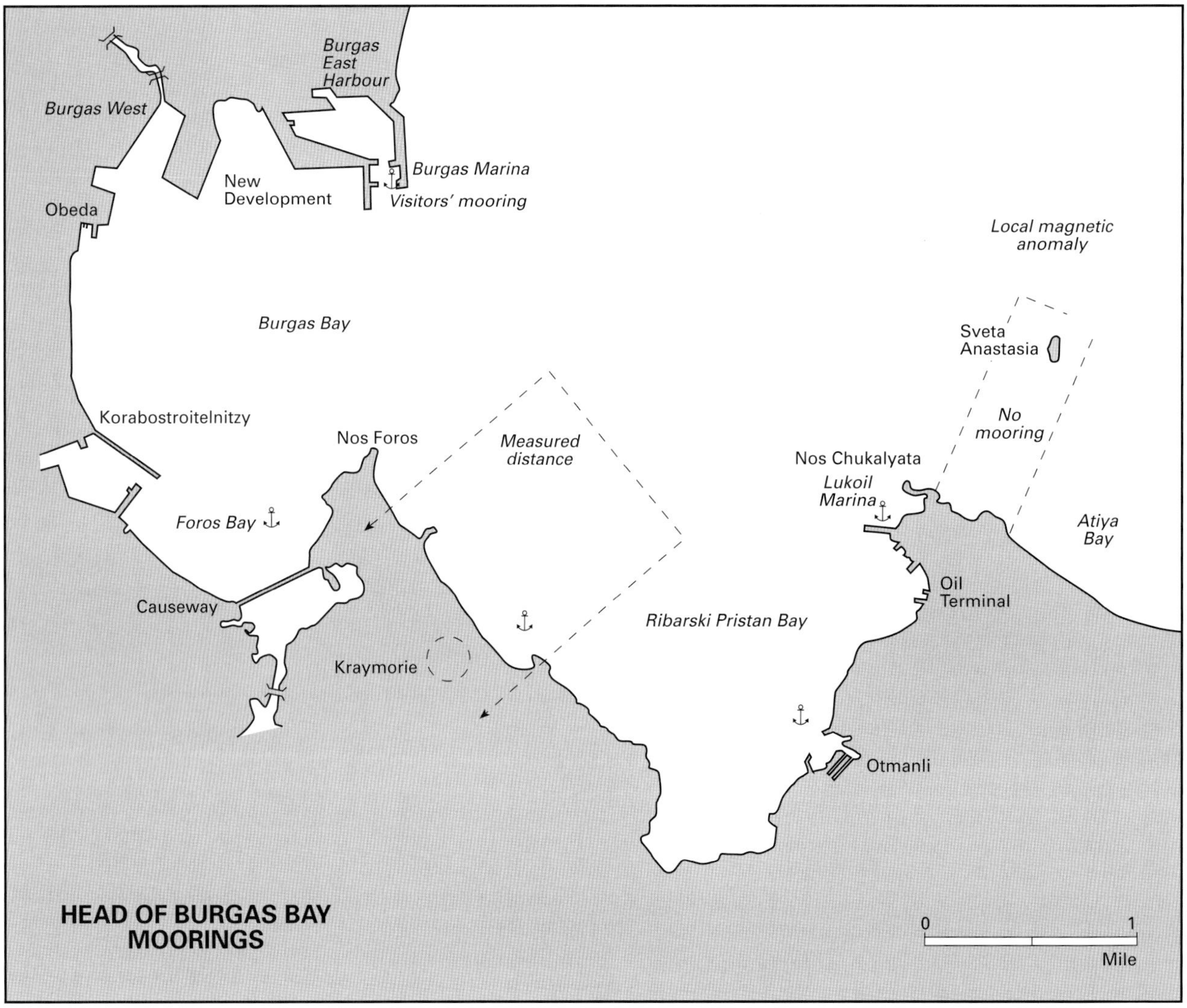

THE BLACK SEA

HEAD OF BURGAS BAY MOORINGS

the landward side of this shore is rolling countryside with trees and fields. To the east and north the scenery changes dramatically with the major port of Burgas.

HARBOURS AND MOORINGS

Chernomorets 42°26´.97N 27°38´.39E

When approaching from the north, Chernomorets is in front of the highest hill in the area, Bakurluka, which has a tower on top.

No electricity exists except at the side with the floating bar, but here it is shallow. Water is limited to supplies from cafés and kiosks. The harbour is full of open fishing boats, and the only place to moor is at the end of the jetty, or there is one other place at the end of the jetty on the outside of the jetty. Situated in a beautiful bay, Chernomorets is popular with tourists as can be seen by the overcrowded beach. There are bars and kiosks on the beach and ample restaurants and shops in the town, which is all low-rise red-roofed buildings.

Sveta Anastasia Island 42°28´.03N 27°33´.14E

At the end of the jetty the depth is 2.2m. It is a pleasant place for a day trip, but not suitable for an overnight stop. There is water at the café, where the guys serving you give the impression that they have not left the island since the days it was a prison.

The island is 8,500sq.m of volcanic rock, eroded by the sea and weather. The old church is well preserved and the other building on the island was used as a

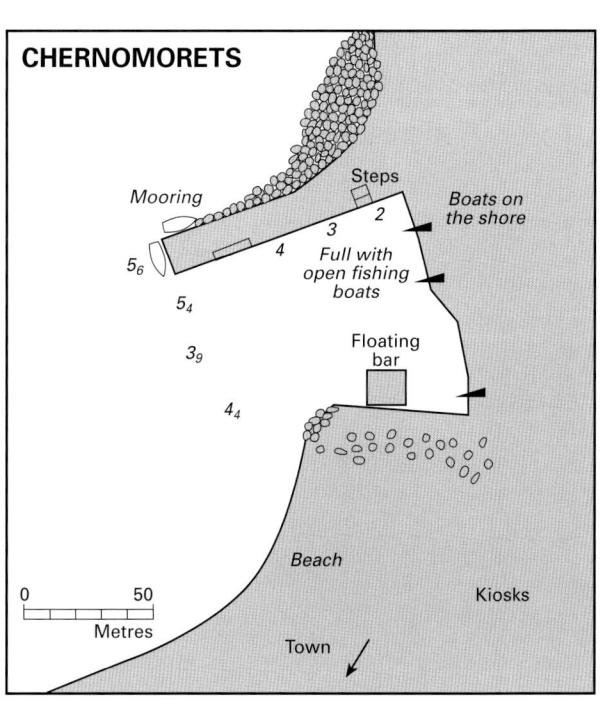

prison for left-wing revolutionaries from 1923 to 1925, and again for anti-fascists from 1943 to 1944. In Communist times the island was known as Island Bolshovik. Cultural and historical remains are displayed in the church.

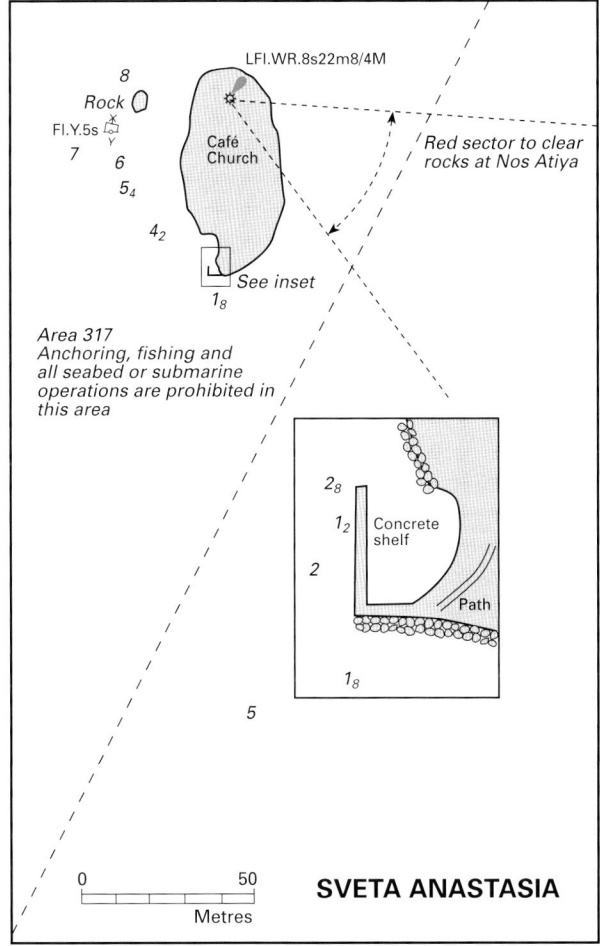

Otmanli 42°26′.3N 27°31′.6E

Most of the small local boats are moored in the well-sheltered canals at the back of the harbour, leaving space at the entrance for visitors. The approach is straightforward from the north, with the only hazards being the mussel farm and fixed fishing nets. The jetty at the south side has subsided in places, limiting the area where mooring can take place, but the jetties provide good shelter. There are no facilities on the jetties.

Two cables to the north of the harbour entrance are two black and white beacons that flash red. This is the lead line for the dredged channel for tankers entering Lukoil oil terminal. On both of our visits here the restaurant at the head of the north jetty was closed, and the one in the ship called *Violet* beyond the south pier would not get a mention in a good café guide. Take your own packed lunch! Local knowledge is needed to find the shops, since they could be located in a garage with no shopfront or advertising. The only clue could be crates of empty beer bottles in the garden.

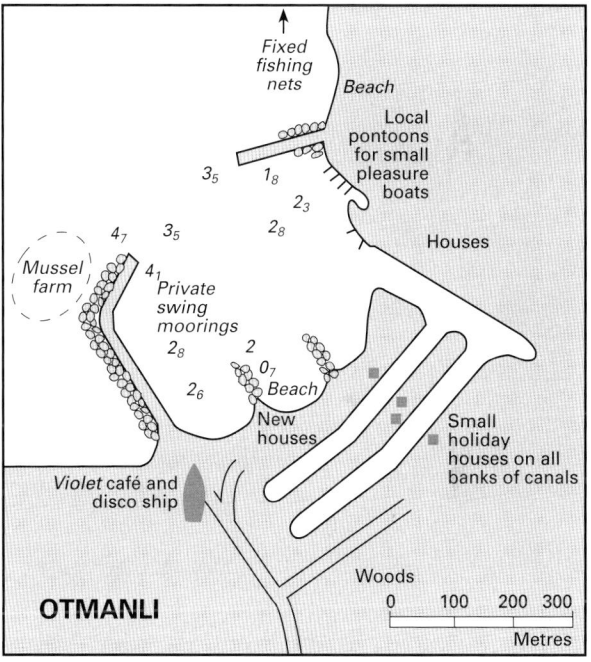

Lukoil Marina

This is for employees of the Lukoil Company. The moorings that are exposed to the westerlies are excellent, but do not expect a friendly welcome. Water and electricity are available. The company's local refinery handles about 7 million tonnes of oil per year, but when we visited this marina they had no diesel. The marina has its own mobile crane.

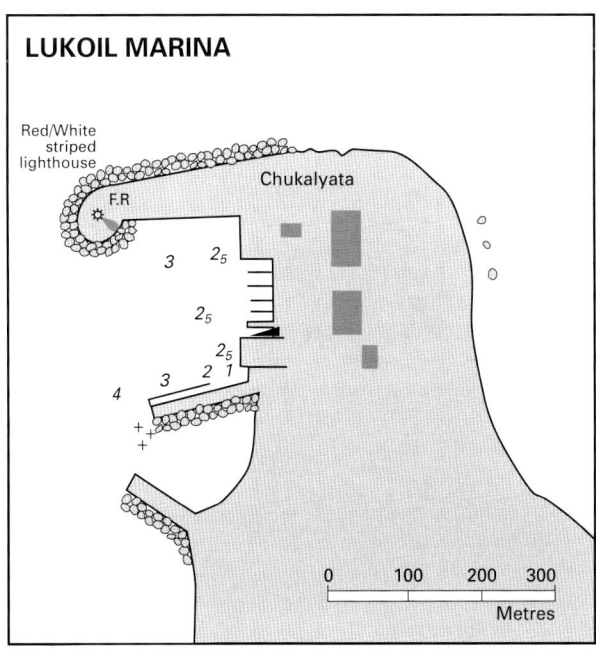

The story of Lubo from Otmanli

Lubo from Otmanli tells the story of 27 October 1987 when, amongst other fishermen, there were many from Otmanli. Two sons were in their small open fishing boat. The father on a larger fishing boat with a radio had heard a weather forecast, warning of a storm heading in their direction. The father saw the sons in the small fishing boat and warned them and the others. Only the sons heeded the warning and headed back to Otmanli. Later that day 27 Bulgarian fishermen lost their lives in the storm. 27 die, on 27 October, so 27 is not a good number in Otmanli. The following week the sons were again at sea in their open fishing boat and they caught a fish that weighed about 300kg.

Although we never experienced bad weather, we have come back to the Black Sea and seen seaweed and flotsam high on the beaches, and been told that the causeway to Old Nessebar has been covered by the sea, and other anecdotal stories such as this.

The sea must be treated with respect; also heed any weather warning.

THE BLACK SEA

Otmanli. Residents' fishing nets

From the town north towards the cape at Chukalyata is 6,000 decacres of thick forest park utilised for hunting and recreation. To the west in the village of Kraymorie, once called Kafka, is the old fortress of Pirgos.

Ribarski Pristan Bay (Zaliv) 42°26´.5N 27°31´.0E

This is reputed to be the best natural anchorage between the Bosporus and the River Danube. There is good holding in mud and it is sheltered from all winds.

Foros Bay (Zaliv) 42°27´.15N 27°28´.29E

This is also a good sheltered bay for an anchorage. At the head of the bay is a causeway. The western end has two small cranes, and local boats were moored in the corner. We approached and moored at the causeway with no problems (we recorded a depth of 2.9m where the chart stated 1.4m). However, on departure near to our arrival route we grounded several times in less than one metre where the chart indicated 2.3 and 2.9 metres. The depths on the chart close into the causeway should be treated with suspicion.

On the west side of the bay to the north of the causeway is the Poda Nature Conservation Area supporting 15 species of amphibians and reptiles, 259 bird species and 18 mammal species.

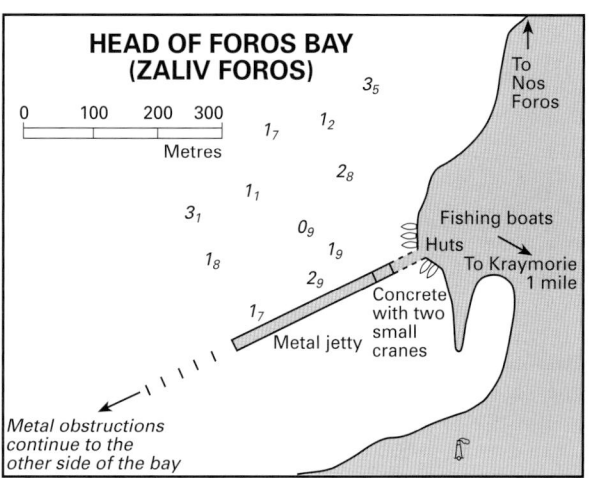

Korabostroitelnitzy 42°27´.6N 27°27´.3E

This is a commercial port and shipbuilding yard. Leisure boats should keep well clear of it.

Burgas West 42°29´.1N 27°27´.2E

This is a commercial harbour handling mainly metals. On one occasion when we had a Bulgarian on board we required fuel, and he said this was the most convenient place in the locality to get a taxi and go to a garage with the cans to get fuel. This harbour can take boats with a draught up to 11m. It has a RoRo and cold storage facilities.

In the bay between here and Burgas East there is major development work in 2006 for a new port.

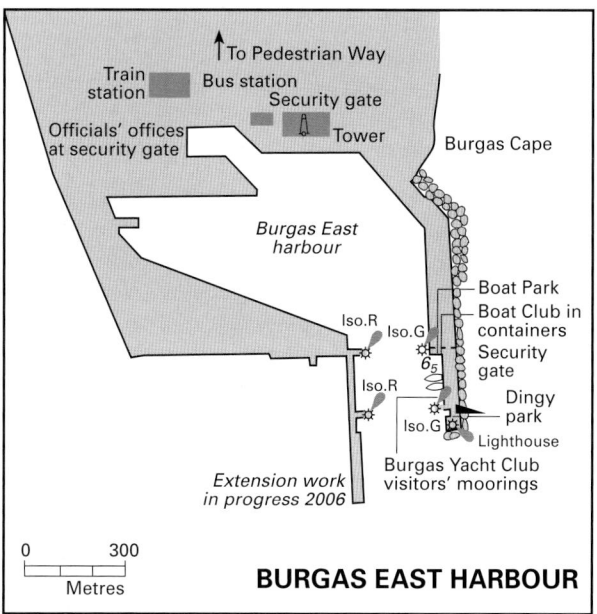

Burgas East

Here they handle bulk cargos such as coal, sugar, ores, ammonium nitrate and there are facilities for oil and chemicals for boats with a draught up to 10m.

Burgas Marina 42°29´.5N 27°29´.0E

On the approach to Port Burgas your arrival should be announced on the radio on Ch 16 or 11 one hour before your estimated time of arrival. The marina is located at the end of the mole on the east breakwater, and is a port of entry. The visitors' moorings have a depth of 6m alongside. All facilities can be arranged: electricity, water, repairs, cranes, lift out, short or long-term stay on shore. There is security on the mole at the end used by the boat club, and at the entrance to the docks, you have to pass down an alleyway between customs on one side and border police on the other side. When the officials check you into the country they take your passport and it is kept in the office on the right hand side as you leave the docks. This is returned to you if you want to go into town, and again surrendered when you return to the docks. Theoretically the security is tight and it should be a good place to leave a boat. What we couldn't work out is that if you have to surrender a passport or have an identity card to get into the docks, and then get the security official to unlock the gate to get into the marina section, how can there be local people at the end of the mole fishing?

Burgas Marina   *Burgas Marina*

The marina manager can be contacted ☎ +359 56 822302. The club use Ch 73.

Mooring charges   1 day   1 week   1 month
Euro
8m   2.95   17.18   68.06
10m   3.68   21.47   73.63
Plus payment for any electricity used
Hard standing fees are half of the above

At present Burgas Yacht Club consists of a few containers. The most useful one has a fridge for a welcome cold beer on a hot day, and the other is a workshop with a lathe, vice, welding equipment, and other useful tools for repair jobs. With major development work being undertaken to increase the harbour size and available facilities, the club are optimistic about getting a new location, and a custom-built clubhouse with a restaurant, bar, jacuzzi, sauna, large workshop, and other facilities, possibly by 2009–10.

All the officials are located in the offices at the gatehouse, in the control tower, or in the first building on the right after you leave the gatehouse. The maritime administration can issue a temporary navigation certificate that permits you to visit all Bulgarian Black Sea ports. The cost is €20.

The mooring located at the harbour entrance gets the wash from all passing boats. The small workboats create more problems due to their speed than the large commercial vessels that enter the harbour slowly.

There are three ship chandlers in town which have the franchise for many international marine suppliers.

Varbanov Yacht Centre, Kraimore Industrial Area,
PO Box 144, Burgas 8000
☎ 089-66-890-80
Email mail@yachtbg.com
www.yachtbg.com
(This is located on the road to Kraimore.)

Vistmar Ltd, 51 Chataldsa Street, 8000 Burgas
☎ +359-56-843676
Email office@vistmarltd.com
(This is located on the main road going west out of town.)

Marina Stores, 30 Kiril and Metodi Street, 8000 Burgas
☎ +359-56-821715, *mobile* 0887 688 889

On leaving the docks, after the square and across the main road you arrive at the pedestrian way. Here and in the small side streets you are spoilt for choice of restaurants and all other facilities. The train station and bus station are located near the gates to the docks.

The largest vessel ever to enter Burgas harbour was MV *Integra Duckling* with a load of 134,000 tonnes of iron ore from Brazil, so it is big enough for super-yachts.

Burgas can trace its history to Thracian times, in about the 4th century BC. It took until 1306 before the name Burgas was used, when it became the administrative centre of the Burgas District. The oldest record is as Purgos, the Greek equivalent of the Latin word Burgos in a poem from the Byzantine poet Manuil Fill and the medieval village on the same site was known as Pyrgos, meaning 'the tower'. The Greeks utilised the port and it has been a seaport and home to many civilisations ever since.

This was the Roman town of Deultum, later changed to Develt, and was founded by Emperor Vespasian as a colony for his military veterans. The present city covers the towns of Kastiacion, Skafida and Rossokastron. The liberation from the Turks came on the 6 February 1878, and the following day the Municipality was declared and ever since the town has prospered. The railway from Sofia arrived in 1890, and a year later the town plan laid out the future for the residential, administrative, educational and ecclesiastical buildings. Prince Ferdinand signed the decree on 1 December 1894 for the construction of the present Port Burgas, and from the official opening on 18 May 1903 the major harbour improvements speeded up the process to make Burgas a rival to Varna. The municipality of Burgas now has 15,000 registered companies and claims to have the lowest unemployment in the country at 4.3% It is an important centre for commerce, transport, industry, education, and tourism.

Five museums are all located to the east of the pedestrian way, as are the main churches, and the sea garden park. The Nature and Science Museum houses 1,200 species of insects and reptiles, and more than 140 species of fish. For those looking for culture there are the philharmonic, drama theatre, puppet theatre, cinemas and opera house. Burgas is known as a town of festivals. It also has sports halls and the most modern stadium in Bulgaria.

Located between Burgas Lake and Atanasovo Lake are ancient saltpans which are still in production today. The salt lakes are a protected area which is important for bird migration. Mandrensko Lake to the south is used for rowing and is also an ornithological reserve.

PASSAGE NOTES
North Burgas Bay (Burgas to Nos Eminie)

From Burgas harbour north the view is of cranes from the harbour and the multi-storey apartment blocks. This gives way to the sandy strip which separates Atanasovsko Lake from the sea, before changing to low-lying coast with fields. After turning east the land starts to rise and become wooded. In this corner up to a mile offshore there are several isolated rocks, the most easterly about a mile southeast of Nos Lakhna.

South of Pomorie peninsula there is danger at Stavro Banka, Krustova Banka, and Pomoriyski Rif (Pomorie Reef). The light on the east mole of Burgas harbour is obscured over these hazards. Stavro Banka is marked by an east cardinal buoy Q(3)10s Whis. Krustova Bank is 1.2 miles southwest of the end of Pomorie peninsula with no marking. East of Pomorie peninsula a black and yellow lighthouse Q(3)10s 12m6M locates Pomoriyski Rif. It is our experience that the reef extends much further south than shown on the chart. Beware of clearing this too far south since you will reach Krustova Banka, which has 3 separate rocks.

Going north Pomorski Lake is fringed by a narrow sand spit, and the main feature is the red and white vertical striped Pomorie brandy and wine factory. There is a fairly good anchorage in the corner of this bay, and the places to avoid are the shoal of about 2–3 cables off Nos Ravdenski and the fixed fishing nets (see Ravda Bay). Between the developments of Ravda and Nessebar, Nos Akrotiriya shoals out a good distance, and also has a fixed net and mussel farm at the point. The low coastal plain continues with hills in the background. To round Nessebar peninsula you must be well offshore to avoid the rocks. A local saying is that you must always see the spire on the tallest church from sea level. If you don't see this you are too far inshore. At night the red sector of the light at the end of Nessebar harbour (Fl.RG.8s10m2M) covers this sector. The natural beauty of the west coast of Neseburski Zaliv (Nessebar Bay) has been obliterated by the concrete of uncontrolled development at Sluncev Bryag (Sunny Beach).

The northern coast is more natural and the wooded hills rise, here developing into stratified cliffs along to Nos Eminie. One major hazard in this bay is fixed nets well offshore and not connected to the shore at 42°41´.91N 27°48´.12E. The bay has good mooring, but is exposed to easterly winds. Nos Eminie can be taken close inshore as it does not shoal much.

HARBOURS AND MOORINGS

Sarafovo 42°33´.4N 27°31´.4E
Tucked in the northwest corner of Burgas Bay, this is a series of seven groynes which are used for shelter by local fishermen. About a mile south is Soka reef and a few other shallows between here and the groynes. There are a few shops and cafés in the town up the hill, and just the odd kiosk on the coast. It is a laid-back town with small family hotels and restaurants. On the opposite side of the main road is Burgas airport.

Pomorie 42°33´.12N 27°38´.4E
Burgas port control CH 11, border police Ch 8

Pomorie is located at the end of a 3.5km long peninsula and a prominent landmark is the hotel in the shape of a boat that juts out to sea. Between the outside harbour wall and 2 red buoys the depth is

Pomorie Reef lighthouse

Akrotiria Nos fixed nets

Sarafovo

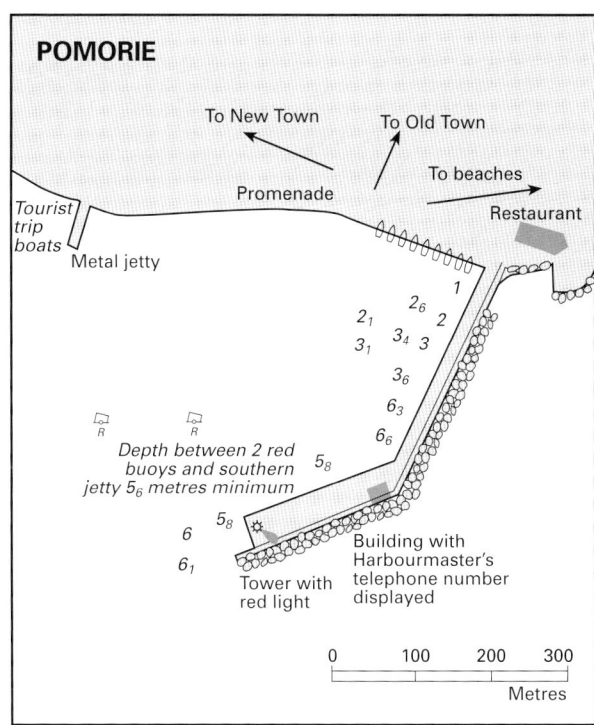

maintained at 5.6m. On the other wall the depth gradually decreases to the shore. There is plenty of space in the harbour. The harbourmaster is very helpful and knowledgeable, speaks good English, and looks forward to welcoming foreign visitors. Electricity and water can be provided. Fuel deliveries can be made by tanker truck. Small repairs can be arranged. The harbourmaster is located in the building on the harbour. If he is not there he can be contacted on the telephone number on the door. He said the charge could be 3.6 leva (€1.8), or nothing (he charged nothing). The metal lattice tower at the end of the jetty carries radio, satellite, and telephone masts and has a permanent red light. Halfway down the mast are floodlights for the harbour, but they are not on all night. The border police may visit on your arrival.

Pomorie Boat Club
Located under the Inter hotel, the harbour is only partially constructed and was up for sale in 2005.

The Thracians regarded this area as a sacred place because of the curative waters in the salty lake in the hinterland. The mud is reputed to be amongst the best in the world, and today the modern sanatorium treats diseases of the bones, muscles, skin, liver and heart, as well as breathing and gynaecological problems. These curative muds were of benefit to the Greeks, who called the place Anhialo. The wetland complex is still important today, and is a partially protected area, with a saltworks museum. The salt, fishing and mining made it an important centre in Roman times, when it also minted its own coins. Inland at Paleokastro (Old Fortress) there are still some remains from this era.

In the 8th century a Barbarian invasion destroyed Anhialo but the Byzantium Empress Irena rebuilt it. Like other towns in the area it regularly changed hands until Amadeus of Savoy and his Knights conquered it and sold it to Byzantium. It was a chief supplier of salt, wine and brandy to the Ottoman Empire, who ruled it from 1453 until the liberation. At this time it was more important in the region than Burgas. Fire ruined most of the town in 1906, and only a few old houses at the east end of the peninsula survive from before this time. Two old churches survive and the Transfiguration

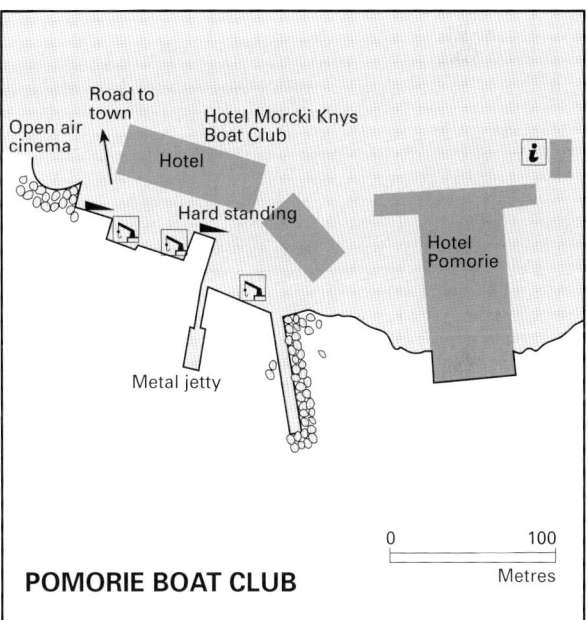

Pomorie small fishing harbour

Church has a valuable wood carved iconostasis. A domed tomb mausoleum from the 3–4th century is the final resting place of a high-ranking Thracian and is located in the area of Kouhata Mogila.

Pomorie is famous for its vineyards, fruit and vegetable growing, and is home to the large Black Sea Gold wine and brandy production unit. (It is possible to tour the factory.) The streets near the harbour have a romantic charm and are a nice place to relax in the open-air cafés and restaurants.

Pomorie small harbours

To the east of the main harbours is a small harbour for local fishing boats. West of Pomorie there are some groynes which shelter some local pleasure boats.

Ravda Bay

A mooring can be picked up in the corner of Ravda Bay near Akheloy harbour. Along this coast are many moles where shelter can be obtained. Most have a good depth, and local boats use some of them.

Akheloy 42°38′.20N 27°39′.08E

There is a small harbour used by fishing boats and local pleasure boats, but without facilities. There are fixed nets projecting from the harbour, but once round them the entry is straightforward. A launching ramp is situated in the corner.

Akheloy, previously known as Anchialus, is based at the mouth of the River Akheloy. It was near here in 917 that Tsar Simeon I defeated the army of Byzantine Emperor Lion Foka, which made Bulgaria the most powerful Slav state in Europe. About a decade ago there was a large storm and flood in this area. This exposed artifacts such as a tiara, coins, rings etc from this era.

A large complex is being built at the head of the harbour. The village is about 1km inland.

Along the coast of Ravda Bay are many hazards. The following are the GPS positions we passed them at:
42°38′.04N 27°39′.09E Floating nets with only small buoys
42°37′.94N 27°40′.28E Fixed nets on poles
42°38′.10N 27°40′.64E Nos Ravdenski Rocks 2–3 cables offshore only covered by 1.5m of water
42°38′.61N 27°41′.43E Nets on poles
42°38′.99N 27°41′.72E Groyne with a small jetty on it
42°38′.69N 27°42′.18E Rock with less than 1m over it
42°38′.39N 27°42′.55E Nets on poles and further offshore a mussel farm which is marked with 2 orange buoys with radar reflectors.

National Sports Academy Marina (NSA Marina)

42°38′.85N 27°42′.31E at the end of the jetty. Ch 77

The mooring is sheltered in all but south to southwesterly winds. The jetty is welded out of railway track, has a platform round it at a convenient height, and 6 sets of steps leading down to it. On approach there is a shallow rocky area around 42°38′.69N 27°42′.18E where we measured depths of less than 1m. The other hazard on approach from the east is the fixed nets and mussel farm off the head of Nos Akrotiriya. This is marked with 2 orange buoys with radar reflectors.

There are no facilities apart from the café up the hill where you can sit and watch young people playing team games on the beach. There is a small shop with minimum provisions near the junction of the small road that goes up the hill and the main road.

Ravda was the site for youth summer camps in Communist times. There is now a building boom, with new hotels and holiday apartments under construction, but the beach at NSA is still relatively undiscovered. When the jetty is being used for training the facilities cannot be used, but at other times the staff welcome visitors. The jetty had a major renovation in 2005 and in 2006 electricity and water were installed on the jetty with a nominal charge for use.

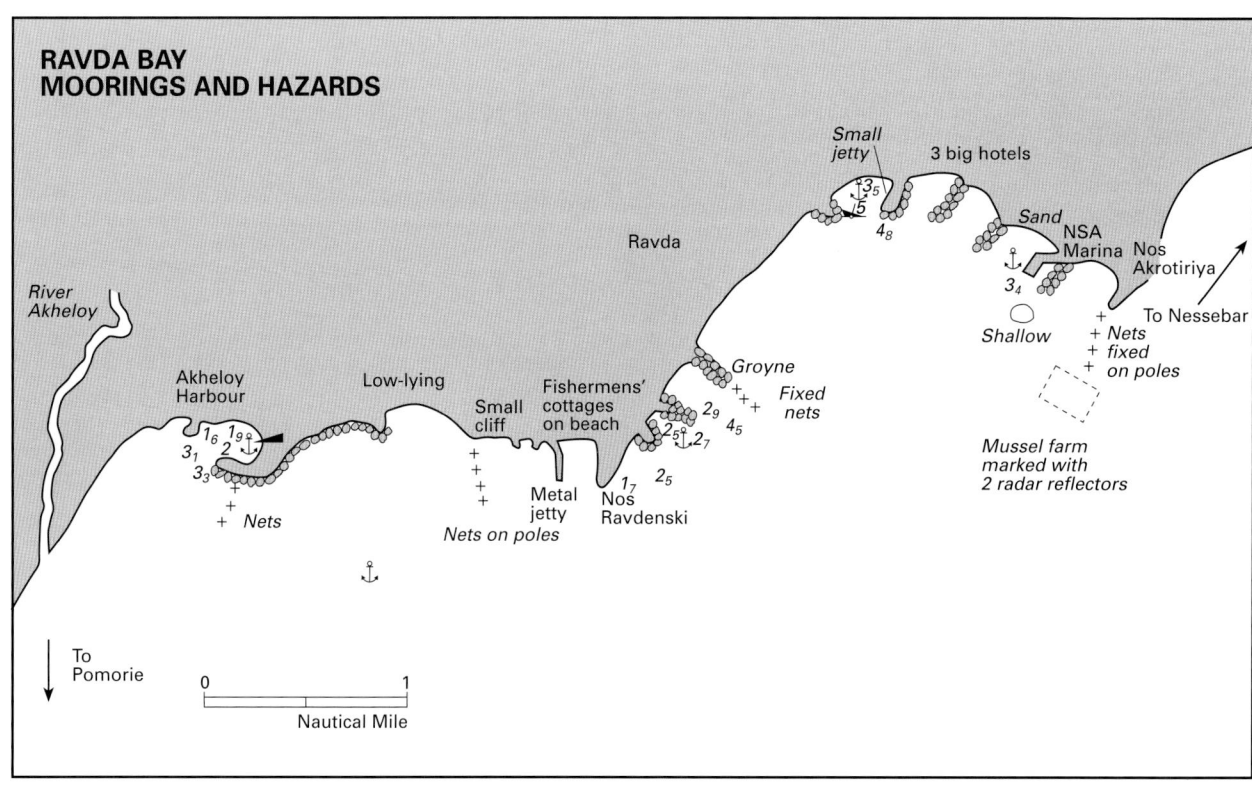

BURGAS BAY

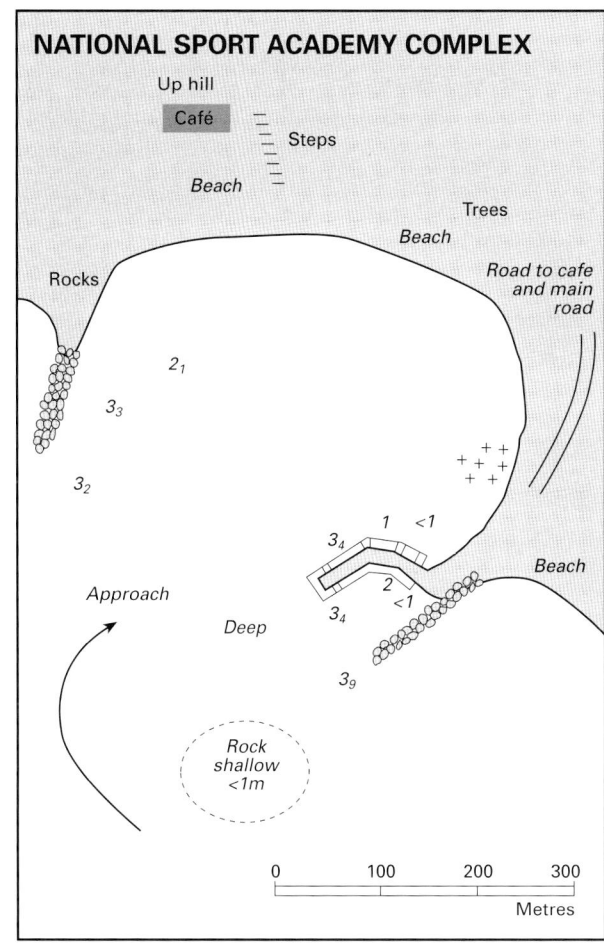

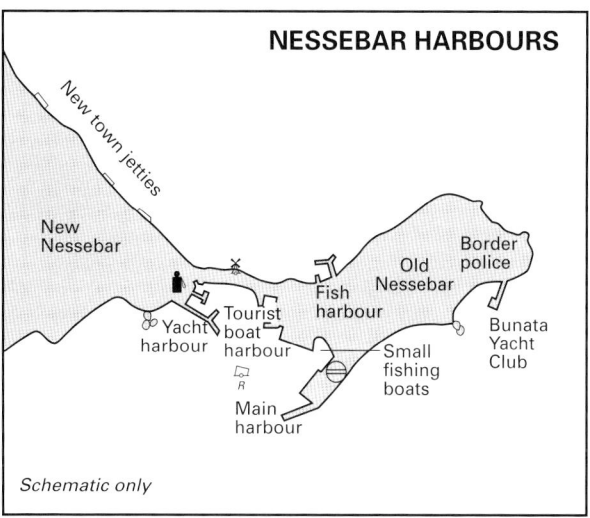

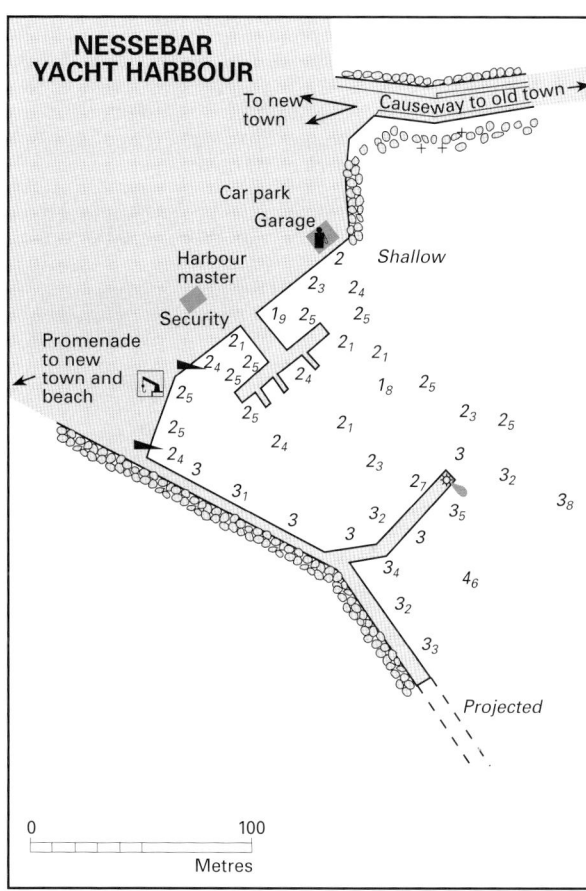

Nessebar Yacht Harbour

42°39'.48N 27°43'.51E at the mooring

There is a wide entrance in front of the causeway that joins old and new Nessebar, and the moorings for recreational craft are at the west end of the causeway. This is the most popular harbour in Bulgaria and is therefore very crowded. Space for a visiting boat may be found at the end of the jetty, but this is exposed. The border police request visitors report to them on arrival and departure on Ch 8.

All the facilities one would require are found in old and new Nessebar. Electricity and water are located all round the harbour. The toilet is at the garage. Fuel is

Nessebar church spire

Nessebar harbours

CRUISING BULGARIA AND ROMANIA 41

available at the garage in the corner. At all Nessebar harbours gas can be delivered. The harbourmaster and security have an office at the gate. The friendly staff, with limited resources are constantly trying to make improvements to the area and the harbour was privatised at the end of 2005 (with the prospect of major development and higher prices).

Boat size in sq metres		30–35	45–56
Price in € per day	1 day	0.36	0.38
	31 days	0.34	0.36
	61 days	0.32	0.34
	91 days	0.30	0.20
	365 days	0.20	0.20

plus VAT at 20%, water and electricity

Nessebar Main Harbour 42°39′.27N 27°43′.75E at the end of the jetty

This is very suitable for super-yachts and is considered the cruise liner terminal for Port Burgas. Water and electricity are available and a visit from a fuel tanker truck can be arranged. The red buoy in the centre of the wide entrance is the port marker for this harbour.

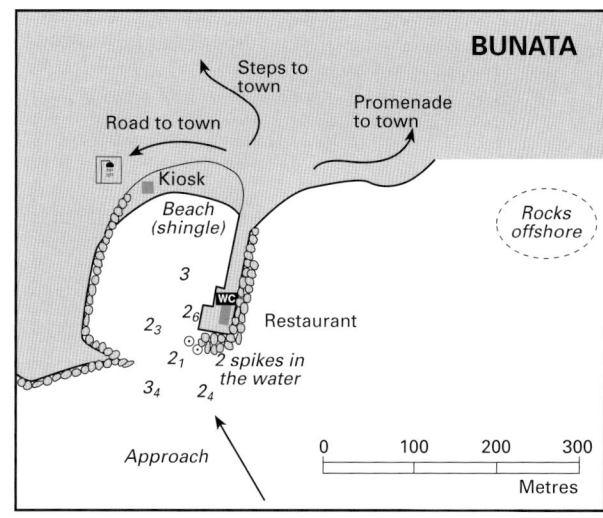

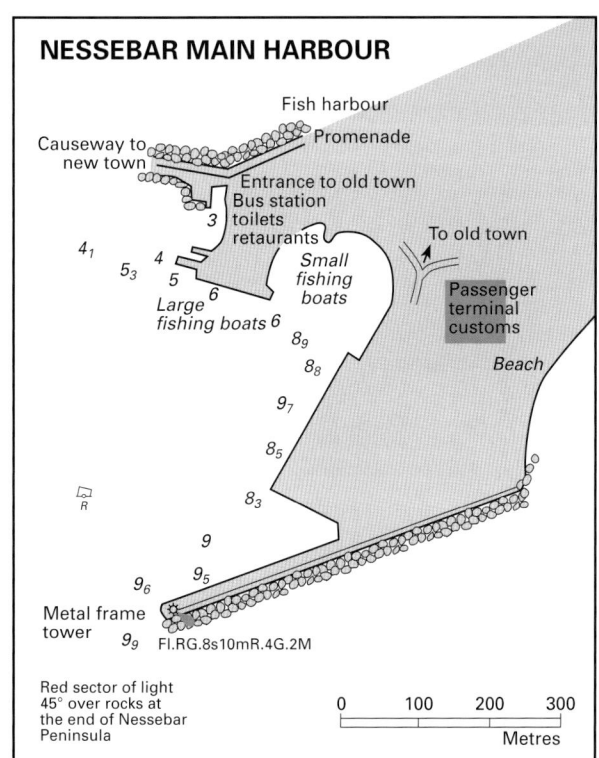

Bunata Yacht Club 42°39′.49N 27°44′.37E

Dangers on approach are the rocks at the end of Nessebar peninsula, and at the harbour entrance there are 2 metal spikes. Water is obtained from the toilets that are adjacent to the restaurant. Mooring is free if you use the bar and restaurant facilities on the jetty. There are many good restaurants up the hill in the old town. This is the quietest mooring in Nessebar; the owner speaks German and welcomes visiting boats.

Nessebar fish harbour 42°39′.656N 27° 43′.907E at the cross on end of pier

Water and electricity are available and a tanker truck can deliver fuel (☎ 089 992 22 55 or 089 832 95 50 to arrange a fuel delivery). The tequila bar gives permission for customers to tie alongside, but it is very noisy. Between here and the new town jetties the fixed nets that start near the centre of the causeway extend well out to sea. On the shore is a large selection of restaurants.

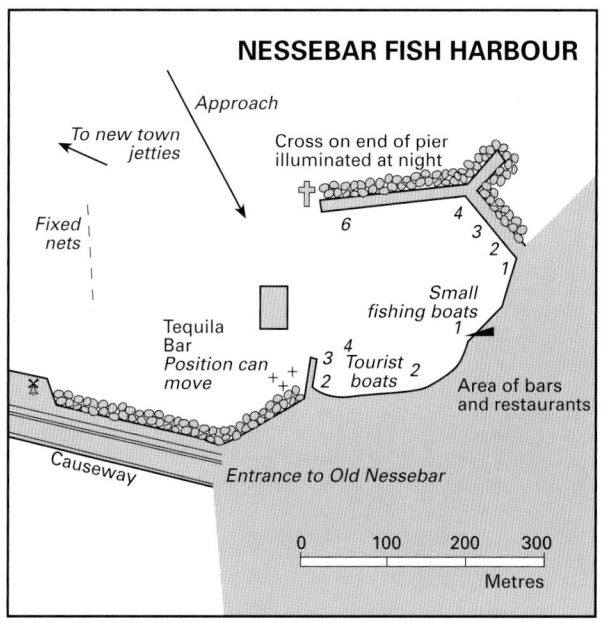

Nessebar main harbour

Nessbar. Local fishing boats in the corner of the main harbour

Nessebar new town jetty in a winter storm

Nessebar New Town
There are three jetties against the promenade on the north side of New Nessebar. They are all newish, with good bollards and wooden fronts.
1. 42°39′.68N 27°43′.48E 48m long
2. 42°39′.77N 27°43′.36E 78m long
3. 42°39′.92N 27°43′.17E 31m long

Between jetties 2 and 3 are rocks just breaking the surface about 100m offshore; the approach would have to be directly from the north and not along the shore.

These are convenient for visiting Nessebar New Town, which, is mostly located up the hill. There are many shops, five of which are hardware stores with a remarkable selection of spares suitable for a boat. Although it does not have the history of Old Nessebar it still attracts a lot of tourists, and has all the facilities they require. From here it is a short walk to the start of Sunny Beach.

Thracian fishermen in the second millennium BC called the town Menabryia (Town of Mena). The Greeks renamed it Messembria and the Slavs called it Nessebar in the 11th century. Connected to the mainland only by a causeway, the town of Old Nessebar had a good defensive position. Fortifications were built and extended by the Greeks, Romans, Byzantium, and Turks. About 680 it became an episcopal centre and in the next two centuries a Byzantine naval base. Kran Krum conquered the town in 812, but in 864 Boris I gave the possession to Byzantium but it was captured again by King Simeon. Bulgarians and Byzantines ruled the town during the second Bulgarian Kingdom, until Alexander I made it one of the most important towns in the Bulgarian state.

Amadeus of Savoy and his Knights captured Nessebar in 1366 and gave it to the Byzantines, but the Turks captured it in 1371. During all these changes it remained important for shipbuilding and the export of wood and corn. After liberation from the Turks it became a fishing port.

The town was designated an architectural and archaeological reserve in 1956, and it was included in the world register of historic sites in 1983. Nessebar has many layers of culture and remains of fortress walls, amphitheatre, aqueduct, Greek, Roman and medieval roads, Turkish bath and windmill are still available to be seen today. Typical Black Sea houses from the 16–19th century (two storeys with the wooden upper storey jutting out) line the narrow cobbled streets. Many of the old houses are now used as museums, restaurants, gift shops, pubs and art galleries. However, Old Nessebar is most famous for its 41 churches. Many of them were built in the Byzantine period (5–6th century) and the Middle Ages (10–14th century).

Nesebărski Zaliv (Nessebar Bay)
The east side is taken up with the hotels of Slunchev Bryag (Sunny Beach). The north coast has smaller resorts. A mooring can be had in this bay, but in the corner between Sunny Beach and St Vlas there are fixed nets.

Slunchev Bryag (Sunny Beach)
This is the largest of the Bulgarian Black Sea resorts. The original plan was for 20sq.m of green area per hotel bed, but now it is less than one. At one stage looking at the coast from the sea, there were so many cranes it gave the impression of approaching a major port. There are some small jetties but they are in constant use by the tourist trip boats and if you go too

Sunny Beach

Main jetty at Sveti Vlas

far inshore some of the local operators can get a bit grumpy. (It is a starting point for many organised tourist trips.) There are many facilities and all types of entertainment and it can offer a lively nightlife.

St Vlas	42°42'.46N 27°45'.49E	1.3m
Robinson	42°42'.09N 27°48'.73E	1.9m
Elenite (Deer)	42°42'.18N 27°49'.18E	1.9m

In these three locations are metal jetties. The depths at the end are specified. They can be used by the tourist boats but there are swimmers in the vicinity of all of them.

Sveti Vlas 42°42'N 27°46'E

This major new marina with six piers of pontoons having a frontage of 300m opened early in 2006. It is equipped with all the latest facilities, including a ship chandler and repair facilities. However, to use it even as a lunch stop you are charged for 24 hours. The cost is 70 stotinki/m² per day.

The Thracian tribe Larisi founded the town in the 2nd century BC and called it Larisa. It got its present name from the patron saint of cattle breeders and merchants. The Turks renamed it Manastir due to the location of five monasteries in the area. After the reunification of Bulgaria in 1886 the town changed its name back to Sveti (Saint) Vlas.

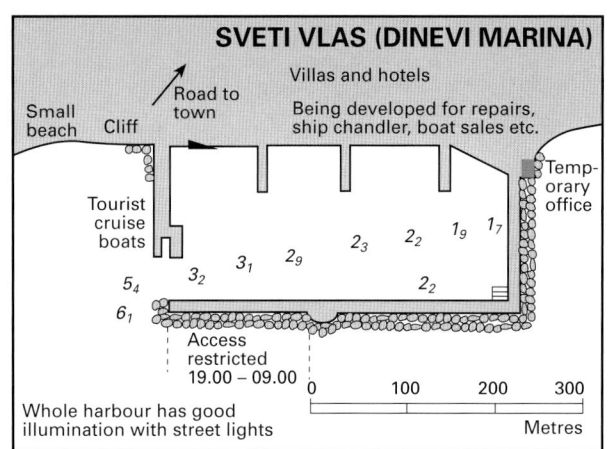

Nos Emenie

This is at the end of the Balkan mountain range, and is reputed to be Bulgaria's stormiest cape. The dumpy round lighthouse displays Fl.6s64m20M

Aemon was the ancient name for the Stara Planina mountain range. To the north of the cape is the town of Emona that was a medieval fort, but was previously also believed to be the birthplace of the Thracian King Rez.

Humble salt: white gold

Salt has always been an essential requirement for food seasoning, as a preservative, as well as for physiological requirements. Early civilisations understood the strategic importance of salt. It could be compared then with products such as gold, silk, or spices; today its importance could be compared to that of crude oil.

For thousands of years Pomorie on the west coast of the Black Sea has been using solar evaporation for the production of salt. The ancient Greeks probably did not have much commercial activity in salt production, but the Romans treated salt gardens as an agricultural activity. Vast quantities of salt were required for their empire, and salt trade routes were established. Salt production continued in the Middle Ages when the method of successive evaporation was developed, and the technique for production is basically the same today. A feature of the production at Pomorie is that there is almost no mechanisation, making it intensive manual work. Although it is essential to put in a presence to reap several harvests in a season, salt farmers usually have a second occupation relating to agriculture or construction.

Conservation of the saline wetlands sustains the local economy and introduces new activities such as ecotourism, the observation of flora and fauna, but principally birdwatching. Another diverse activity is exploiting the muds and minerals from the salty lakes for therapeutic treatments. This gives a contribution to the preservation of the traditional know-how of salt production and safeguards the cultural heritage.

'A salter works somewhere between the earth and the sea. A salter is a mix of gardener, seaman, magician and they produce a unique sea-garden cultural landscape.'

Nos Emenie to the Romanian border

Charts
Admiralty
2230   Constanța to Kefken Adasi
2285   Varna and approaches
2283   Maslem Nos to Nos Kaliakra
Turkish
10A   Western Black Sea
17   Mis Kinbun to Nos Kaliakra
18   Nos Kaliakra to Istanbul Boğazi

PASSAGE NOTES
Nos Emenie to Nos Galata (Varna Bay)

Nos Emenie cliff has a small stone lighthouse Fl.6s64m20M at the point. The Stara Planina mountains terminate here, producing steep stratified cliffs that fall away into the sea. They gradually decrease in height and become wooded until there is a break in the cliff at Obzor, where the Dvoynitsa River flows into the sea. Byala harbour is tucked in the bay before Nos Sveti Atanas and is the only harbour on this stretch of the coast. On top of the cliff at Nos Sveti Atanas there is another small stone tower lighthouse (Oc.R.7s38m12M) with a metal structure on top.

North from Byala the grey cliffs give way to long sandy beaches surrounded by hills with scrub and trees and continue until just north of the River Kamchiya. Intruding in this is Cherni Nos at 42°56′N 27°54′E where a local magnetic anomaly is reported, and there is a wreck about half a mile offshore. The only other prominent feature on this stretch of coast is a high metal jetty at 42°57′.66N 27°54′.07E and this has 2 metal structures offshore.

At the mouth of River Kamchiya (43°01′.4N) there is silting up to three-quarters of a mile offshore. The light here may no longer be functioning. Cliffs covered with woods stretch to Nos Galata where, in the northern sector, are some sandy bays that are popular with the locals. There is a prohibited entry area for about half a mile offshore from 43°03′.8N where there is a metal jetty to 43°06′.5N Gas pipelines come ashore here and just to the north.

Before Nos Galata, with light Fl(3)15s62m25M, the chart indicates a measured distance of 3703m, marked by 2 pairs of 2 towers. This cape which is showing signs of erosion can be taken close inshore to enter Varna Bay.

Nos Emenie

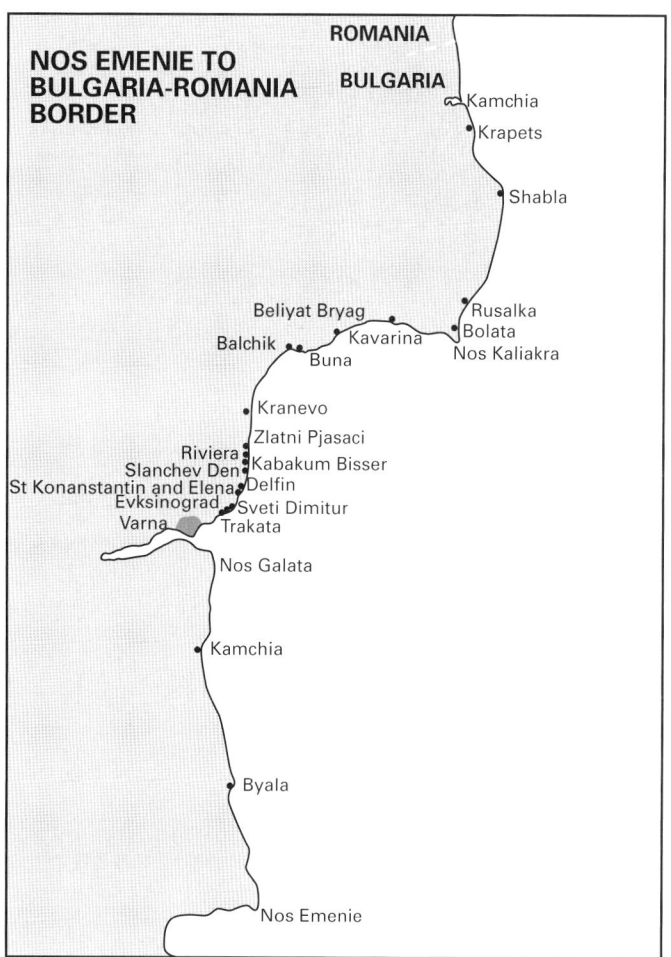

HARBOURS AND MOORINGS

Byala 42°51′.2N 27°53′.7E
The harbour is to the south of Nos Sveti Atanas, but the town is seen from the sea to the north of the cape. There are no hazards on approach. The hazards of Byala are the shallow silted entrance, which between our two visits had changed position and depth considerably. Once round the bar there is a good depth

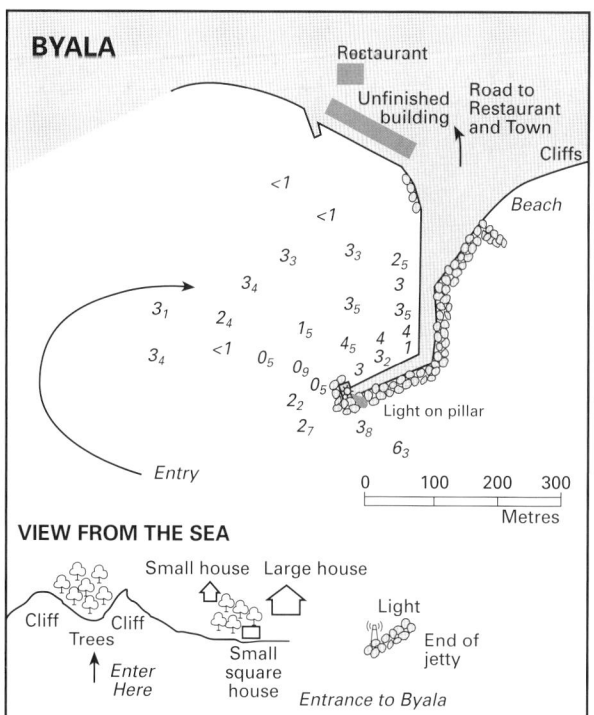

Byala

inside. The local fishing boats were entering well to the west of the harbour.

Everywhere down the jetty side are lots of stray ropes, which are not being used as moorings. Once moored, this is compensated for by the friendly staff at the restaurant, and friendly police. There is a tap at the jetty but no electricity. The border police visit on arrival. The best restaurant is the one at the head of the harbour.

Our first visit here was a fiasco. There was only a tight space between two fishing boats and we decided to nose in bow-first. The stern anchor was dropped, and when we looked up there were already two border police standing on the harbour. When they shouted at us we suspended the operation and the wind caught us and the bilge keel caught on a rope. We pulled ourselves back and freed it. Gradually we eased our way into the mooring, and threw the bow rope to the police, who very helpfully secured it, then checked the passports and the crew list and made some notes. Before departing they pointed to the restaurant at the head of the harbour and said it is good. We took a walk up the hill and through the vineyards into the village, which is a few miles inland.

On our way back, a police car with three police stopped and they told us to get into the car. They advised us that Varna border police has said we had to move to Burgas. We advised them that we didn't think it was prudent to sail in the dark and that we had not yet managed to follow their advice and visit the restaurant. They had a discussion on the radio with Varna, who then said we could stay, and leave early in the morning. The police then drove us to the restaurant. Halfway through the meal the friendly police arrived again. Varna border police had changed their mind and we had to move. We advised that it was even more unsafe to move now since we had had a drink and hadn't finished the meal they recommended. Varna police agreed we could finish the meal.

The police drove us back to the boat and said we could stay in the harbour if we moored 25m away from the jetty. Just as we were moving away the radio burst into life. Varna again, with new instructions, that we could stay the night after all. In the morning three border police arrived and the clearance was done very quickly. The boat was pulled back on the anchor rope but again we caught on a rope that we could not get clear of. After half an hour the police got into a rowing boat and cut the offending rope. Once on our way, we decided to keep further away from the jetty since on entry the depth near the jetty was just over one metre. Nearer the centre of the harbour mouth it is even shallower and we grounded in less than a metre of water.

Byala is located in the neighbourhood of the ancient Greek fortress of Aspro, founded in the 3rd century BC. It was a border town between the Bulgarian Principality and Eastern Rumelija before the reunification of Bulgaria in 1885. In the town is an ethnographic museum and a rural house displaying traditional items and customs.

Kamchia

The nature reserve straddles both sides of the river for 4–5km and inland for 20–25km. The woodland in this strip is known as Longoza and was formed after the glacial period when the ground became covered with dense vegetation. It is the best example of this type of tropical forest vegetation in Europe and is jungle-like, with creepers and roots penetrating the water. It can only be seen by taking a boat trip up the river through the nature reserve, where there are 40 types of trees and bushes, 40 types of fish, and 156 different bird species, including the rare black stork. (A modern complex was built here in Communist times.)

Varna East 43°11′.5N 27°55′.3E

This is a port of entry and authorities should be contacted on Ch 16. Visiting yachts should tie up at the yacht club just inside the entrance to Varna east dock. Someone from the yacht club will probably meet you and direct you to a mooring; otherwise tie up at the end and search for an official. They will notify the harbour authorities, customs and border police who may visit the boat to carry out the formalities. Stay with the boat until they arrive.

There are good secure moorings on the east pier that has a gate at the end guarded by club staff. On the west pier there is no gate or security. Water and electricity are available and there are toilets and showers in the yacht club that is located at the head of the moorings. Small repairs can be carried out in the club workshop. The club bar is shut on Monday and Tuesdays.

Club members can arrange for a fuel tanker to visit the boat, otherwise take a taxi and cans and visit the

Varna marina

NOS EMENIE TO THE ROMANIAN BORDER

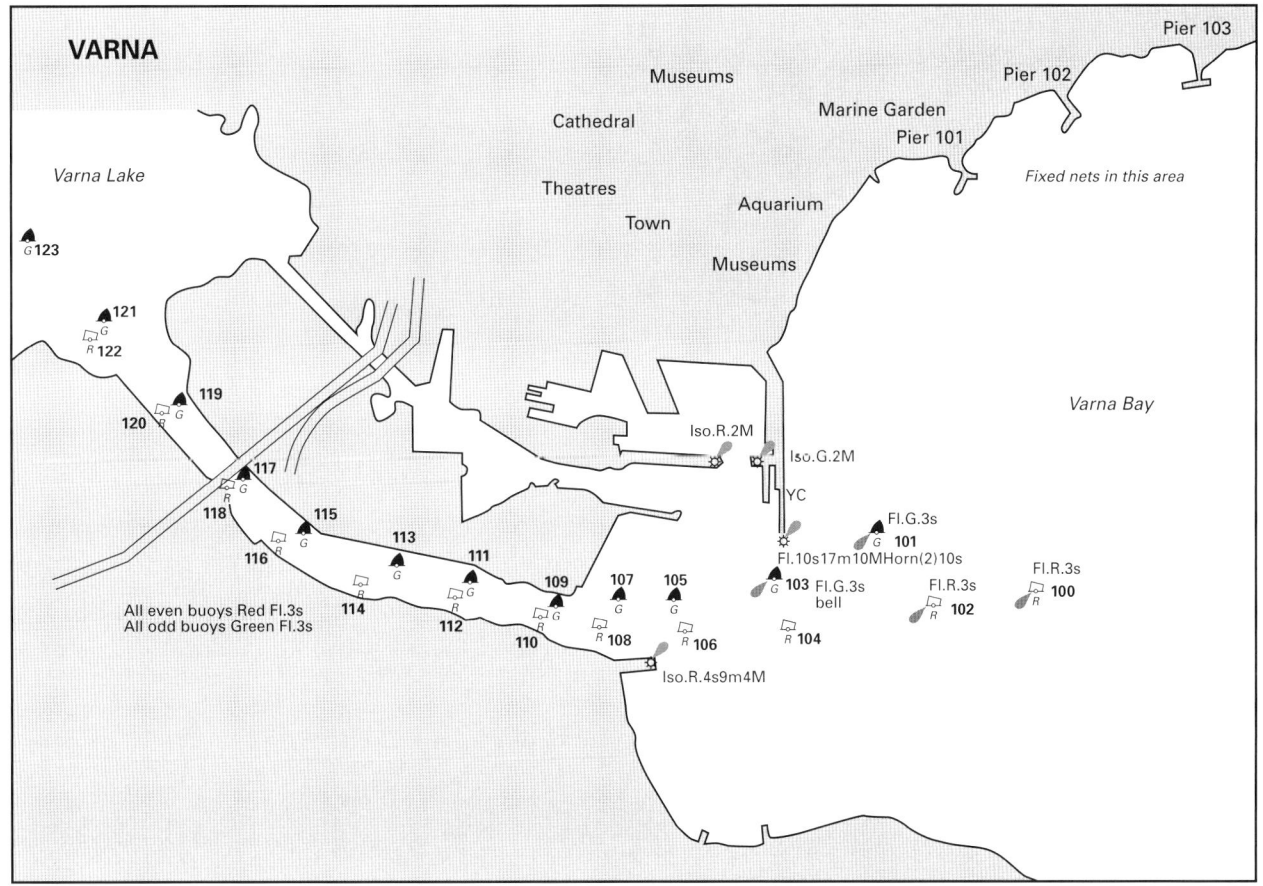

garage. There is a refuelling boat based in the commercial port for large quantities of fuel.

The cost is approximately €50 cents per metre per night (but will probably be increased), paid to the yacht club in leva. For an 8-metre boat for one year the cost is about €200. If this is the first port of entry the port harbourmaster gives you an invoice for US$25, which you must go to a bank to pay. The receipt from the bank must then be taken to the harbourmaster. We tried to pay this at the first bank we came to and they wanted $27 to do the transfer, making the total $52. If you go to the same bank as the port uses there is no transfer fee and you pay only $25.

Varna radio: all ship's calls are transmitted on Ch 26.

There is a ship chandler and Marina Store in the building behind the boat club (☎ 52 69 20 24, *email* imbg@lalizas.com, www.lalizas.com). Across the road from the entrance to the harbour is the other ship chandler. Transcommerce yacht shop, 27 Bul. Primorski ☎ 052 60 36 37 www.yachtshopbg.com.

At the passenger terminal is the bus stop for the number 48 bus that takes a meandering route but gets to the town centre. The restaurant behind the yacht club has a nice atmosphere and background music. There are other restaurants near the harbour entrance, but in town the choice is overwhelming.

Thracians inhabited the area in 4000BC. (From 280 graves on the north bank of Varna Lake 3,000 objects have been excavated, making these the oldest gold objects found in Europe.) It became an important port in 585BC when the Greek city of Odyssos was founded. It was a trade and agriculture centre minting its own coins, and was later conquered by the Romans.

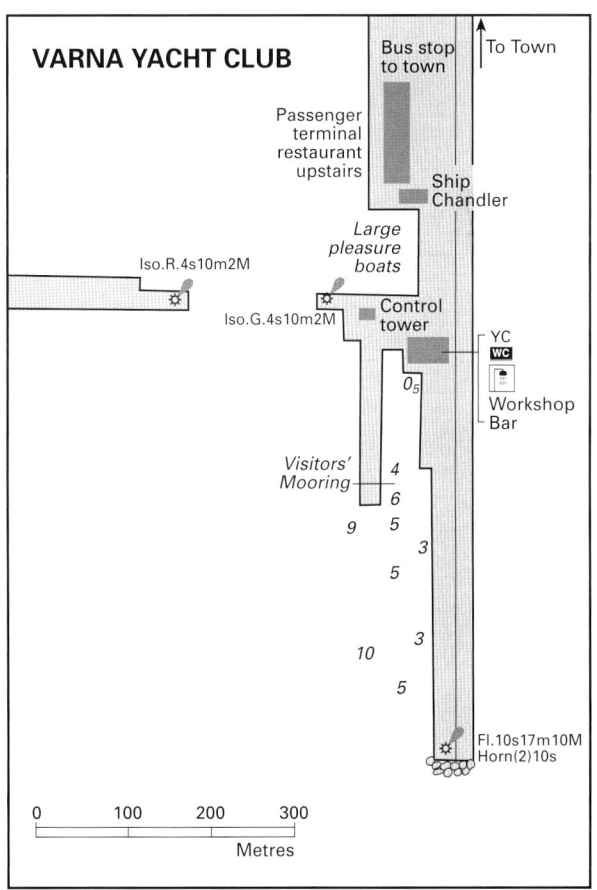

THE BLACK SEA

Varna channel

Varna harbour, a boat club on Varna Lake

In AD586 the Avars destroyed it. The Slavs then took over the area and gave it its present name of Varna (meaning Black One), and continued to develop the port. In the 8th century it was part of the first Bulgarian state and became a centre for the Christian faith. It was an important port in Byzantine times before a decline during the Turkish occupation; the Tartars plundered it in 1389. Varna was at one time a cholera-ridden Ottoman garrison town. Major General J R Hume of the British troops passing through here on their way to the Crimean war described the place as 'no paradise', 'a wretched place with very few shops'. (He would not recognise it today.)

In the Russo-Turkish war of 1828–9 the town was occupied by the Russians, but returned as agreed in the Odrin Peace Treaty, until the Russian army again liberated it in 1878. During the 19th century the town prospered and there were incomers of various nationalities. The railway link with Russe in 1886 connected Varna with the Danube. Today the port typically handles 18 million tonnes of cargo per year.

Outside the capital Sofia, Varna has the largest collection of museums in Bulgaria. The archaeological museum is based in the former girls' high school: on display are probably the oldest examples of gold jewellery, from 6,000 years ago, which were found in a

Varna folk festival

Varna Navy Museum

Varna Cathedral

Chalcolithic near Varna. This supports the theory that metalworking techniques were independently developed in Bulgaria. There is a magnificent collection from the Thracian, Greek, and Roman periods.

The National Revival Museum is in the former Church of Archangel Michael. In the Ethnographic Museum is a display of goods from occupations as diverse as fishermen and shepherds. Costumes from various regions of Bulgaria are displayed.

The City Historical Museum portrays the historical life of the city, and is located in the oldest surviving house in Varna built in 1851 for the Belgian Consulate. It was later used as a hotel and a prison. Located in Varna's first public hospital is the Medical History Museum. This gives some macabre displays including 10th-century skulls with holes drilled in them, as well as a collection of old instruments.

The Marine Gardens, which were laid out at the end of the 19th century, are based on Austrian Baroque Palace Gardens. This is the largest public park in the Balkans and located in it is the Naval Museum. It displays the *Druzki* 'Intrepid' which, by sinking the Turkish cruiser *Hamidie* off Cape Kaliakra in 1912, achieved Bulgaria's only naval victory. The Aquarium is in a building with a unique façade, covered in ivy, and along with the Natural History Museum, Zoo and Dolphinarium, exhibits the flora and fauna of the Black Sea.

The ruins of Eastern Europe's largest Roman *thermae* dating from the 2nd–3rd century AD are located in Varna, as are mosaics from the same era. In the northwest of the town is the Park of Fighting Friendship where, mounted on top of a Thracian Tumulus, is a monument to commemorate the battle of Varna where 30,000 crusaders led by King Ladislaus III Jagiello were defeated in 1444 by advancing Turks.

The Cathedral of the Assumption, built in 1884–6 was modelled on the Cathedral at Saint Petersburg and is second in importance only to the Alexander Nevsky cathedral in Sofia, designed by the master-builder Gencho Kunev in honour of the liberation from the Turks. In front of this is the old clock tower from 1880.

The Church of the Holy Virgin dates from 1602 and displays valuable icons dating back to 1646. Another important venue is the Palace of Sport and Culture. The Temple of Wine is a museum shop where, in the cellar, is the base of one of the towers of the first stronghold of the antique town of Odesos, which was built over a Thracian settlement dating from the 4th century BC. It also stocks one of the best selections of malt whisky in the country.

There are many educational institutions, including four higher, giving the town a population with 20% students. This gives the town a lively nightlife, most of which is located to the south and east of the town centre. The entertainment is diverse, with cinemas, opera house, jazz clubs, discos, a puppet theatre, etc. A jazz festival and a film festival usually take place in August.

There are boat clubs under the Asparukhov Bridge and in Varna Lake, but foreign boats are not permitted to visit the bay.

PASSAGE NOTES
Varna to the Romanian Border

From Varna to Nos Sveti Georgi (light F.R.19m6M) there are many fixed nets. Going north there is a reasonably flat mountain range covered with woods, which becomes more undulating the further north it goes. The coastal plain opens out and there is a succession of summer tourist resorts until Zlatni Pjasaci (Golden Sands). Between 2 and 3 miles northeast of Nos Sveti Georgi and extending half a mile offshore is Monastery (or Chingani) reef. Depths of water over them are 0.9m to 1.2m, and the area for a further half-mile seaward is also shallow. You are recommended to stay 1.5 miles away from the coast here. From Monastery Reef to Balchik, about 11 miles to the northeast, the sand can shoal out from half to one mile offshore in places, giving depths of less than 4m and even less in some areas. Offshore from Rivera is a BYB Q(3)10s Whis which marks the extremity of a group of rocks and the shallow area.

After Golden Sands the beaches disappear and there are cliffs that continue until Kranevo. On the cliffs is the Nos Ekrene lighthouse (not operational) located at 43°19´.22N 28°03´.63E . There are 4 sets of fixed nets between 43°17´.92N and 43°18´.45N.

From Kranevo to Albena, with its distinctive triangular and wedge-shaped hotels, there are sandy beaches which give way to wooded hillside. These hills continue until Balchik, which is at the western extremity of the grey-white chalk cliffs. The end of Balchik pier is marked with a light (Fl.R.5.5s10m8M) and the west breakwater has a flashing white light. On either side of Balchik harbour are fixed nets. From here to Kavarna, there is only one small harbour for shelter.

Kavarna has a triangular chalk hill with a deep ravine. At the end of the pier is a light on a black metal pole. Between the harbour and Nos Kaliakra the high limestone cliffs turn red and have a sheer drop into the sea. On top of them are 9 prominent radio masts. From Kavarna to in front of the radio masts there were 3 sets of fixed nets and several areas of mussel farm with no markings. A trawler was also laying lengths of nets with almost no marking and leaving them to drift unattended. It would be wise to stay at least a mile offshore in this area.

Nos Kaliakra light is Fl.5s68m21M(0.7s light, 4.3s off) and the headland is fringed by a reef extending at least 1 cable offshore. Nos Kaliakra headland is a distinctive reddish crag up to 70m in height and jutting well out to sea. From here to Nos Shabla the cliffs retain their red colour before turning grey and gradually decreasing in height.

After the cape going north a local magnetic anomaly is reported. Offshore from Rusalka in the vicinity of 43°25´N are many rocks. The cliffs become a mixture of red and grey, and this is a desolate area with no buildings on the clifftops. About halfway between Nos Kaliakra and Nos Shabla headland is Kamen Bryag (Stone Coast). At Tyuleiovo there is a break in the cliff with a small natural harbour. From Tyuleiovo village to the north there are rugged grey cliffs with many caves, which then become low land before Nos Shabla. The Nos Shabla light is prominent on a red and white painted octagonal stone tower with Fl(3)20s36m17M.

North from Nos Shabla the cliffs give way to sandy beaches until south of Krapets where low cliffs have woods on top. The reef from Shabla to Krapets extends well offshore, and a wrecked boat has already found the rock less than a mile north of the lighthouse. We had one depth reading of 2.4m about a mile offshore.

North of Krapets the land is slightly elevated with a low plateau which is inclined to the sea, and further north this gives way to sand dunes rising to 18m and a width of 600m. This area of the coast is closed due to schemes to prevent erosion and is a protected area under a UNESCO reservation scheme. Half a mile offshore from Nos Kartalburun there is rock with 2.1m over it, and from here to the Bulgarian-Romanian border at 43°45´N 28°35´E up to one mile offshore the depths could be less than 3m.

HARBOURS AND MOORINGS

Trakata 43°13´.03N 27°58´.79E

This is a traditional fishing village with a hazard of fixed nets just inside the entrance. There are fixed nets on the outside of the harbour extending to 43°12´.87N 27°58´.89E It has minimal facilities but there is a restaurant where the small track leading down to the village meets the main road at the top of the hill.

Evksinograd 43°13´.03N 27°59´.22E

This is a good sheltered harbour with a light (F.R.5s) at the end of the jetty.

The palace, built for Prince Aleksander Battenberg the first royal sovereign in Bulgaria, started construction in 1886 and was reminiscent of a French

Trakata

Evksinograd

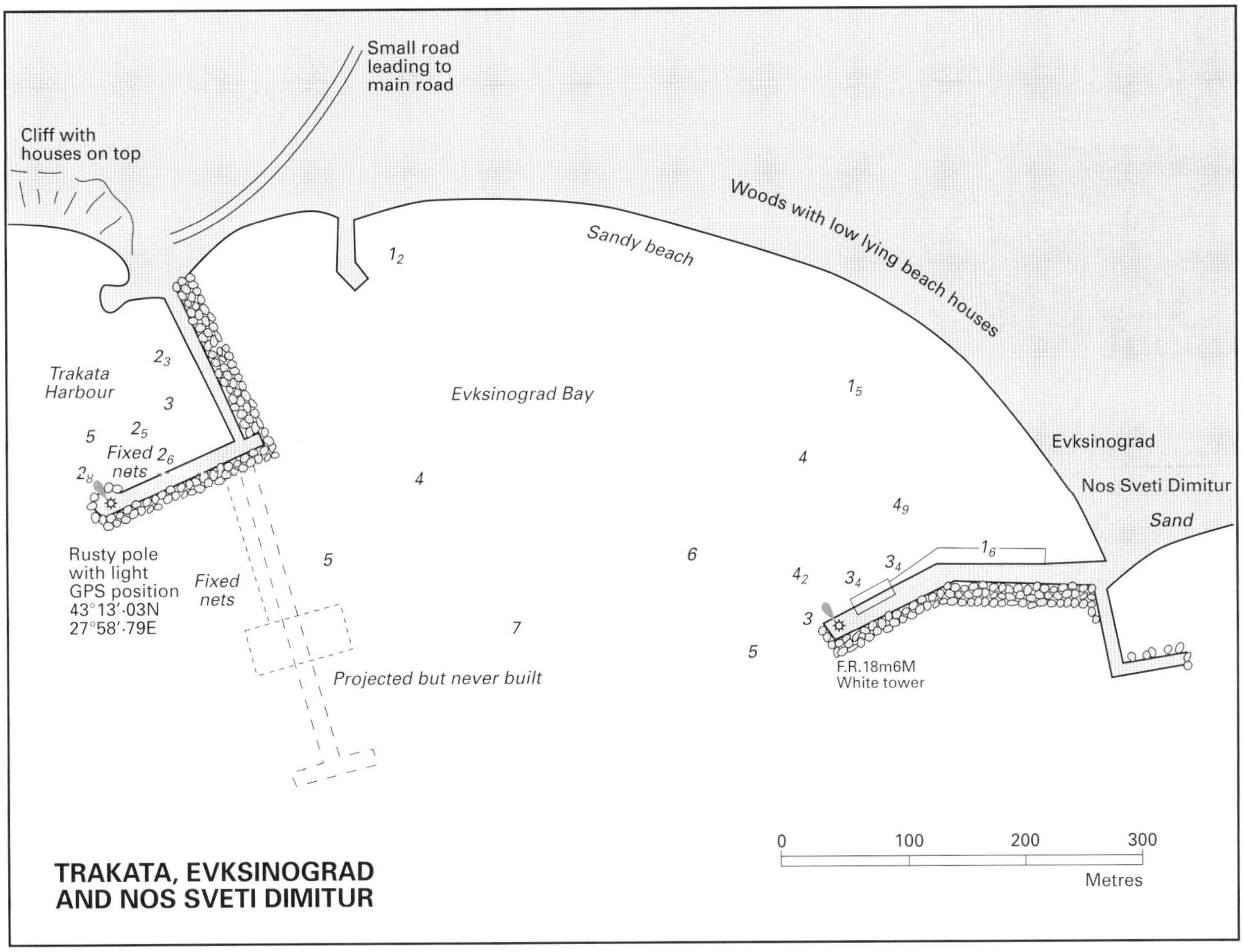

TRAKATA, EVKSINOGRAD AND NOS SVETI DIMITUR

18th-century palace. It was originally named Sandrovo from the Italian Alexander Sandro. The architects were the Viennese architects Rumpeil Meir and the Swiss architects H Meyer and N Lazarov. The prince's successor Prince Ferdinand renamed it Evksinograd and it was later used by Tsar Boris. Down by the seafront he had botanical gardens laid out, which included rare and exotic plants shrubs and herbs.

In 1821 the captain of a ship that capsized in a storm managed to get ashore here and escape into the harbour. He had a chapel built on the shore and dedicated it to St Demetrus. In Communist times it became the holiday home of the Politburo, who built themselves a luxury beach-complex complete with health clinic, sports hall and bowling alley. They had all their individual beach-houses connected by secret tunnels to the 'nerve centre' bunker. In the grounds are vineyards, whose grapes were used to produce superb wines and brandies that were only available to the Politburo. The present government still uses the place for holidays; when the government officials are in residence the harbour cannot be used.

Nos Sveti Dimitur 43°13′.1N 28°00′.2E at the entrance

This is almost attached to Evksinograd. There are good depths in all areas and no hazards. The whole area was deserted, with no boats or any signs of life. There are no facilities.

St Konstantin and St Elena (formerly Druzhba)
43°13′.42N 28°00′.70E

This is the name of the resort, but the marinas take on different names. Here and at other resorts major hazards are swimmers, airbeds, pedalo boats, and

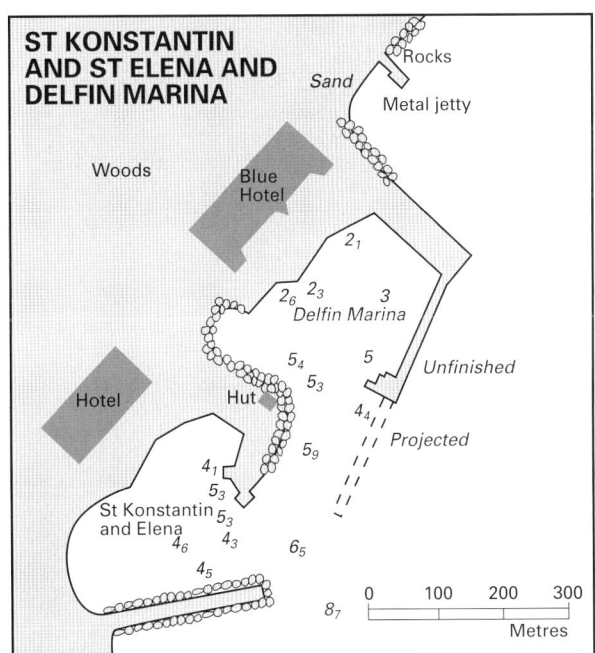

anything else that floats. This is the oldest resort on the Bulgarian Black Sea coast, with construction being started in 1908. Its original function was to house patients with tuberculosis but in 1955 the town, which had many trades union rest homes, was opened to western tourists. It is named after a local monastery that functioned at the beginning of the 18th century.

THE BLACK SEA

Delfin Marina

Delfin (Dolfin) Marina 43°13'.45N 28°00'.81E

A blue hotel with a lot of glass is the prominent marker for this harbour, which has been under construction for many years without any sign of progress. It still provides adequate shelter, and many tourists facilities are available. There are sandy beaches, and trees surround the hotels.

Slânchev Den (Sunny Day)
43°14'.85N 28°01'.79E at the entrance

There is a sand bar at the entrance, but it is deeper inside. Water and electricity can be made available at one side of the harbour, which is located just to the north of Sveti Konstantin and, with its own beach, is nicely nestled in oak and cypress woods. There is a new hotel being built in the corner of the harbour.

Kabakum Bisser Beach beside the resort of Pisatel
43°14'.85N 28°01'.78E

Care should be taken here not to take up a mooring which is used by tourist trip-boats. There are two hazards of fixed nets, one just outside the harbour and the other sometimes located just inside the entrance.

The hotels are on the beach and the houses are perched on the hillside and on the clifftop. Apart from the usual tourist facilities on the excellent beach, they advertise jet-skis, water-skis, surfing, banana-boat rides, and pedalo boats.

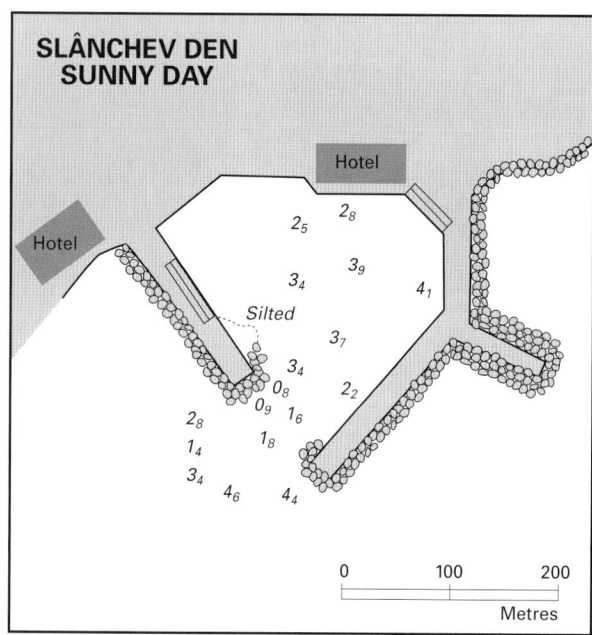

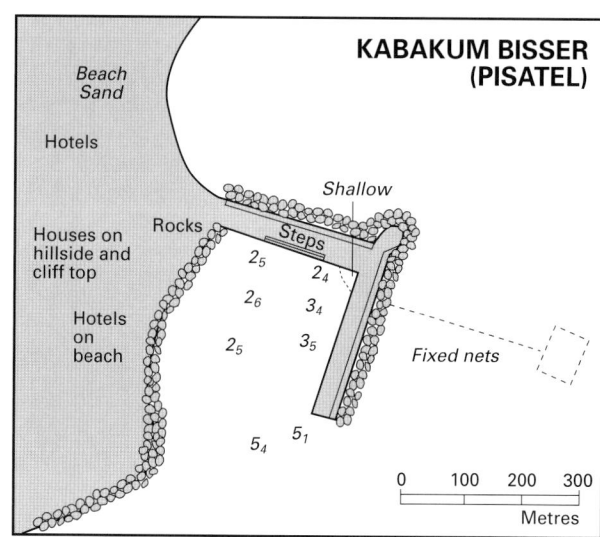

Slânchev Den

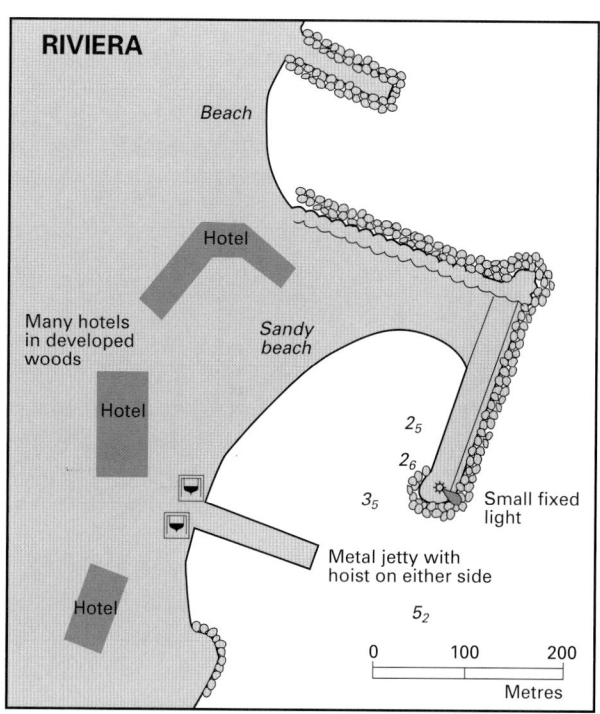

52 CRUISING BULGARIA AND ROMANIA

NOS EMENIE TO THE ROMANIAN BORDER

Riviera

Golden Sands

Riviera 43°16´.48N 28°02´.64E at the entrance
This is a compact little harbour with a small fixed light at the end of the breakwater. There is water and power on the pier. On the metal jetty there is a hoist for small boats. The sand is filling up the northern corner, leaving space for only 2 or 3 boats.

This is at the southern end of Golden Sands, but assumes a different name. It is located at the foot of a natural wooded hillside with centuries-old trees, and is much quieter and less busy than its northern neighbours. A big hotel is an ex-government residence but today offers balneological treatment and has other uses for the mineral springs. There are the usual tourist facilities of bars, discos and restaurants. From here to Golden Sands the hazards are, swimmers, airbeds and small fast powerboats.

Zlatni Pjasaci (Golden Sands) 41°18´.05N 28°03´.10E
The hazard on approach is Aladzha Monastery Rock which is marked with an E Card buoy at 43°16´.6N 28°04´.3E. Here is one of the few places with pontoon moorings that also has power and water. The building at the foot of the jetty houses the harbourmaster, showers, toilets and a small ship chandler. If what is required is not available the owners have their main shop in Varna and they may be able to supply from there. They may also assist in finding someone to do repairs. There is a garage a few metres behind this building for fuel supplies, and kiosks, bars and restaurants are all around for other supplies.

Halfway along the harbour wall on the seaward side are fixed nets. The mooring cost is approximately €1 per metre per night.

Located between the trees which surround the area in deciduous forest of oak, ash, hornbeam, maple, lime and other species, are 4km of safe, picturesque, golden sands and a concrete jungle of hotels. One oriental plane tree which is over 200 years old is 23m high and more than 4m in diameter. It is these woods that are the natural habitat for wild boar, squirrels, deer, turtles, tortoise, and many other species and which is being destroyed by mindless people with short-term ambitions for indiscriminate development.

This centre offers over 120 different kinds of medical services and various programmes such as mud treatment, anti-stress, arthritic, cosmetic and balneotherapy. There are plenty of tourist and sports facilities, bars, restaurants, discos, parasailing, water-skiing, scuba diving, 22 outdoor swimming pools, one indoor mineral water swimming pool, 22 tennis courts, a bowling alley, riding, and children's playgrounds.

To the northwest is an aquapark. About four kilometres from Golden Sands in the Hanchuka Forest is the Aladzha Monastery (which in Turkish means 'multi-coloured'). The caves were occupied in the Stone Age and the Dark Ages. A Christian church was founded about the 5th century and the monastery in about the 13th century. The faded remains of what were once brightly colored murals still exist in the first and second galleries, and the museum display includes some 5,000 year old items from the Chalcolithic Necropolis on the west side of Varna.

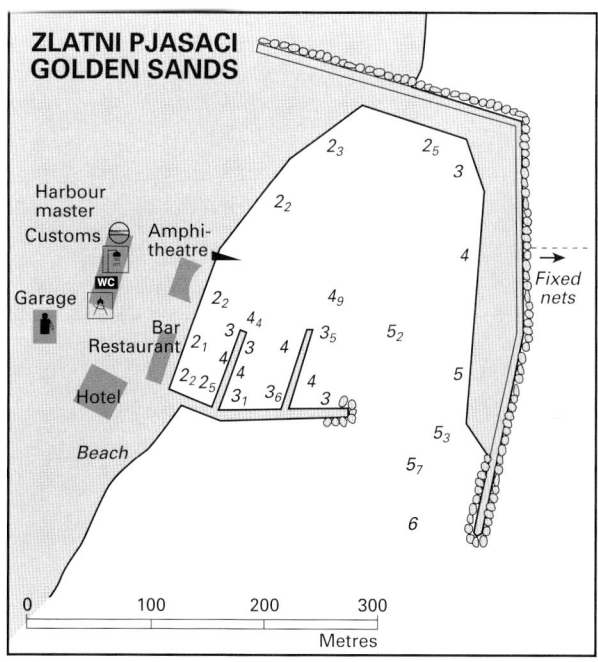

THE BLACK SEA

Kranevo (Cranevo) 43°19′.55N 22°04′.15E

There are three small harbours used by fishermen, but they will welcome foreign boats. They advised that it is best to moor in the most northerly harbour the deepest, as their huts overlook it and they can keep an eye on the boat. There are no facilities at the harbours, but Kranevo beach and town are about half a mile to the north where there are adequate facilities at less cost than in the neighbouring resorts. With its vast beach and curative mineral waters it is undergoing swift growth into a competitive tourist destination.

The Roman town of Ekrene was on the plateau just south of the present village and the harbour was called Kaneia. This could be a starting point for a visit to the Aladzha rock monastery. The present name of the town is taken from *Kraneia*, meaning fortress.

Kranevo

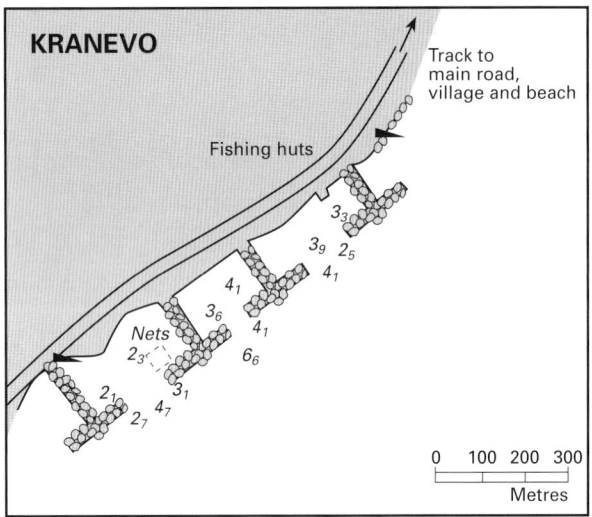

Balchik (Baltchik, Baltjik)
43°24′.20N 27°28′.09E

The light on the east breakwater (LFl.R.5.5s10m8M) is red (the opposite of the normal convention). The west breakwater light is flashing white. VHF is Ch 16. Yacht harbourmaster is Ch 6.

Balchik is responsible for the area between Albena and including Kavarna. The moorings for visiting boats are in the west side of the harbour. This is a port of entry and full customs and border facilities are available from Monday to Friday. Electricity and water on the harbour, the main tap being on the north-south pier. Water can be plumbed in on the other pier, at a cost, and if staying for a long time. In the harbourmaster's office at the foot of the west pier there are toilets and showers, but in 2006 this area was being developed and the location may change.

The cost for a 7m boat is about €4.5 per night plus the cost of electricity used. The cost for the same boat staying for a season is about €140, but is paid in leva. Local boat-owners are friendly and have their own contacts who can assist with repairs, and payment for their time is modest.

To refuel the boat ask the local boat-owners or the harbourmaster to arrange for a fuel tanker lorry to come to the pier. Future plans for the harbour are to utilize the natural mineral water, which comes out of the ground at 19°C, and provide bathing facilities near the foot of the pier. This water is not suitable for drinking, but another planned development is to distribute drinking water to a variety of locations around the harbour.

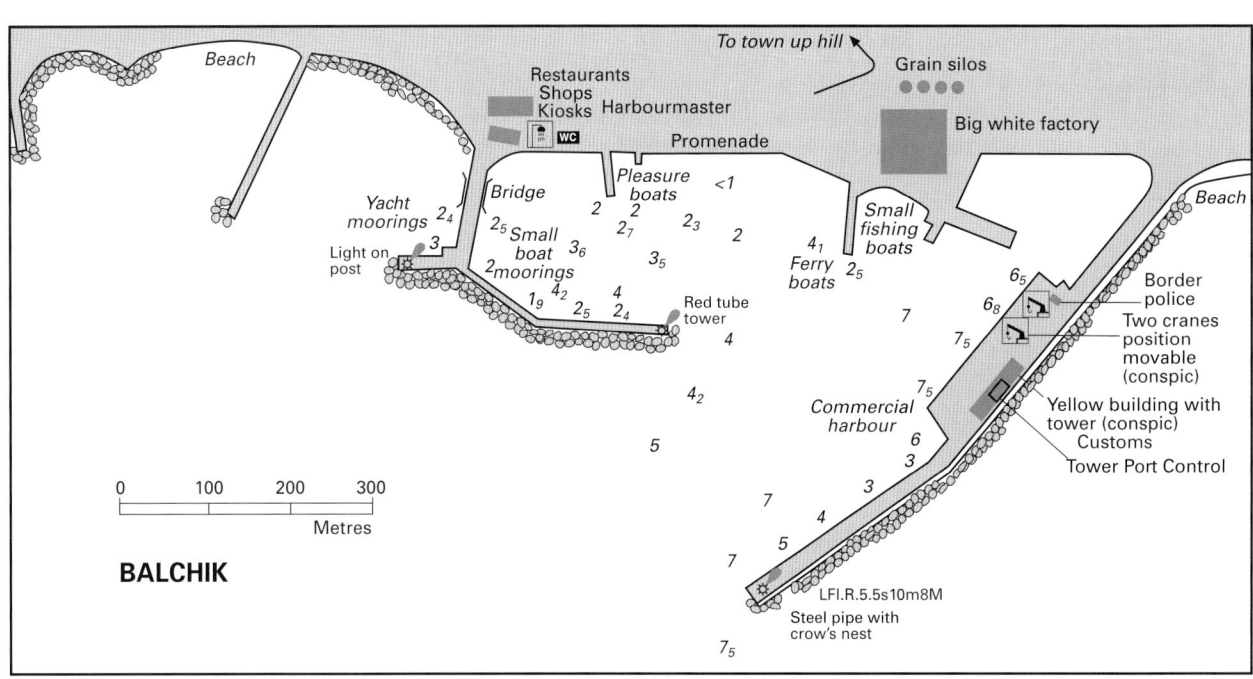

Balchik

Balchik Summer Palace

There is a good selection of restaurants close to the harbour along the waterfront and in other parts of town. The large grain silos on the shore are a good navigation landmark but are an eyesore. There are fixed nets on both sides of the harbour. The price for permission to sail is paid to the main harbourmaster and is 40.44 leva, about €20. The boat must be taken to the east harbour, where the customs and border police have their offices, to do the clearance before leaving.

The town was founded by Milesians in the 6th century BC when they called it Krounoi ('the springs' or 'source'): the Milesian colonists believed Aphrodite the Goddess of Beauty was born here out of the sea foam. The view of Balchik from the sea inspired Ovid to write 'O white stone town, I salute for thy unique beauty'. The history museum has a marble statue of Dionysos, the God of the vine and feasts. It was after this god that the town had its next name Dionysopolis, which also appeared on the coins that were minted here. The legend is that a wooden statue of the god was washed ashore in a storm, and this was the sign to change the name of the town and to erect a temple.

The Romans made the town an important fortress until Barbarians overran it. In the 6th century AD a tidal wave destroyed the town and the harbour silted up. The town was then rebuilt up the hill. Bulgars occupied the town for 400 years, building their own fortifications, which were destroyed by the Turks. A feudal lord, Balik Baltchik, gave the town its present name in the Middle Ages. Later the town developed as a corn trading and export centre.

After the Balkan war, which finished in 1913, this area was annexed to Romania. After 1940 Balchik was returned to Bulgaria and now has a diverse population including Greeks, Bulgarians, Turks, Tartars, and Romanians. There are poor beaches here.

The ethnographic complex displays exhibits from the various trades, traditional costumes, and replicas of a town and village house. The church of St Nikola, (the patron saint of seafarers) which was built in 1865, was restored in the 1980s to commemorate the 1,300th anniversary of the Bulgarian state. The art exhibition gallery in a former school displays traditional, Impressionist and contemporary art. The history museum explains the town's name changes and its role through the centuries to the second world war.

During the era under Romanian control the Summer Palace of Queen Marie of Romania was constructed 2km west of Balchik in Oriental, Gothic and Bulgarian style. She was the granddaughter of Queen Victoria, and was born in England. The palace called Tenka Yava (Quiet Nest) was built as a love-nest for her Turkish lover from 1924–31: a minaret was incorporated in the house to inspire him and to please both her Christian and Muslim subjects.

The botanical gardens which surround the house have 600 varieties of trees, cacti and plants. Europe's second most important collection of cacti with over 250 species, and Bulgaria's tallest cactus at 7m, nicknamed the hedgehog, are located in the botanical gardens. Queen Marie also planted her favourite lilies from the Isle of Wight in the grounds. Going down to the sea are six terraces, one for each of the queen's children. In the grounds of the palace are follies such as Roman baths, a chapel, a rose garden, and a water mill. The stones for the church were brought from Crete and the earthen jars from Morocco. The queen's heart was buried here while this was still a Romanian town. The Union of Bulgarian artists now uses the pavilions as a rest home.

THE BLACK SEA

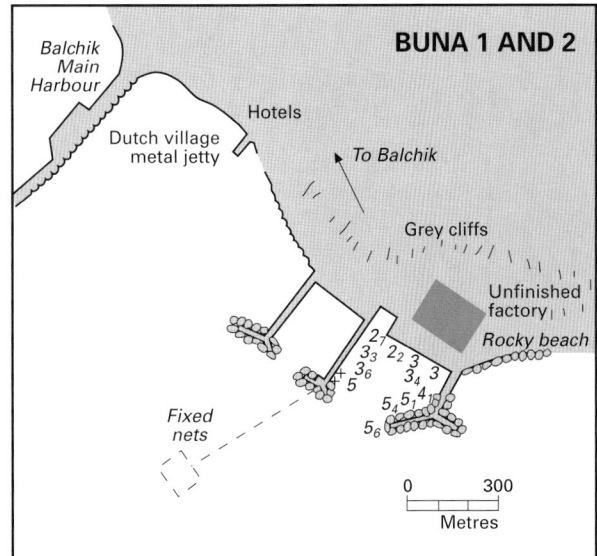

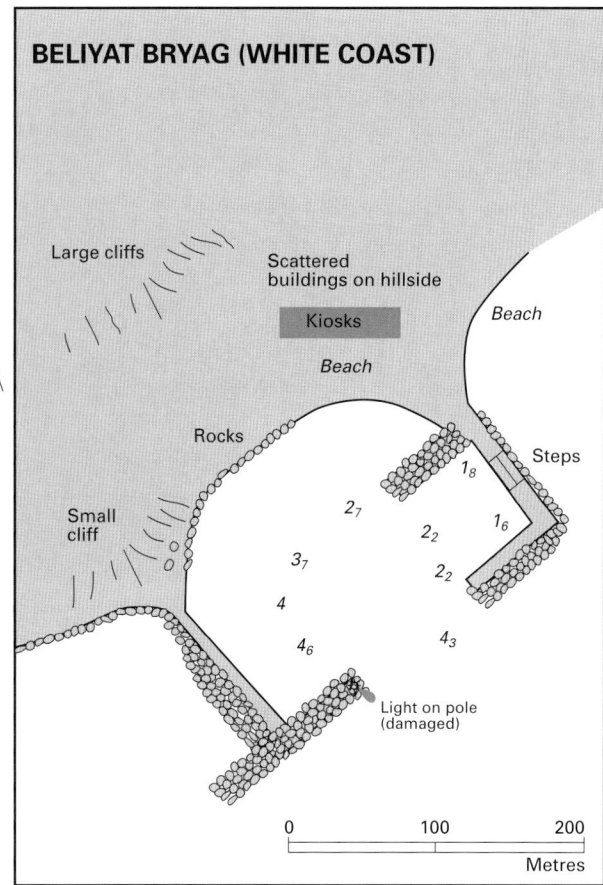

Buna

Buna 1 and 2 43°23′.85N 28°10′.50E

This is a harbour complex where work has commenced but never been completed. Most of the harbour area has deep water, but there are no facilities so you must walk into Balchik. Beside this there is a large derelict factory, started by the Russians for water purification.

There are fixed nets projecting from the end of the central pier.

Beliyat Bryag

Beliyat Bryag (White Coast, Laguna, Bialiata)
43°24′.17N 28°14′.14E

On approach from the east the entrance to the harbour is hidden until almost opposite it, due to a small headland. There are fixed nets to the east of the entrance. Electricity for lights is on the east jetty, but there is no sign of a socket. Water is available in small quantities from the kiosks. This is a small quiet resort with basic facilities, but it does have a villa to rent which is done out in grand Communist style.

Kavarna 43°24′.66N 28°21′.38E

A large triangular-shaped limestone cliff is the landmark to aim for and the harbour entrance is to the east of this; entry can be made with a bearing of due north. The mooring for pleasure boats is to the east side of the harbour, beside the fishing boats, where there is good shelter. An alternative is to anchor in the bay and get good shelter from the breakwater.

There is power and small quantities of water on the jetty. For large volumes of water the locals advised the use of a tap, which is located between the grain silos and a hut with a red roof; however, there is no good mooring close to this. There are toilets and showers at the beach in the harbour. Fuel is ordered at the garage and they deliver it to the boat. The lighthouse at the end of the east breakwater on a white pillar with a crow's nest flashes white Iso.5s12m5M.

On the beach there are a disco, café, and snack bars. For the main town, which is located up the hill, take the road up the hill, go under the tunnel then turn right to reach the pedestrian area. This is a distance of 3km (1.8 miles) from the harbour.

The town has existed since Thracian times. In the 5th century BC the Greeks established the fortress of

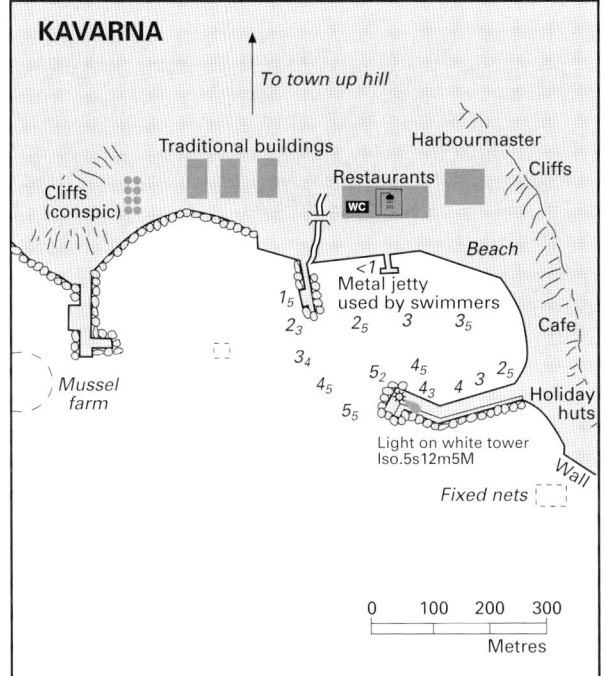

Kavarna. Distinctive white cliff landmark

Kavarna

Bizone (probably as competition to Krounoi, one of their many colonies along the Black Sea coast). A severe earthquake destroyed the town in the first century BC. It was rebuilt up the hill by the Romans, but was destroyed again by invading Tartar tribes. Again it was reconstructed.

The Turks captured it in 1393. In the 1340s a noble called Boyer Balik declared it an independent state stretching south to the River Kamchiya. It suffered damage in the Russo-Turkish wars of 1828–9 and 1850; again it was rebuilt. In 1877 Bashibazouk (an army of Turkish volunteers noted for lawlessness and cruelty) burned the town to the ground and 1,200 inhabitants lost their lives. During the first and second Bulgarian kingdoms it was the administrative centre of Dobrudja.

Finally, the town has been rebuilt and is a centre for fishing and agriculture, since it is located in rich arable land that produces grain and animal fodder. The town has changed its name several times, being known as Karvounska Hora, Karvouna, Karbona and eventually Kavarna. Today the port handles medium-sized passenger and cargo vessels, with one of the main exports being grain.

There is a town museum that has some Thracian remains and tells the story of the town's history. An art gallery and archaeological museum are also located here. A former school is now the ethnographic museum and the classrooms are done up like small town-houses from the 19th century.

Nos Kaliakra (Beautiful Headland)
43°22′N 28°28′E

The light on this headland is Fl.5s67m21M: the reef at the point of the headland extends at least one cable offshore. Kaliakra controls from the border to Kavarna and is on Ch 8.

The fortifications of Tirisis date from the 4th century BC and were enlarged by the Romans, who called the town Tetrasiada. The Byzantines knew it as Akre and they dug shafts from the clifftop down to the sea in the 4th century so that supplies could come from the boats direct to the fortress. It was in the Middle Ages that it got its present name Kaliakra. There are many ruins on the headland and a museum is located in one of the caves. The Muslim myth surrounding one of the caves is that it is the grave of Sari Saltuk, a hero who came to kill a seven-headed dragon, which would free the Sultan's two daughters. The Christian myth is that the cave is the grave of Saint Nicholas, the patron saint of seafarers, and who directs fishermen to the fish. There is a small village near here called Sveti Nikola.

Out at the very point of the headland is a small chapel, but before reaching it you pass a memorial to Fiodor Fiodorovic Ushakov (1745–1817) a prominent marine commander: 'Here at Cape Kaliakra on 3 July 1791 the squadron under the command of Admiral Ushakov gained a brilliant victory by defeating and putting to flight the Ottoman Empire squadron. In 2001 he was canonised by the Russian Orthodox Church'.

There are three legends associated with the cape. The first says that forty Bulgarian maidens tied their hair together and jumped into the sea from the cape, chosing to commit suicide rather than be captured by the Turks and be converted to Islam. The second legend is that it was the hiding place for the treasures of Lyzimah, who was the successor to Alexander the Great. The third is that Saint Nicholas ran down the cape to escape capture from the Turks. He was, however, captured and killed. To mark his symbolic grave there is a small chapel at the end which was restored in 1993.

Between this cape and Nos Maslen is the home of one of the world's rarest animals, the Black Sea seal. In 2004 there were only 5 or 6 specimens left.

Bolata 43°22′.9N 28°28′.3E

This was previously used by the border police and navy fast patrol boats, but has now been abandoned, probably due to silting. This has produced an excellent beach, but made the southern jetty unusable, with less than half a metre of water at the end. The other jetty further in the harbour has 2m depth at the end and is a sheltered place to moor away from the other jetty. There are no buildings or facilities, and the narrow road at the head of the bay winds its way up to bleak steppe land on top of the cliffs. Divers use the bay and claim there is interesting underwater flora and fauna, and day-trippers have also discovered it.

In the hinterland is one of the last areas of uncultivated steppe left in Europe. Most of the plants here are protected by law and therefore cannot be picked. This is the Kaliakra reserve, steppe ecosystem, coastal limestone cliffs and marine territory. There are 240 rare and endangered plants and animals in the area, including the Kaliakra catchfly and Kaliakra thistle. It is also a nesting area for Calandra lark, short-toed lark, stone curlew and pled curlew. Offshore is home for the monk seal, which is threatened with extinction. A few kilometres north after Tyuleiovo there are about 40 caves cut into the cliffs; most have smooth walls with holes dug into them. The entrances are rectangular and inside on the walls are primitive cave paintings.

Nos Shabla

This is the most easterly point in Bulgaria. Right on the point, construction of a harbour has been started but never completed, with some of the reinforced concrete blocks still lying on the land. The entrance is 43°32′.4N 28°36′.5E giving some protection from the north. The metal jetty to the south is in a dangerous condition and provides no protection from the east or the south. There is a shallow part at the centre of the entrance. This jetty was probably used for taking oil away since just inland are numerous beam engines for oil extraction. The town has minimum facilities. On the cape is the oldest lighthouse in Bulgaria (Fl(3)20s36m17M) built in 1856 and distinguished by its red and white strips. The cape is the nesting place of 100,000 wild geese.

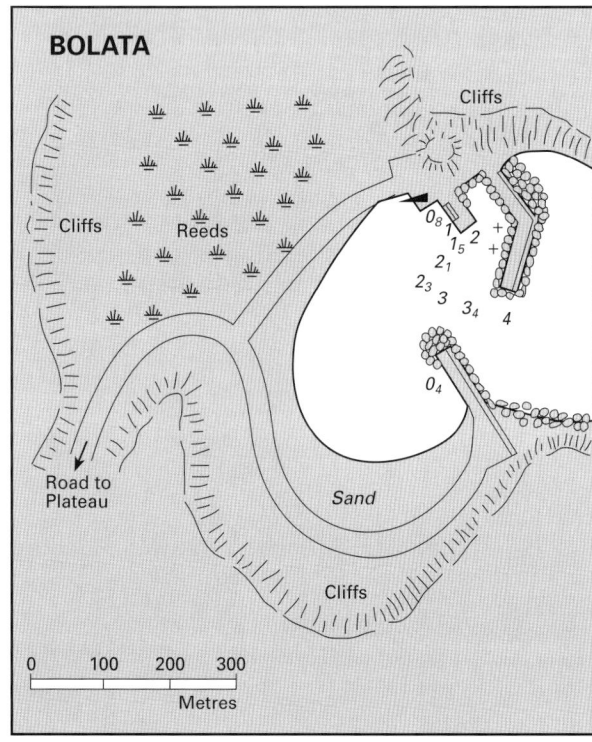

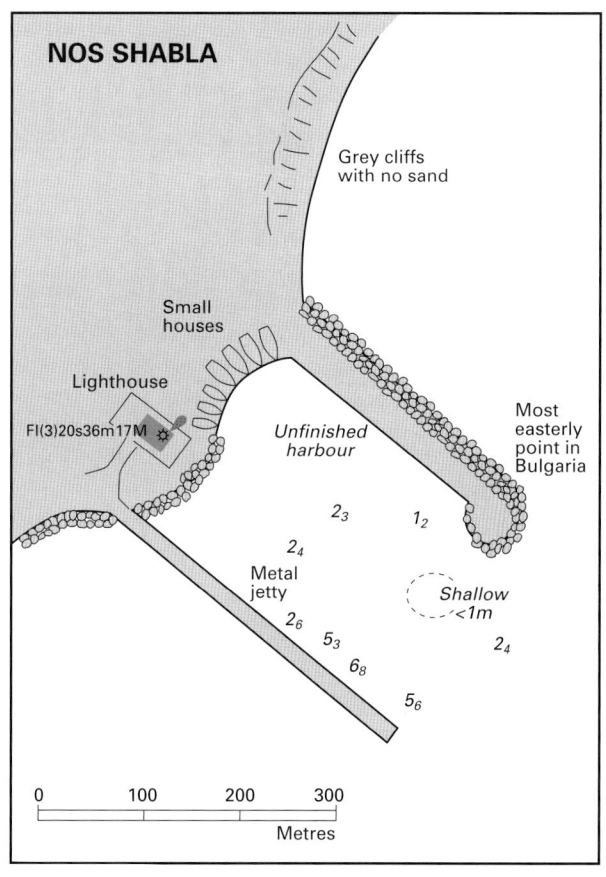

Rusalka (Roussalka, Russalka, Rousalka) (Mermaid)

Situated in Taukliman Bay (Bay of the Birds), this quiet holiday village was founded in 1968, but unfortunately since this time the number of bird species has declined. It has facilities such as tennis, swimming, scuba diving, windsurfing, and an underwater museum a few metres offshore that can be visited by scuba-divers. The advertising brochure gives yachting as one of the activities, and there is a small jetty behind the rocks. Some small yachts moor in the bays sheltered by the rocks. Offshore is very rocky.

Shabla lightouse

The village of Shabla is inland about 5km from the cape. The area has been inhabited by Thracians, Greeks and Romans, reached a peak of prosperity in Byzantium times, and has suffered a subsequent decline. Shabla Lake goes down to 9.5m in depth, and is semi-salty, and next to it is Shabla Touzla, which provides mud for therapy.

Krapets

This is a small fishing village where tourism is only just starting to develop. The fishermen drag their boats up on the beach as there is no harbour. To study the rich history of the area you would have to moor in front of the village, where there is a good holding on a sandy bottom, but with no protection from the elements.

Kibela Temple is the oldest prehistoric necropolis in continental Europe and is 2,500 years old. This was discovered on an island in the nearby Dourankulak Lake. Archaeologists have excavated a stone settlements near the temple believed to date from 5400 to 4100BC. Historical remains from various periods are now exhibited in the museum in Dobrich. The area is also famous for the diversity of bird species in the surrounding lakes and the deserted beaches.

The border between Bulgaria and Romania is reached at 43°45′N 28°35′E.

For Divers

From Nos Kaliakra to just north of Nos Shabla is an area appreciated by divers.

Off the point of Kaliakra is a well-preserved metal cargo ship which divers can penetrate at 45m. Just to the north of this is a metal cargo steamer of unknown origin lying in 7–12m of water. Further north is a group of metal wrecks at 12m. Towards Shabla, 5m down is a 17–18th-century wooden battleship and also in the vicinity are scattered fragments of 2 or 3 wooden battleships from different eras, between 4–9m. Near Nos Shabla is the *Kostas*, a Greek cargo ship that divers can enter at 7–12m. Also in the vicinity is a second world war German cargo ship that was sunk by a Russian submarine and is lying in 7–13m water. Offshore from Nos Shabla is a second world war Russian submarine at 60m and a second world war Russian submarine type ST in 59m of water. Divers have never visited either of these submarines and the flora and fauna of the Black Sea can be studied in their natural surroundings. South of Nos Shabla are many underwater unexplored caves also of interest to divers., also at Tyuleiovo is the Monk Seal cave that is 108m deep. Kamen Briag area has many caves, most of which are unexplored. At Nos Kaliakra is the Bats' Cave. Although this short stretch of coast has a high concentration of interesting things for divers there are also other wrecks and caves at other locations on the western Black Sea coast.

ROMANIA

The Black Sea Coast

Charts
Admiralty
2213   Gura Sfîntu Gheorghe to Dnistrovs'kyy Lyman
2230   Constanţa to Kefken Adasi
2232   Constanţa to Yalta
2282   Plans in Romania
2284   Portul Constanţa and approaches

Turkish
10A   Western Black Sea
17   Mis Kinbun to Nos Kaliakra

Romania's Black Sea coast stretches 245km (152 miles) from the Bulgarian border to Ukraine at the Danube Delta.

The weather forecast in English for this area is broadcast on Ch 12 just after 1000 and 2200.

The border town of Vama Veche is in a sandy bay. At the north end of the bay is a conspicuous wreck, with fixed nets further north. There are other unmarked nets in the area. The low sand dunes continue for another 4 miles until Mangalia.

HARBOURS AND MOORINGS

Mangalia

The entrance is at 43°47′.98N 28°35′.65E
Tidal range is 0.3m

The light on the northeast breakwater (Fl.4s23m10M Horn Mo(M)17s) is on a grey framework tower 43°47′.95N 28°36′.12E. The light on the southeast breakwater (Fl.R3s15m5M) has a cupola on a grey stone and concrete building at 43°48′.0N 28°35′.7E. Port Mangalia's main light (Fl(2)5.5s72m22M) is a little inland on a white pyramid stone tower at 43°48′.67N 28°33′.60E .

The approach to the harbour is 270°, with those going into the harbour staying north of 43°47′.5N and those leaving Port Mangalia to the south of this. Port authorities, customs, port control, border police and harbourmaster can be contacted on Ch 67. After entering the harbour turn to port and moor in front of the oil storage tanks with Transbitum written on them. The customs and immigration are located in the faded purple and white building next to the tanks. All of the above authorities arrived very quickly after we moored; you are expected to stay on board until they arrive. They filled in all the forms themselves, only leaving us to sign and stamp them. It was a very quick process. You are then issued with Mangalia Port immigration rules.

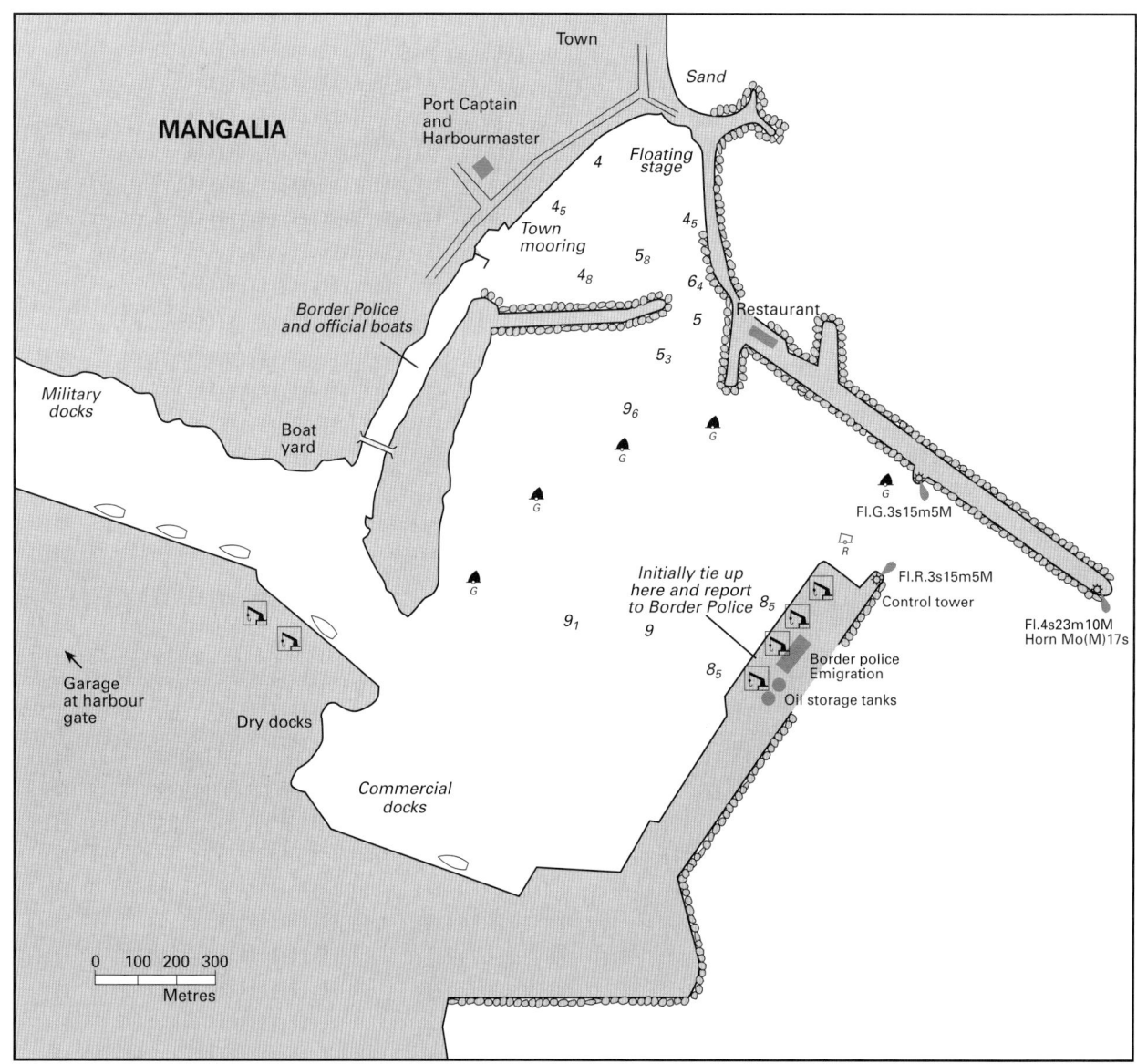

Mangalia lighthouse

They then gave us two options. One was to moor near the entrance beside the fishing boats; this was very secure since the public have no access to this part of the harbour. If we moored here the customs officer offered to drive us to the town and we could get a taxi back. The first time here we took this option, and not only did they drive us to the town, but took us on a conducted tour in their official car. Two things they did not mention were that even a taxi is not permitted to enter the dock area, and that it is a long walk back. The second was that there would appear near the boat a long train with trucks filled with scrap metal, which would be unloading all night, with a grab crane which dropped the metal on the quayside making a tremendous noise.

Our other option for mooring was in front of the town, which is very convenient for shops and restaurants, but they advised that security is not good here. (We took this option on the next visit and before we had the mooring ropes tied there were four children climbing all over the boat.) The plus side is that many Romanians take their evening stroll along this waterfront, and many will be curious about the boat, and you may have some interesting discussions with them.

This mooring is at 43°48´.4N 28°34´.9E and the port control and harbourmaster do their paperwork at this location. The young man from port control will ask you many questions about your boat: this is not for bureaucratic reasons, but it is his hobby. (He has a beautifully laid out book with details of every visiting boat, and after work he will draw in your national flag and perhaps a drawing of your boat.) One hour before departure you should contact the port authorities. On one occasion on departure it was not so easy to find the officials; for two and a half hours there was no answer to the radio. A fisherman finally took us to the border police office, which is located on the first floor at the south end of the white and purple building near the harbour entrance. He then telephoned the others, who soon appeared. They then asked us to sign a declaration that they had arrived within fifteen minutes from the first radio call to them.

The easiest way to contact them before departure is to go to the 'captain port Mangalia' office at B-dul 1 Decembrie 1918, Block M4-prater. This is right across the road from the town mooring. After getting clearance from port control you have to sail to the purple and white building to complete formalities with customs and immigration.

There is a garage at the harbour entrance for fuel.

Many tourists are attracted to this quiet attractive spa town. Sapropel mud from the nearby Techirghiol Lake, sea water, sulphurous and mesothermal water are the main elements that have turned Mangalia into a resort famous for its balneology clinics which can cure many ailments.

Mangalia was the ancient Greek colony of Callatis, but its present name is derived from the Byzantine Greek name Pangalia or Pancalia meaning 'the most beautiful'. Ruins of ancient Callatis were found when excavations were being carried out for the foundations of a new hotel. The basement of Hotel President is laid out like a museum, displaying baths, walls, and sewers.

The Esmahan Sultan Mosque (1570) is located on a pretty garden just south of the town centre. This elegant mosque with a single minaret is surrounded by a Muslim graveyard. A Scythian tomb discovered in 1959 unearthed fragments of a papyrus in Greek that is the first document of its kind to be found in Romania. The incineration tombs of the necropolis of the 6th century Callatis citadel can be seen today. The archaeological museum has artefacts from the Hellenistic epoch, fragments of stone sarcophagi, etc.

A string of hotels lines the beach and in the area are many tourist facilities such as tennis courts, discos, cinema, bowling, clubs and restaurants. The town harbour is close to all these facilities, which are just to the north. In the southwest corner of the harbour is a naval base and in front of this is the main commercial harbour with the successful shipyard of the South Korean company Daewoo. All of this means that if you choose the secure mooring at the end of the harbour, there is a journey of over 5 miles into the town around all of this.

Two miles north of the town is a purebred Arabian stud farm, where tourists can enjoy rides by the beach.

PASSAGE NOTES

North of Mangalia there is a proliferation of tourist resorts, mainly named after the planets. Trees are a backdrop to the tourist hotels and the arcades and stalls on the promenades above the sandy beaches, where there are the tourist facilities of restaurants, nightclubs, casino and discos. There are a number of breakwaters, some illuminated, which will give some protection from northerly and southerly winds, if there is sufficient depth. There are no places to tie up to in any of them.

Some of these breakwaters are located as follows:

43°49´.7N less than one metre, 200m offshore
43°50´.5N 1.3m at the entrance
43°50´.6N 1.5m at the entrance
43°50´.9N More than 3m near the southerly breakwaters in front of Hotel Onix at Jupiter. There is less than 1m near the northern breakwater.
43°52´.9N 2 sets of breakwaters

The summer resorts continue until 43°53´N when the scenery changes to low brown cliffs which are only broken by Costinesti. This section of the Romanian Black Sea coast lacks natural harbours.

Costinesti

Originally a small fishing village but now an 'in' place for young people who want 24-hour partying and lots of sports facilities such as basketball, aquatic sports and scuba-diving. The village also arranges theatre and film festivals, and various types of concerts.

At 43°57´.6N 28°39´.5E is a conspicuous wreck, and to the north of it are fixed nets. A local magnetic anomaly is reported in this area.

Cape Tuzla

The lighthouse at 43°59´.5N 28°40´.1E with Fl(2)9.7s 62m20M 191°-vis-014° (183°) and an auxiliary light F.R.57m6M 162°-vis-192° (30°) and a Horn Mo(T)30s, is based on a green metal framework tower with white bands. Beside it is a radio mast painted red and white. From south of the lighthouse opposite to a metal sign with white horizontal strips it is very shallow for a good distance offshore. The sand can be washed about and it can be shallow for up to a mile offshore for the next few miles going north. Adding to this hazard there are many sets of poorly marked fixed nets in this area.

Continuing to Constanţa there are grass-topped muddy cliffs mixed with breaks in between where there are sandy beaches and tourist resorts. The cliffs decrease in height and the cranes and buildings of Constanţa can be seen.

Cape Tuzla

Constanţa 44°10´N 28°39´E

The main light (Fl(2)29.8s87m24M) at 44°09´.50N 28°37´.91E is located on a white pyramidal concrete tower with a blue cupola.

The other light (Fl.4.5s24m10M and Horn Mo(C)30s) is located on the northeast breakwater on a grey granite tower 44°08´.63N 28°40´.45E.

At the entrance to the port is a traffic separation scheme marked by 2 red and white buoys LFl.10s, and there are other lights with a visibility of up to 5 miles.

Sixty per cent of Romania's imports and exports transit through Constanţa, the main products being ore, coal, oil products, grains, chemical products, rolled metals, cement, building materials, edible oils, molasses, vehicles, general goods and containers. The largest port in Romania has 133 berths and a total quay length of 28.5km, with more due to be built. Constanţa is an interface between Europe, Asia and Russia, trans-shipping containers and crude oil. From here the crude oil from Russia and Asia can transit on its way to central and Western Europe by pipeline. The other goods go on the barges and use the river and canal system.

The only reason a recreational boat would visit here is for entry to the River Danube–Black Sea canal.

For mooring, Port Tomis, just to the north, is reserved for pleasure boats and is nearer the town centre.

For entry into Constanţa Harbour or Port Tomis the port control and harbourmaster should be contacted when 12 miles away, or one hour before the estimated arrival time, both on Ch 67.

Radio Constanţa is on Ch 16. There are several possibilities for repairs. There are quayside refuelling facilities in Constanţa harbour, but only for large quantities.

For history and visitor attractions see under Port Tomis Marina below; this is the recreation boat harbour for Constanţa.

River Danube–Black Sea Canal

Unless time is an issue, a more interesting route is through the Danube Delta. (To cut 400km off the journey from the Black Sea to the River Danube the 64.2km canal from Cernavoda to Constanţa at the seaport of Agigea can be used.) Facilities can be arranged at both ends of the canal for yachts to lower or erect their masts. The air height for bridges over the canal is 16m. The canal is 90m wide and handles an average draught of 5.5m and a maximum draught of 7m, allowing a navigation speed of up to 12kph.

With an average depth of water in the river Danube at Cernavoda, there is only 5m to drop to the Black Sea water level. This is accomplished by two locks, one at Cernavoda and the other at Agigea at the other end. Both locks are in pairs 310m long and 25m wide with a depth of 7m. When the wind is over 16m/s the locks do not operate. Mooring in the canal is not permitted.

Seagoing ships of up to 5,000DWT or convoys of up to 6 barges with a maximum weight of 18,000DWT can be accommodated. This is the equivalent of 900 trucks of 20 tonnes, or a train of 360 carriages each of 50 tonnes. The canal is projected to carry 75 million tonnes of freight annually, and is the first link in the trans-European waterway between the Black Sea and the North Sea at Rotterdam via the rivers Danube, Main and Rhine, and the Rhine-Main-Danube Canal.

The cost for use of the canal is length x breadth x draught x €1.5 with a minimum price of €100.

For boats with a length up to 15m no pilot is required; from 15m length upwards it is necessary to have a pilot that cost €150, and two hours notice should be given before arrival at the canal entrance.

The working VHF channel for the Agigea lock is 74.

Near the waiting place for the lock at Agigea is a supermarket. Nothing much can be seen when transiting the canal and after Agigea the cutting is 8.5m deep with only scrub on the banks. The cutting decreases at Poarta Alba, which has a small basin with 2 cranes. A mooring can be had here. At 44°13´.05N 28°23´.05E is the entrance to the Midia Canal, with the banks becoming lower and some countryside being seen. Medgidia harbour, which is noticeable with 3 cranes and a large industrial complex, is the recommended stopping place, if required. There are two holding pontoons, one on either side of the harbour entrance. The one to the east that is inside the port security is recommended. The one to the west has no security. Medgidia is the only place on the canal with any life: there are promenades, which appear to be popular with the local walkers and fishermen, a museum and a big mosque. The rolling countryside continues until Cernavoda. The working channel for the Cernavoda lock is 14.

The canal, which cuts through the Dobrogea platform was envisaged in the Roman period. Work started in 1949 with the labour being provided by criminals, peasants who did not co-operate with the collectivisation programme, critics of the Communist Party, the youth brigade, and others. Between 10,000

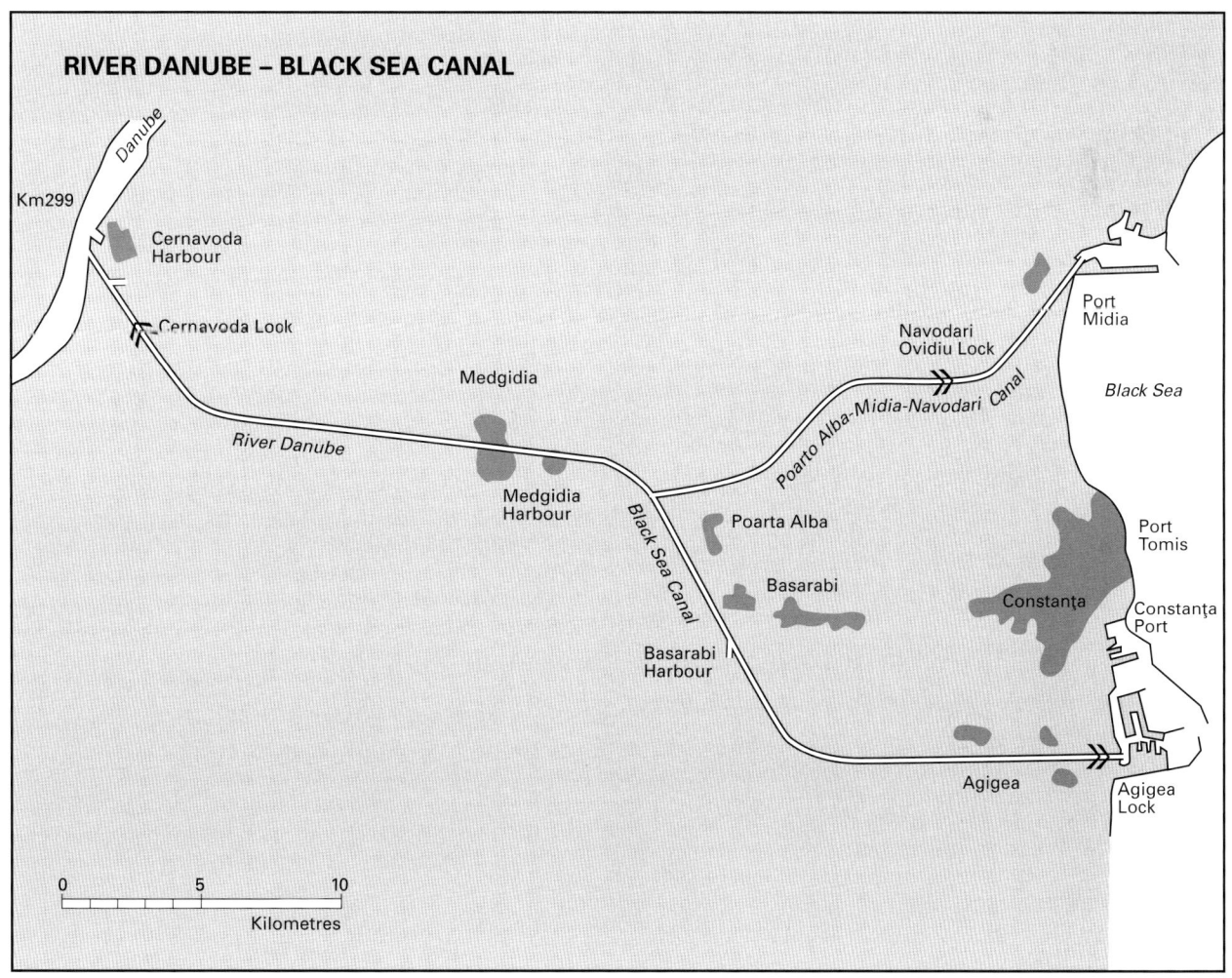

Midia Canal entrance

and 200,000 people lost their lives in the 4-year period until the project was abandoned, and in this period it was called 'the canal of death'. The project was restarted in 1976 and completed in 1984.

During the construction of the canal the amount of soil and rock excavated was 294 million m³. (For comparison, the amount excavated during the construction of the Suez Canal was 275 million m³ and Panama Canal 160 million m³.) This was the costliest engineering project in Romania's history, and it also involved building 150km of access road, upgrading 80km of rail track and erecting 36 major bridges. Three new port facilities were developed along the canal:

Cernavoda, to handle 7 million tonnes per year
Medgidia, to handle 11.5 million tonnes per year
Basarabi, to handle 1 million tonnes per year.

POARTA ALBA–MIDIA–NAVODARI CANAL

This canal is a branch canal joining the river Danube-Black Sea canal at Poarta Alba. Work began on this 26km canal in 1983 and was completed in late 1987, and 87 million m³ of soil and rock were excavated during its construction. The canal runs northeast through two natural lakes to the new port of Midia on the Black Sea. The two new ports of Ovidiu and Luminita were also constructed.

Ovidiu, with over 13,000 inhabitants, is a place where wealthy citizens from Constanța retire to.

The twin locks at Navodari Ovidiu are 145m in length, 12.5m wide and 5.5m deep. The canal is 45 metres wide and has a draft of 4.5 metres.

THE BLACK SEA
Coast Port Tomis Marina
44°10′.58N 28°33′.87E at the entrance

This is well marked with lights on the east breakwater: on a green mast Fl.G.3s10m4M, and on the west breakwater on a red metal mast Fl.R.3s10m4M. The eastern breakwater has been extended, and the new entrance is now further south. A high round building, a blue glass building and a mosque are conspicuous from the sea.

Port officials Ch 67. Radio Constanța Ch 16.

This is a good sheltered harbour for pleasure craft. Mooring will be against the seaward wall and the position will be given by the harbourmaster who has an office after the restaurant. At the south end of the jetty is a security box. The guard here or harbourmaster will phone for the officials. They arrived promptly, were very smart and carried out their duties in a very efficient manner.

Danube. Black Sea Canal, Agigea entrance

Port Tomis marina

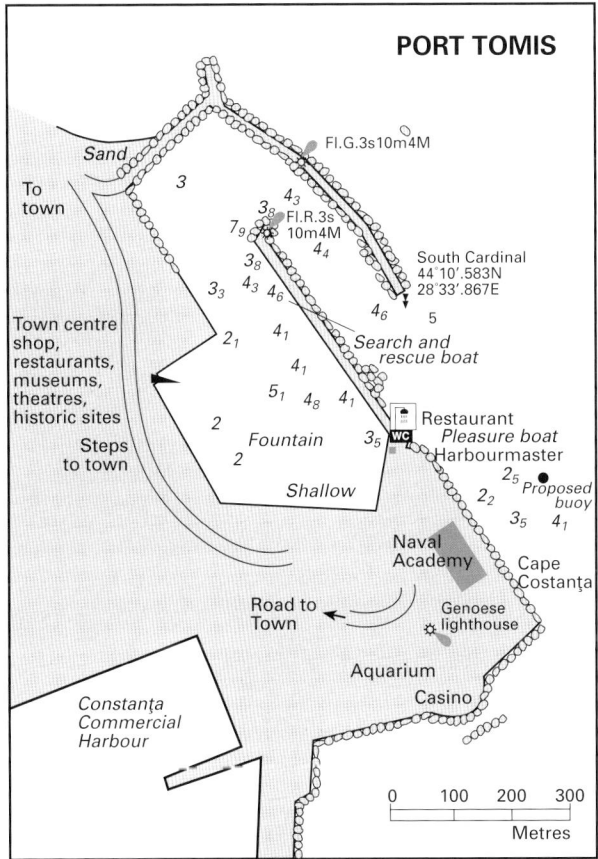

Showers and toilets are beside the security box and restaurant. The weather forecast can be printed off from the internet in the harbourmaster's office. Water and electricity are available on the harbour.

The only problem we encountered was getting diesel (*motorina*). Arrangements can be made for a fuel truck to come to the harbour, but the locals did not encourage this since they said it was too expensive. They preferred to organise a car that cost a bottle of brandy (approximately €3). However, the first garage did not sell diesel, the second and third had run out, the fourth was shut, so finally we got it at the fifth attempt. Even the local taxi drivers complain that many garages do not sell diesel or run out. The harbourmaster can advise which garage has stocks of fuel and arrange a car for transportation. For large quantities of fuel there is a fuelling bay in Constanţa harbour.

For repairs ask the locals who have boats here and they will introduce you to their contacts since there are many possibilities.

Charges in Euros per metre per day

Day	Week	Month	3 months	6 months	1 year
1	0.7	0.5	0.33	0.25	0.2

plus VAT and electricity consumed

One hour before you intend to depart the officials should be contacted on Ch 67, and they will visit the boat to complete the formalities.

In the evenings border police and security patrol the harbour. Most of them spoke English, and we had an interesting chat with them. A search and rescue boat which is manned full time is based here.

Constanţa has an international airport, mostly used by summer charter flights, but it is only 2 hours away by train from Bucharest, and could be a location for a crew change.

Looking south is a forest of cranes at the commercial harbour. To the west is the main town, and to the north are popular beaches with the usual tourist kiosks and facilities that line the shore.

Constanţa has been a seaport since the 6th century BC. Greek colonists built the city of Tomis and the town was associated with Jason and the Argonauts when they were searching for the Golden Fleece. The town prospered under Roman rule and many statues, foundations, walls, and monumental architecture can still be seen today. When Constantinople was the capital of the Eastern Roman Empire, Tomis was rebuilt by Constantine the Great, who changed the name to Constantina in honour of his sister.

Constanţa's spiritual patron is the Roman poet Ovid who was exiled here by Emperor Octavian Augustus in AD8 and stayed until his death in AD17. Here he wrote some of his most important works. The Genoese developed the harbour and built the first lighthouse in the 13th century, and it stands to this day. During Turkish occupation that lasted until 1877 there were no significant improvements, except for the railway to Cernavoda that opened in 1860. Re-attached to greater Romania in 1878, the port started to flourish after King Carol I decreed it should be a principal seaport and seaside resort. During both world wars it was destroyed, but rebuilt again between 1956–58. Since 1978 there has been substantial expansion.

Constanţa. Ovidiu Square (named in honour of the town's spiritual patron) and national museum of history and archaeology

Constanța. Genoese lighthouse

The Archaeological and National History Museum houses objects from Hamangia and Gumelnita cultures, and beside it lies a multicoloured mosaic from the Roman period covering 700sq.m. The maritime museum traces history from pre-Greek times to the present day. Modern Romanian paintings are hung in the art museum. There are museums of folk art, military history and natural sciences, and the Ion Jalea museum of sculptures.

Turkish rule gave the city the Mahmoud II Mosque in 1822. It is in Byzantine-Egyptian style with Romanian influences. Near the harbour the casino is in Baroque French style with Rococo elements and was started in 1909 for Queen Elisabeta (1843–1916). It has a restaurant and terrace overlooking the sea.

Opposite it is the aquarium with 4,500 species of fish and fauna from the Black Sea, the Danube Delta, and the Dobrogean lakes, and nearby is the lighthouse. There is also a famous dolphinarium, home to intelligent and playful dolphins, and a planetarium. Conveniently located up the steps from the harbour are theatres, cinema, shops, banks, and many restaurants.

The mayor has major ideas to make Port Tomis an important marina with pontoons and other facilities for pleasure boats, and plans a 'touristic' terminal to be available for cruising boats. The entrance to the harbour will change in the future. The length of the breakwater will be increased, with hundreds of stable legs each of which weighs 4.5 tonnes and consumes 1.88m³ of concrete.

Mamaia

Mamaia is just to the north of here. It is the largest resort on the Romanian coast with 60 hotels and no shortage of restaurants, casinos, discos, etc. For the more energetic there is sub-aqua diving and paragliding, water skiing, tennis, basketball, archery, mini-golf, and sailing. There are also good facilities for small children. The 8km long beach has good sand and one area dedicated for nudists. There is a groyne at the south end of the beach providing some shelter, suitable for a lunch stop, and popular with the locals.

Just north from Constanța at 43°13´.5N 28°39´.7E there is an obstruction marked on the chart. The depth is believed to be about 3.5m.

Port Midia

A satellite port of Constanța, Port Midia is for commercial traffic only. It is the terminal for the northern branch of the River Danube–Black Sea canal. The working Ch is 67.

The entrance light (Fl.5s25m10M) is on a metal structure with a white concrete tower at the end of the offshore breakwater at 44°19´.31N 28 °41´.76E. At the head of the breakwaters on white concrete towers are red and green lights flashing 5s and visible for 6M.

The Cape Midia lighthouse (Fl.5s36m17M) is at 44°20´.85N 28°41´.06E. This is on a white cupola on a metal framework tower with red and white bands.

The low hills in the background die away after Midia. To Sfîntu Gheorghe the shore is low and the lagoon complex of Lake Sinoie and Lake Razim is separated from the Black Sea by two long grinds. Twelve miles NNE of Midia is Chituc beacon, a black and white metal structure. In front of this marked on the chart is 'danger area'. The only dangers we noted were that it was shallow in many areas well offshore and there were badly marked fishing nets. There is no mobile phone coverage on some sections of this coastline.

Portita (Portitei) 44°40´.5N 28°59´.3E

The lighthouse (Fl.9s22m10M) is located on a black metal tower with a red platform with white bands. There are three groynes where some shelter can be obtained.

The only other features in this area are at Zaton (44°48´.2N 29°35´.6E) where there is a black and white square metal structure, and slightly inland at 44°51´.5N 29°35´.6E where there is a disused lighthouse.

Eight miles inland the town of Histria (Istria) was settled in 657BC by Greek traders and was the first Greek colony on this coast. It was a key commercial port, superseding Tomis (Constanța) before the silting of the harbour led to its decline. This gives an indication of the amount of silting that takes place in this area. Greek and Roman remains are displayed in the archaeological museum of this ancient fortified village.

On the chart the bar L-le Sacalinul Mare at 44°48´N 29°33´E appeared to be a good place to moor behind to get some shelter. The 2m depth extends about 2 miles out from the end of the bar, and on the seaward side about a mile out to sea. Behind the bar the depth soon drops to a metre. A canal enters the sea behind the bar and we found it impossible to even reach this, due to lack of depth. All along the seaward side of the bar there were many fishing nets, but here they were reasonably well marked with poles and rags. To the north of the bar is the Sfîntu Gheorghe arm of the River Danube and where it enters the sea there is a change in the colour of the water.

River Danube meets the Black Sea

Mouth of Sfîntu Gheorghe (St George) Channel
44°53'.5N 29°37'2E

Sfîntu Gheorghe lighthouse (Fl(2)7.2s48m19M with fog signal) is located on a solid silvery metal tower about 1 mile inland on the northern bank of the river. Also on the northern bank about 2 miles upstream is the village of Sfîntu Gheorghe. The position of the sandbanks at the mouth of the river is constantly changing. This arm does not get the regular dredging that the Sulina arm does and the depth over the bar has been reported to be as shallow as 1.5m, although the shallowest readings we typically got were around 3m. Upstream after this the depth can vary up to 20m in depth. There are many fishing nets in the vicinity of the river mouth.

Sfîntu Gheorghe 44°53'.71N 29°35'56E at the mooring
See the chapter on the Romanian Danube, below.
From here to the Sulina Arm the land is low-lying with sandy beaches. In the sea are many nets that are badly marked only with plastic bottles. One rule of thumb about all of the Romanian coast is that if you see fishing boats pulled up on the beach, there is a good chance there will be nets in the water.

Sulina 45°09'.2N 29°38'.3E
See the chapter on the Romanian Danube, below.

Sulina Canal

Navigation notes for entry into the Sulina Canal from the Black Sea

The principal navigation aid is the Sulina light (Fl(3)16.2s49m19M Horn Mo(SU)30s) on a white stone tower, with a red cupola at 45°08'.9N 29°45'.6E.

Navigation Ch 16. Tidal range nil. The Sulina canal is closed for navigation at night.

When approaching from the seaward side it is featureless flat land, but there are some prominent landmarks in Sulina. On the southern shore of the canal there is an 18.5m lighthouse where the depth over the bar is displayed in feet. One and a half cables away WNW there is a church and a water tower 1.5 miles further west. Also conspicuous is a power station WSW of the lighthouse.

The depth at the end of the buoyed channel could be much shallower than shown on the charts. Dredging and development work regularly takes place in the approach channel, and light buoys may be moved.

Position yourself in safe water in the vicinity of the No. 1 light buoy at 45°08' 01N 29°47'.7E (RW Fl.6s). On an alignment of 301° there are beacons standing on the elbow of the northern breakwater. The front light (yellow day mark, black strip) is at 45°09'.9N 29°43'.4E. The rear light (Fl(3)16.2s19M) has a yellow day mark and a black strip 220m NW of the front light. This leads along the centreline of the channel passing between pairs of light buoys that are also marking the entrance to the channel. Following 301° will give a passage across the bar and between the two breakwaters that project about 5km out to sea. The breakwater heads are marked by square concrete towers 5m in height. The lights were destroyed in 2003 and by 2006 had not been replaced.

When it is dangerous to enter, or a vessel is leaving Sulina for the Black Sea, a blue flag is flown from Sulina old lighthouse. When this flag is flying no vessel should enter from the sea. It is kept open by icebreakers and the most likely time for ice is in February and March. The main period for fog in the area is December and January.

III. THE RIVER DANUBE

GENERAL

The River Danube is part of Europe's important Trans-European waterway system. It links the Black Sea to Central, Western and Northern Europe via the Rhine-Maine-Danube canal and the River Rhine to Rotterdam, giving a navigable length of 3,515km and making it the longest inland waterway in the world. For the connection between the Mediterranean and the Black Sea it also links with the Rhine-Rhône waterways. The Danube has been important for merchants, travellers, warriors and peacemakers for thousands of years and has been a cultural and economic link and at many times of great strategic significance. About 500 million people are served by the waterway.

At its source on the eastern slopes of the German Black Forest the altitude is about 915m and at Ulm, where serious navigation commences, the altitude is about 460m. The River Danube crosses or forms the border of ten countries: Germany, Austria, Slovakia, Hungary, Croatia, Serbia and Montenegro, Romania, Bulgaria, Moldova, and Ukraine. Four capitals are located on its banks: Budapest, Bratislava, Budapest and Belgrade. It is the natural boundary between Romania and Serbia for 230km, Romania and Bulgaria for 472km and Romania and Ukraine for 120km. 1,075km of the river are in Romania on the northern bank, and Bulgaria, on the southern bank, includes 472km of riverside.

The Danube is also rich in biodiversity with mountains, gorges, river valleys, enclosed seas and delta. There are five protected areas on the main flow of the Danube. The two which are in the Romanian sector, are Portile de Fier (Iron Gates) Nature Park and the Delta Dunarii (Danube Delta) Biosphere Reserve, part of which is also in the Ukraine. In Bulgaria there is Srebarna Lake, Belene Island complex, and Ibisha Island.

Fishing is an important source of employment and a major source of income for inhabitants along the riverbank. The fish is also a major supply of protein for the population.

Being an international waterway passing through many countries, The Danube is known by different names in the countries it flows through. This should be kept in mind if referring to different charts, maps or books.

Germany and Austria	Donau
Slovakia	Dunaj
Hungary	Duna
Serbia/Bulgaria	Dunav
Romania	Dunărea
Ukraine and Russia	Dunay

This section of our guide presents each country separately, since if you want to go from one side to the other it is necessary to go through all the customs and border police formalities to check out of one country, then go through them all again to check into the other country. This can be a swift process in Romania, but might take days in Bulgaria. It is hoped this should all change now that both countries are in the European Union.

NAVIGATION

Navigating the River Danube is a different experience to sailing on the sea or canals. The sheer volume and speed of water is mind-boggling and has to be experienced to be appreciated. It is difficult to imagine that at 2,858km long, and with 2,424km of it navigable, it is only the second longest river in Europe and 25th longest in the world. (The longest river in Europe is the Volga 3,530km (2,193 miles).) The catchment area of 817,000km^2 covering 8% of Europe's surface is also second only to the Volga's drainage area of 1.3 million km^2 (536,000 miles^2). Where the River Danube comes into first place is in the volume of water. The River Volga, with typically 2,160m^3 of water per second, does not compare with the Danube's average 6,200m^3 per second. This volume of water exceeds that of all the rivers combined that flow into the North Sea.

All of the Romanian and Bulgarian portion of the River Danube is navigable. The Danube Commission recommended depth from Braila upstream is 2.5m, although occasionally it can go lower than this in an exceptionally dry season. After Silistra Romania is on both banks of the river until the River Prut, where Ukraine is on the northern bank.

The last 175km from Braila is navigable for sea-going vessels, and is called the Maritime or Lower Danube with a maintained depth of 7.32m (24ft) on the Sulina Arm. The Romanians call this section Dunârea De Jos. The seaports of the Lower Danube in Romania are Braila, Galati, Tulcea, and Sulina. In Ukraine there are the ports of Reni, Izmail and Kilija.

The river divides into 3 main arms to form the Delta. The central arm is the Sulina arm and this is the international waterway. Other arms are considered as Romanian or Ukrainian inland waterways and permission is required to sail there. Late in 2005 visa requirements were relaxed and tourism is now encouraged. The lower bridges are back upstream in

Danube fishermen

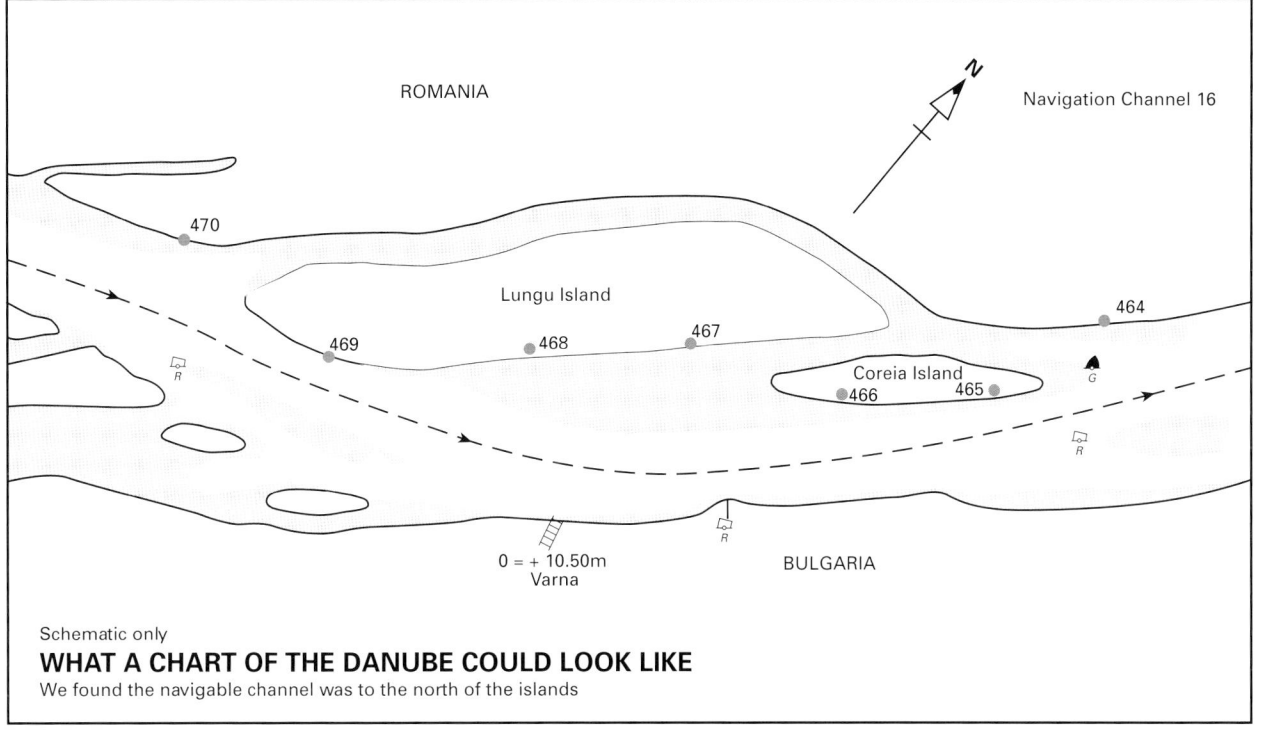

WHAT A CHART OF THE DANUBE COULD LOOK LIKE
Schematic only
We found the navigable channel was to the north of the islands

Hungary with Ujpest Bridge at 7.66m and Komarno 7.75m air height. The recommendation is to give an air height of 9.10m and all bridges should be altered to obtain this.

Three hundred tributaries enter the Danube, of which about 60 are navigable. The largest tributary is the River Prut in eastern Romania which drains from the Carpathian Mountains. In the west of Romania and also draining from Ukraine, Hungary, Serbia and Montenegro and Slovakia, is the River Tiza, the second longest tributary of the Danube. Romania has a further 615km of navigable rivers and canals, but there are none in Bulgaria.

The construction of the Iron Gates Barrage in 1972 removed a major barrier to navigation, but in the Romanian section there is also a dam and locks at Prahovo.

The official charts from the Danube Commission are A4 in size and are like a flip-chart, with each page covering about 9km. Even with the latest charts the silting can change dramatically, even to the extent of the channel going between an island and the riverbank where the chart has it as silted up.

The Romanian and Bulgarian section is very poorly buoyed compared to further upstream. The torpedo buoys are much smaller than those upstream and many are washed out of position and can be seen further downstream washed up on the river bank. There are markers on the riverbank indicating which side the channel is on, but sometimes these are obscured by vegetation. When the land comes steeply down into the river it should be deep and where there is vegetation and grass at the water's edge, it is probably shallow. The deepest channel will generally be on the outside of a bend where the current is greatest and has eroded the bank and riverbed away. If in doubt watch where the local boats go and follow them.

There can be a substantial difference in the river width depending on the volume of water. At low water between Vienna and the Iron Gate the width can be 600 to 1,800m at low water and at high water 11 to 48km wide. At The Cauldrons in Romania the width is reduced to 180m. The extreme differences in depth between high and low water is reported to be at these locations: The Cauldrons 7m, Turnu Severin 7.5m, Braila 6m, Tulcea 4.5m, Sulina 1.7m. The depth of the water also affects the current. The mean speed to the west of The Cauldrons is 2–3kn but in a high flood it is reported that it could be 8kn. At Tulcea the flow rate is 0.5kn in very low water and normally never exceeds 3kn. The maximum speed ever observed here is 5.25kn. The depth can change on a daily basis. Generally the highest water is in April and May, and the lowest water is in September and October.

Signs
In some places it is signed to navigate on the opposite side of the river. Other signs indicate no overtaking. The signs are shown below.

Right of way
Boats going downstream have the right of way as boats have more control when going upstream. Ferries, barges or tourist boats may be going across the river. The pleasure craft must always give way to the working vessel. Care should also be taken when there are fishing boats since they may have nets out. Overtaking is permitted only when the river is wide enough and it is appropriate to do so.

Radio
The working channel is given on a sign on the riverbank. Listen in to this and, even if you don't understand the language, the fact that there is radio traffic indicates that there are other boats in the vicinity.

Night navigation
Don't navigate at night or in severe weather conditions.

INTERNATIONAL WATERWAY SIGNS

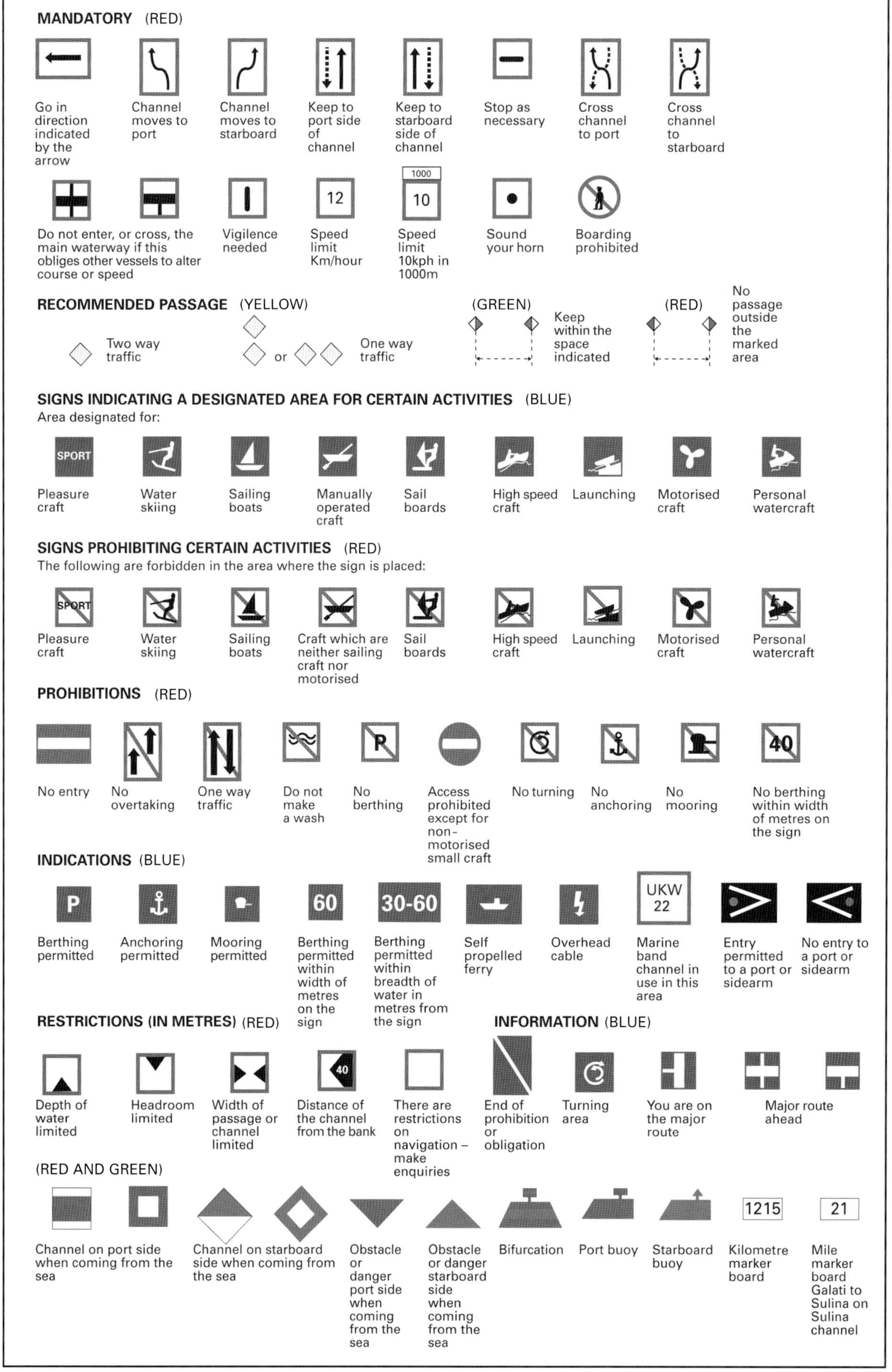
MANDATORY (RED)
Go in direction indicated by the arrow
Channel moves to port
Channel moves to starboard
Keep to port side of channel
Keep to starboard side of channel
Stop as necessary
Cross channel to port
Cross channel to starboard
12
1000
10
Do not enter, or cross, the main waterway if this obliges other vessels to alter course or speed
Vigilence needed
Speed limit Km/hour
Speed limit 10kph in 1000m
Sound your horn
Boarding prohibited
RECOMMENDED PASSAGE (YELLOW)
Two way traffic
or
One way traffic
(GREEN)
Keep within the space indicated
(RED)
No passage outside the marked area
SIGNS INDICATING A DESIGNATED AREA FOR CERTAIN ACTIVITIES (BLUE)
Area designated for:
SPORT
Pleasure craft
Water skiing
Sailing boats
Manually operated craft
Sail boards
High speed craft
Launching
Motorised craft
Personal watercraft
SIGNS PROHIBITING CERTAIN ACTIVITIES (RED)
The following are forbidden in the area where the sign is placed:
SPORT
Pleasure craft
Water skiing
Sailing boats
Craft which are neither sailing craft nor motorised
Sail boards
High speed craft
Launching
Motorised craft
Personal watercraft
PROHIBITIONS (RED)
P
40
No entry
No overtaking
One way traffic
Do not make a wash
No berthing
Access prohibited except for non-motorised small craft
No turning
No anchoring
No mooring
No berthing within width of metres on the sign
INDICATIONS (BLUE)
P
60
30-60
UKW 22
Berthing permitted
Anchoring permitted
Mooring permitted
Berthing permitted within width of metres on the sign
Berthing permitted within breadth of water in metres from the sign
Self propelled ferry
Overhead cable
Marine band channel in use in this area
Entry permitted to a port or sidearm
No entry to a port or sidearm
RESTRICTIONS (IN METRES) (RED)
40
Depth of water limited
Headroom limited
Width of passage or channel limited
Distance of the channel from the bank
There are restrictions on navigation – make enquiries
INFORMATION (BLUE)
End of prohibition or obligation
Turning area
You are on the major route
Major route ahead
(RED AND GREEN)
1215
21
Channel on port side when coming from the sea
Channel on starboard side when coming from the sea
Obstacle or danger port side when coming from the sea
Obstacle or danger starboard side when coming from the sea
Bifurcation
Port buoy
Starboard buoy
Kilometre marker board
Mile marker board Galati to Sulina on Sulina channel

International waterway

The Danube Conference at Belgrade confirmed that the Danube is an international waterway with the commission headquarters in Budapest. This was established by United Nations Convention No 518 regarding the Regime of Navigation on the Danube signed at Belgrade on 18 August 1948. The spirit of the agreement is 'Desirous of providing for free navigation on the Danube in accordance with the interests and sovereign rights of the Danubian States and in order to strengthen the economic and cultural relations of the Danubian States among themselves and with others nations'. This agreement applies to the navigable part of the River Danube between Ulm and the Black Sea with the outlet to the sea through the Sulina canal.

We had a copy of this convention on board in English and during a border dispute with Romanian and Bulgarian officials, the Romanians radioed to their HQ for a clarification in Romanian. After the translation was received they agreed with our interpretation and the matter resolved. The Bulgarians however, claimed the United Nations Convention did not exist. This resulted in a four-day delay, a court case and the British Embassy in Sofia classifying it as a 'Serious Diplomatic Incident'. Today the responsibilities of the commission are dredging, hydrotechnical activities, signalling on the navigable channel, hydrographical measurements, regulations for navigation, pilot services, salvage, fire fighting, and icebreaking.

NAVIGATIONAL DANGERS

Weather

With almost no warning strong winds can start, but they can also die down just as quickly. In the gorge section, particularly if the wind is blowing right up the gorge, waves of over 2m can be encountered. On more open sections a series of choppy waves give an uncomfortable sail. Mist, particularly in the morning, can be dense, with almost zero visibility stopping even the commercial traffic. Severe rainstorms are often accompanied by strong winds and start with almost no warning. Although it would sometimes make sense to stop, it is often not practical.

Commercial boats

These can be ocean-going boats as far inland as Braila, or huge barge trains with nine barges and a pusher unit. Local captains know of recent changes in sandbanks and river depths and to the inexperienced

Danube in a swollen state

pleasure boater some of the routes they take may not be the obvious ones. The barge trains need to position themselves for corners, so again they may appear to be out of position. Coming downstream the barges can move at an incredible speed and a constant lookout to the stern is essential. After being caught out once, we fitted a car rear-view mirror. The main rule is: all the barges are bigger than you and are often trying to manoeuvre in narrow or difficult conditions, so keep well out of their way. Other working boats could be involved in dredging, bridge building or maintenance, lock or riverbank renovation or piling. Keep out of their way and don't cause any wash.

Debris

Submerged logs can damage propellers, the hull or the gearbox. Polythene bags or other items can block water intakes.

Currents

Localised currents could be up to 12kn. Care needs to be taken to line up the boat correctly to go through bridges, or manoeuvre into the correct position to go alongside pontoons.

Anchoring

In many areas the bottom is gravel and there is no good holding. Some areas have mud or sand and a good mooring can be had. The best place is the downstream side of an island.

Shallow water

Sandbanks and depths change regularly and you should always be aware of this.

Ice

This is not normally a consideration for holiday boaters, but for year-round sailors it must be taken into account. Some years the Danube does not freeze over, but the earliest date of the river being closed to navigation due to ice was 7 December, and the latest date was 23 February. The earliest date for navigation recommencing was 18 January and the latest was 30 March.

HISTORY

This could have been the first river to be navigated by humans. It was used for thousands of years before the Greeks and Romans came to the area. The Greek records show that the Celts used the River Danube when their main trade was in salt, hides, iron and amber. The Celtic civilisation from 700–800BC had territories known as Danuvius, a name that eventually extended to mean the whole river, in the area covering modern-day Austria, Switzerland, Southern Germany, Southern Poland, Czech Republic and Slovakia.

Danu was the Celtic Mother Goddess whose name means 'the divine waters from heaven'. Danuvius to the Romans was the god who protected their fleets on the River Danube. On the banks of the Danube at Lepenski-Vir in Serbia there is evidence of a developed village with farming and domesticated animals, pottery and sculptures dating back 8,000 years. The Greeks called the river the Ister and described it as the mightiest river in the known world.

The river has acted as a natural boundary between empires, being the natural northern boundary of the Roman and Ottoman Empires. The Romans were the only people to control the whole length of the River Danube from its source to the Black Sea. They used it as a supply route in their campaigns, such as those against the Dacians in Romania. They built harbours and shipyards, which produced the galleys for the fleets, each of which would consist of 40 to 60 vessels.

After the collapse of the Roman Empire the trade continued to increase. Charlemagne's campaigns to the east used the Danube as a supply route and a defensive line in the 8th century. The Crusaders used all or part of the river on their route to the Middle East. Turks used the Danube as a supply route on their expansion west when they reached as far as Vienna in 1529. The Erste Donau Dampfschiff Fahrts Gesellschaft (First Danube Steamship Company) had its first steamship, the *Franz I*, in 1829. The company expanded to operate 180 craft and became the world's largest inland carrier.

The Vienna Congress of 1815 declared there should be free navigation on international rivers. In 1856 the Congress of Paris at the end of the Crimean war stipulated that the River Danube should be an international waterway. Two commissions were set up whose function was to carry out improvements and maintain navigation. The Treaty of Berlin at the end of the Russo-Turkish war in 1878 redrew the national boundaries. At the Delta the Kilia branch became part-Russian and part-Rumanian and the other two branches were totally Rumanian.

The Treaty of London in 1883 established the European Commission of the Danube, which did a lot of work to improve navigation. Trade was seriously disrupted during the first world war. In 1919 the Treaty of Versailles declared the Danube to be an international waterway as far inland as Ulm. This was broken between 1936 and 1945 when Germany controlled the river. After the second world war the Kilia branch was put under the control of the Soviet Union and the Iron Curtain split the river between east and west.

> 'Danube' is a popular name for restaurants in the area, and many ships have been named after the river. The *SS Danube* was the first vessel to sail through the Suez Canal in 1869. It was built in Leith where both the owner, Donald McGregor, and Captain Mann came from.

Danube Delta typical house

The Danube Delta (Delta Dunarii)

Formed over the last 16,000 years, the Danube delta is the last great wilderness in Europe and includes 479 lakes. It splits into 3 main arms, the northerly one known as Chilia, the centre as Sulina and the southerly Saint George. The Delta covers an area of 5640km² with 4,470 of those being in Romania and the balance being in Ukraine. It is composed of two large areas, the delta itself and the lagoon complex Razim-Sinoe (99,000ha).

The delta itself can be considered as 2 main parts. On either side of the Sulina arm is the fluvial delta, with numerous lakes. To the north some of the larger ones are Merhei, Bambina, Matita, Fortuna and on the other side the lakes are Rusca, Gorgova, Isac and Izlina. South of the Saint George's arm the largest lake of all is Dranov. The second area is the fluvio-maritime delta which includes the bank ridge tops like Letia, Caraoman, Săraturite and Ivancea, and lakes such as Roşu, Lumina and Puiu.

It is estimated that the delta increases by about 40m annually. This is due to the depositing action of alluvial materials carried down by the river, estimates of which vary between 30 and 70 million tonnes per year. (It would require a train with 750,000 wagons to remove this deposit.) The area is constantly changing due to action of the river and the sea. During the low water season 60–65% of the area can be water, and up to 90% of the area can be underwater in a high flood season. Only 9% of the delta area is permanently above water. The average amount of water flowing out of the Danube calculated over the period 1981 to 1990 was 6,200km² per sec and at the floods in April 2006 it was 15,800 cubic metres per sec, the highest recorded in 111 years. This raised the water level to 10.5m above the normal level.

The Danube Delta is one of the richest and most diverse nature reserves in the world. It is a natural marshy water maze and is the largest continuous marshland in Europe with dense undergrowth, forest, swamps and reeds. Reeds which can grow 5m high cover 1700km² making it one of the largest such expanses in the world. It is a mecca for birdlife, with 300 resident species attracted by this luxurious vegetation. It is a critical transit area for migrating birds, with five migration routes, which cross over the delta, the most important one being the Pontic Way used by flamingo, geese, ducks, gulls and terns.

This is an ornithologist's dream where you can spot, among other birds, pelicans, stilts, storks, falcons, swans, eagles, pratincoles, pigmy coromonts, ibis, herons, snipe and cranes. Birders report they can see up to 100 different species in a day.

It is also a fisherman's paradise, with 160 species of fish. Fishing is only permitted in certain areas with a permit issued by AJVPS (the Association of Sport Hunters and Anglers) in Tulcea and at some hotels. The main times for fishing are 15 March–15 April and 15 August–1 November. Fishing is totally prohibited from 15 April to 15 July. The best catches are after the

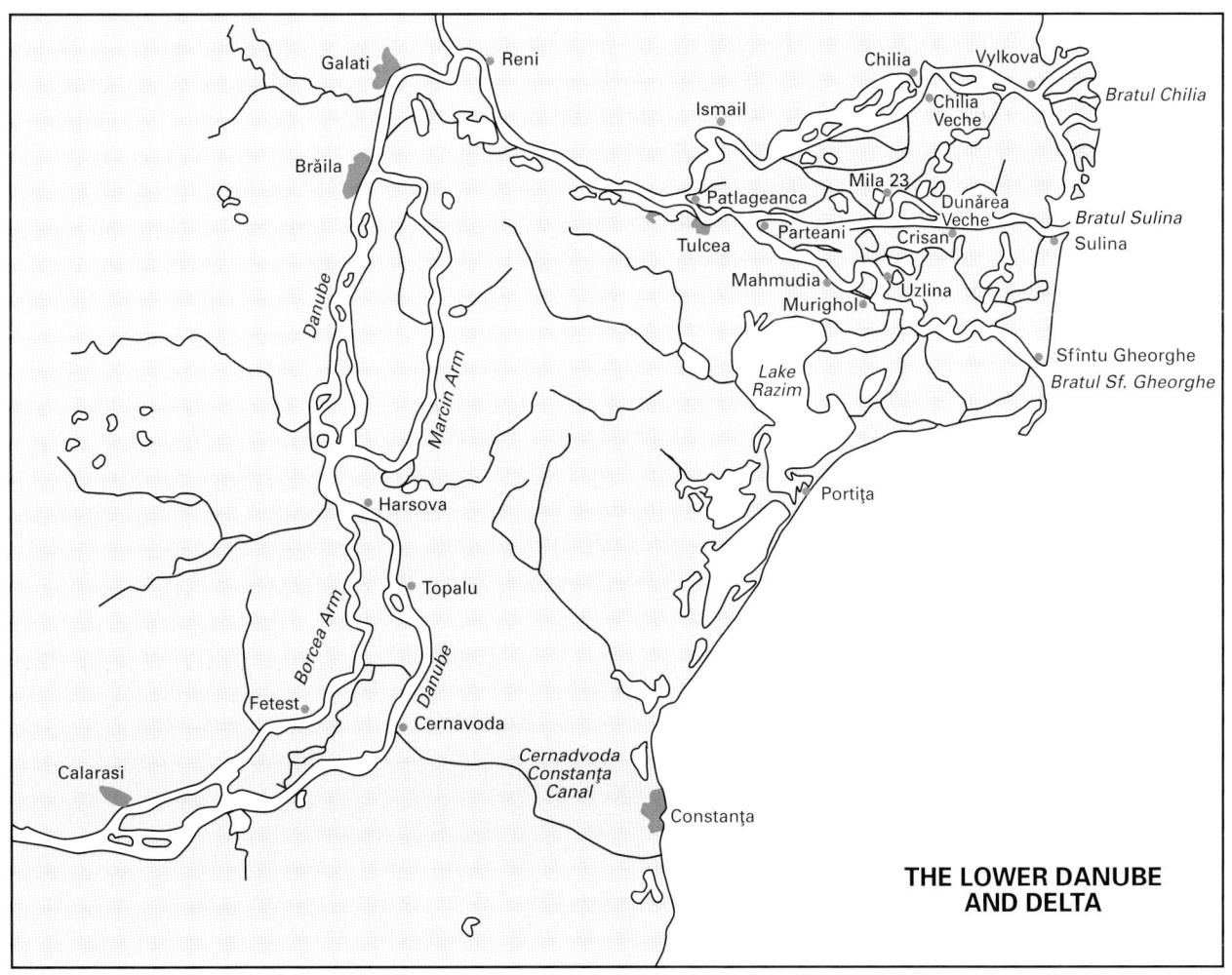

THE LOWER DANUBE AND DELTA

early spring floods. When the water recedes, bream, carp, pike and pike-perch are left in the pools and lakes. Other fish include sturgeon, swordfish, zander, mackerel and sardine. The value of the fresh fish caught is worth up to €5 million per year. It is estimated that in the delta birds consume 8,000 tonnes of fish per year.

There are areas reserved for hunters, and permits are obtained from the same places as anglers. Other areas are reserved for water sports

In the forest are rare reptiles and over 800 plant families. There are types of vipers that can give a deadly bite. There are no poisonous insects, and the risk of malaria from mosquitoes is minimal, but they can be annoying.

The Danube Delta has been inhabited since ancient times and there are many archaeological sites. It has been a major trading centre and crossroads for human migration. Neolithic art from 7,000–5,000 years ago has been found here, and there are remains of Iron Age settlements from 3,200–2,500 years ago.

Not all the population are typical Romanians: some are Lipovenians who are migrants from the Volga Basin in Russia. Peter the Great tried to modernise the Orthodox Church practice, even changing the translations in the Gospels and ordering the faithful to shave off their beards. Those dissenters who could not accept the changes to their Orthodox Religion and did not swear allegiance to the Tsar left Russia, crossed the Ukraine and arrived in the Danube Delta. Their leader was a monk named Philip who renounced military service, marriage and the priesthood. Today the Lipovenians are the fishermen here but in other parts of Romania they are skilled craftsmen, farmers and factory workers. The name Lipoveni is derived from *lipo* meaning lime, or linden tree, since their religious icons were painted on wood from this tree.

The delta is protected under the administration of the Danube Delta Biosphere Reserve Authority (DDBRA). Eighteen protected reserves constituting 580,000 hectares are effectively off limits to tourists. It was also declared a National Biosphere Reserve in 1990 by UNESCO. This world heritage site is the world's third most important wetland site after the Amazon and the Nile Deltas. It is recognised by the RAMSAR convention, which covers 600 wetlands through the world. Thirty types of ecosystems in the delta make it a natural museum of biodiversity.

The best way to see the delta is in a small boat and this can be arranged with local fishermen or at the hotels.

Prices for renting a boat at Hotel Uzlina
Prices in Euros

	Up to 4 hours	Up to 8 hours
Rowing boat	10	15
Rowing boat plus guide	23	32
60hp motor boat plus guide (boatman)	45	62

You pay additionally for fuel used and meals for the boatman. It is not possible to rent a boat without a Romanian boatman.

The inhabitants of the villages in the Delta preserve many old customs and traditions. Lipovenian boatmen believe that if someone whistles while standing in the boat, this is a bad omen. Often the best currency here is brandy, vodka or one of the local spirits.

Sfîntu Gheorghe harbour

River Danube navigation
Romania

Km1075
The River Nera flows from the Transylvanian Alps and merges with the Danube and forms the border between Serbia and Romania on the east bank at 44°49´.3N 21°.20´.1E. Transylvania is the Latin for 'beyond the forest' and this is where Bram Stoker based his story of Dracula. From here to Braila the maintained depth is 2.5m and after Braila the maintained depth is 7.32m.

Km1072
The first township is Bajias which only has a flimsy wooden jetty in front of a café. This has just over 1m at the end.

Km1059
Veliko Gradiste 44° 46′N 21° 31′N (in Serbia)
Population 6,300
This was the site of the fort of Punicum. Before entering Romania, formalities to leave Serbia have to be cleared at Veliko Gradiste.

It is advisable to start the clearance procedure early in the day as it could take many hours to complete. You will need the daylight to find a mooring afterwards, since from this point onwards you have to stay on the Romanian side of the river. From here to km1040 the flow rate of the river is very slow.

Km1047
Moldova Veche
Moldova Veche is the location of Romanian customs, who can be contacted on VHF Ch 16. There is a good pontoon to moor on to. On going ashore we met three officials who, after a quick look at the passports, said, 'Go!' and within a few seconds we were in Romania. We could not convince them to put a stamp in the passport as proof that we had stopped there. This is the smartest and fastest working group of officials you will meet in this part of the world. This is the former Romanian pilot station for the Iron Gates and is located in a poor agricultural area. The town was once fortified by the Turks.

From entering Romania and for a distance of 130km the Danube flows through a series of gorges with interesting geological structures. The first is the Golubac ('pigeon') Gorge with a width of 400m before opening out into Liupkovska ('sweetness') Valley. The second gorge, Gospodin Vir ('the lady's whirlpool') is towered over by the Sokolovac ('the hawk') with a height of 590m and the river only 200m wide before entering Dolnji Milanovac (lower valley) and opening out to become 2km wide.

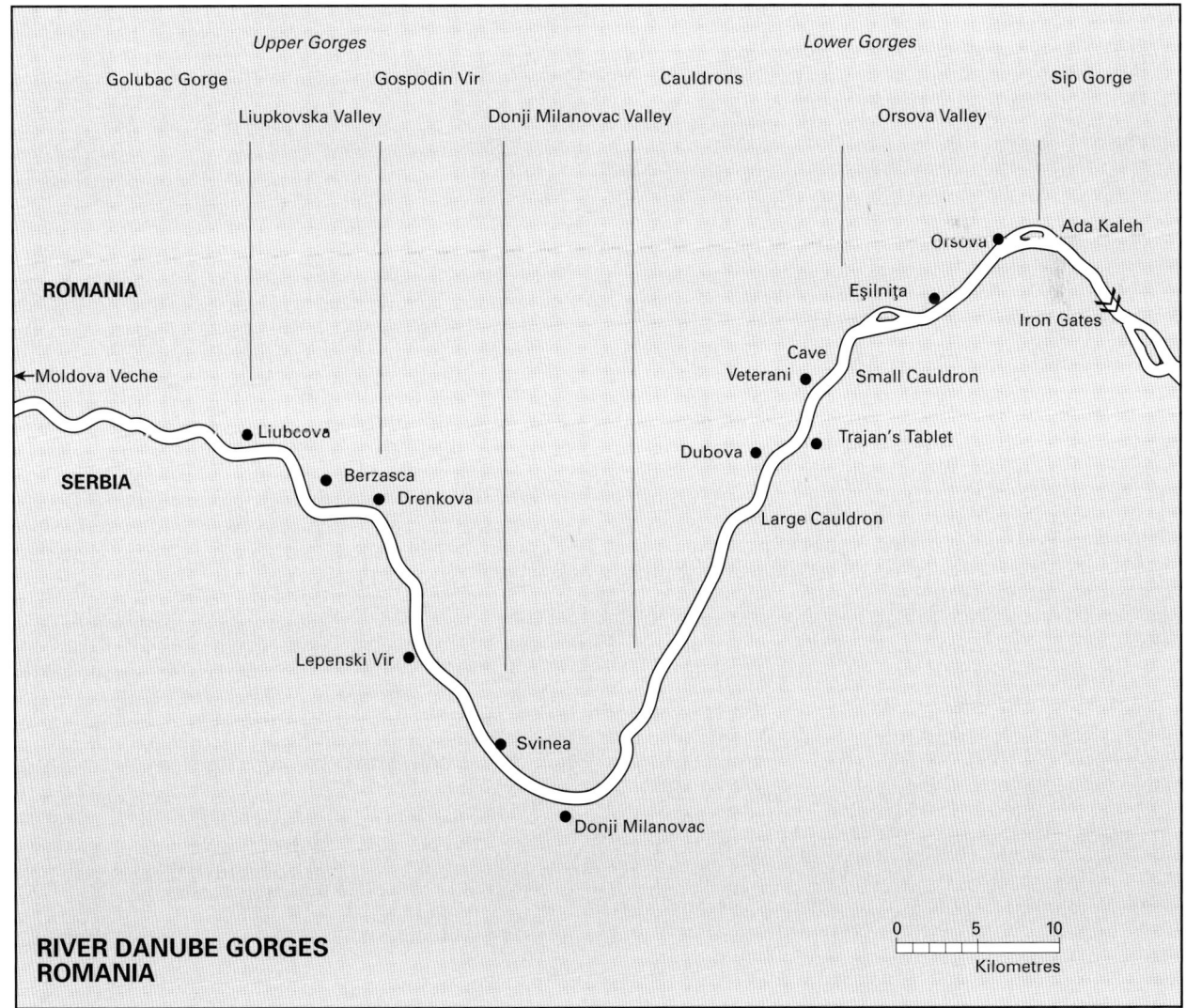

By km975 there is the third gorge which opens out in two places known as the Large and Small Cauldrons. The Cauldrons are also known as Cazanele Mari and Cazanele Mici by the Romanians and called Djerdap or Kazan Gorge by the Serbs. The Cauldrons are overshadowed by Veliki Strbac (768m) and Mali Strbac (Stirbatu Mic) mountains rising to 626m. The width of the river narrows to 180m and the depth we measured was greater than 70m, but it is reputed to have depths over it 80m. The Orsova valley is sandwiched between here and the final gorge called Sip.

The whole of the gorge and Iron Gate area is a proliferation of archaeological sites.

Km1016
Drenkova

The jetty here today is used mainly for exporting wood and has 3m depth alongside.

This was formerly a pilot station before the Iron Gates Dam was built. Some passengers left here and went overland and joined another boat further downstream.

Km1000

Near Svinița there is almost no flow in the river.

Looking back into the mouth of the Small Cauldron

Km973
Veterani Cave

The cave here was believed to be the sanctuary of the Dacian god Zamolxis.

In 1682 General Veterani and 400 of his troops held out against the Turks for 45 days before they had to surrender due to lack of food, water and ammunition.

A similar thing happened in 1788 when Lieutenant Colonel Voith held out for 21 days against the Turks. The Turks were so impressed with their bravery they allowed the Austrian solders to return home. Today, because of the increase in the water level the cave can only be visited by boat.

Km970
44°39′2N 22°15′.4E

There is a gulf between the Cauldrons where the village of Dubova nestles. We suddenly encountered a gusty Force 3–4 westerly funnelling up between the steep hills and giving a choppy sail. It died down as quickly as it started and the calm returned, only to be repeated a short time later.

Km960
Eşilnița 44°41′4N 22°21′3E

Rather than stop at the drab industrial town of Orsova it is more interesting to stop at Leselnita (Eşilnița). In this bay there are a lot of new buildings with tourists in mind and in future there will be more choice, with signs of new pontoons being installed in 2004.

The Doru Oniga guesthouse has an excellent pontoon with water and electricity and the use of a shower in one of the rooms. The mooring is free if the bar and restaurant are used. To reach it is a nightmare, having to pick your way through many fishing nets only marked by plastic bottles (in some cases only half-litre ones). One bonus is the possibility to sit on the balcony and look across the reservoir and back into the Cauldrons.

New building at Eşilnița

Km955

The Orsova Depression is formed where the River Cerna flows into the Danube. This area is now flooded as the reservoir was formed when the Portile de Fier (Iron Gates) dam and lock system was constructed. Orsova Bay has Miocene deposits with conglomerates, limestones, marls, clays and sands which are covered with alluvial deposits (sands and gravels).

These tectonic conditions give important reserves of ferrous ores and non-ferrous ores (barite, bentonite and feldspar), chromium and granite, which have been exploited at Toplet in the valley just north of Orsova.

Km954
Orsova Town
Population 19,000

At the mouth of the Cerna River in the original town there are traces of the Daco-Roman settlement of Dierna (Tierna). This was important in the reign of Septimiu Sever (193–211) as a strategic fortress to protect navigation. There is also evidence of an earth fortress from the 9th and 11th centuries. In the 14th century a stone fort was constructed and this was captured by the Turks. It was later occupied by the Austrians. On the 1 December 1918 it was returned to the Romanians who promoted it to a town in 1923. Before the flooding it was a quarantine and pilot station for this section of the river.

Unfortunately all of this was flooded with the construction of the Iron Gates dam. The northeast limit of the old town has become the southern limit of the new town, which included the townships of Jupari, Tufari and Comarnic and now spreads 7km along Cerna Bay.

Orsova is the most important port in the Danube Gorge area and is an industrial town with the economy based on the port, shipbuilding, mineral extraction, timber processing, engineering production and thermo-electric power station.

The vegetation in the area is common oak, hornbeam, beech, and manna-flowering ash and the agricultural cultivation of potatoes and some cereals.

Just downstream from Orsova was the island of Ada Kaleh. Work on the island fortress started in 1691 and was completed in 1737 and because of its strategic importance it earned the nickname 'Gibraltar of the Ottoman Empire'. Today it is covered by 69.5m of water.

Km950
Bahna River
Until 1918 this was the border between the Austria Hungarian Empire and Romania.

Km944 to Km942
Portile de Fier (Iron Gates) Lock
44°39′.2N E22°24′.4E

Before approaching the Iron Gates Lock contact the lockmaster by radio who will then give instructions. In our case this was to tie up at the end of the pontoons that project upstream from the lock. A few minutes after tying up a pilot came to the boat with the instructions to wait until a large barge convoy of nine barges and a pusher unit, which was due in about an hour, was in the lock. He stayed with us until we were in the lock and he kept in touch with the lockmaster by radio. The large convoy had difficulty getting into the lock, being blown by the wind and hitting the side. There was a lot of cursing over the airwaves; the pilot translated all that was being said and the Ukranian barge captain was unaware that we were hearing all. He wanted to blame our presence for the accident, while the lock captain blamed his incompetence for not taking into account the wind.

We were instructed to go into the lock behind the barges. It takes just under an hour and a half to go through the two locks and drop 33m before you continue downriver.

The morals from this part of the voyage are:
1. Keep well away from barges; a recreational boat is dwarfed by the size of these vessels.
2. Follow the instructions of the lock captain. If they are not clear ask for a repeat, and if there are language problems put a question to the lock captain that can be only answered by a yes/no answer, and make sure all instructions are clear.
3. Take into account the wind. since it can also affect pleasure craft.

At one time it was essential to have a pilot on board to navigate this section, which was only possible when there was high water. It had the reputation of being a narrow hazardous gorge with whirlpools, currents and rocks just below the surface. At this section substantial deepening and widening were undertaken in 1896, but

One of the huge locks at Portile de Fier

it did not become easily navigable until August 1969 when the locks were finished and in May 1972 the dam and hydroelectric power station were completed.

The increase in water level flooded as far upstream as Belgrade, drowning the original town of Orsova and the Roman road through the gorge. This road was constructed by drilling holes into the cliff face and inserting beams that formed the support for a fortified carriageway. A 19th-century Hungarian road was also lost with flooding (along with towns and villages and some ancient monuments, some of which were moved up to higher ground). Eight thousand people from the former Yugoslavia and 14,000 Romanians were relocated. All communications – road, railway, electric distribution cables and telephone wires – had to be built on higher ground.

Iron Gates, (Portile de Fier, Djerdap Power Station)

This is a huge dam and double lock system on both the Romanian and Serbian sides. The hydroelectric power station produces 2,100 megawatts of electricity per year that is shared by both countries. Their share represented (at the start of construction in 1960) the equivalent of the total annual output from the then Yugoslavia and 33% of the total annual output from Romania.

The dam made an incredible improvement in the passage time in this area. Previously tugs were used to pull barges through this section, taking an estimated 4½ days. From our entry into the first lock to the exit of the lower lock it took 1 hour 26 minutes.

STATISTICS FOR THE DAM AND LOCK
Width across the river   1278m
Two locks, one each on the Romanian and Serbian side
Max height of boats into the lock   70m
Length of locks   310m
Width of locks   34m
Depth of locks   4.5m
Drop in height   33m

This is adequate for a pusher tug and 9 barges of 1,000 tonne each plus several pleasure boats.

The dam now serves a major purpose it was never designed for: there are huge amounts of rubbish and flotsam in the river which are trapped by the dam, and the river is certainly more pleasant and safer east of the dam. Another effect of the dam is that some flora and fauna disappeared and different species of birds now inhabit the area.

Serbian side of the river

There are some places of interest on the Serbian side of the river, but if you have to check out at Veliko Gradiste you have to keep on the Romanian side of the river and can't visit them.

Km1040
Golubac (Golubex)

This is a small coalmining town.

The castle, built to guard the entrance to the Iron Gates gorge, was built on the rocky outcrop in the 14–15th century, on the site of the Roman fort Columbarium. Despite being the scene of many battles the fortress's 7 towers are well preserved and represent one of the finest medieval fortresses in Serbia. The town was rebuilt on higher ground after the flooding for the Iron Gate Dam.

Km1021.5
Dobra

This used to be the Serbian pilot station for boats going downstream and was also a guard post. The village was relocated further up the hill due to the flooding.

Km1004
Lepenski Vir

Important archaeological discoveries uncovered an 8,000-year old town of trapezoidal wooden houses from the Neolithic period, and evidence of farming and fishing from about 6400BC. Research published in 2004 dates human remains to 9000BC, giving further proof of Neolithic civilization spreading from the Danube through Europe. It has a small museum where there are sandstone carvings.

Km992
Donji Milanovac (Donli Mianovic, Majdanpek)

Another town rebuilt higher up the hill. There is a pontoon mooring and it is convenient for shops, water, restaurants and the garage for fuel is nearby.

Km964
Trajan's Tablet (which has also been relocated higher up)

'This celebrates Emperor Caesar overcoming the hazards of mountain and river and opening the road'. The Emperor Tiberius, who ruled from AD14–37, started the road and it was completed by Trajan (AD98–117), about AD103. The monument was damaged by Serbian fishermen who used it as a fireplace. Trajan was the second of the so-called 'five good emperors' and was also the first non-Italian to reach that position. He was best known as a soldier in the Dacian Campaign and resettled Dacia with Romans and incorporated Dacia in the Roman Empire.

Km956.5
Tekjip, (Tekija, Taekjip)
44°41´.2N 22°24´.4E

Pontoon mooring with shops and restaurants in the vicinity. Another town rebuilt on higher ground.

Km934
Kladovo (Claudia)

This has a small shallow harbour and a floating restaurant. There is a customs post here for boats coming from Romania. Originally a Roman fort, its main function today for the workers from the Iron Gates dam to stay.

Romanian side of the river

Km930
Dobeta Turnu Severin
44°37´.0N 22°39´.3N
Population 104,000

This is the capital of Mehedinti County and is surrounded by hills and built on terraces on the banks of the Danube. It has good communications, being based on the European highway E70, and is a major port.

The city, known as Drobetae in Roman times, was a prosperous military and political centre due to its strategic position with the harbour, road and bridgehead on the north Danube bank. It had the status of Municipium during Hadrians time in AD124 and became Colonia when Septimiu Sever (AD193–211) ruled. Archaeological exploration has uncovered ornaments and monuments from this period.

Trajan is said to have built a bridge across the Danube near here about AD103–105 with a length of about 1,155 metres, the largest in the Roman Empire with 20 arches. The town and bridge were destroyed by the Huns in the 5th century but the town was rebuilt by Justinian (AD527–565). There is little trace of the bridge and there is a programme to recreate a similar bridge to check the feasibility of this. It is said that there are two stone supports remaining on the Romanian side and one on the Serb side, with the possibly of others under the water.

In the Middle Ages it changed its name to Turnu Severin, meaning northern tower, after a tower that was builtt by the Byzantines. In 1972 took on both names and is now known as Dobreta Turnu Severin. By the 13th century it was the political centre of Banat and was later occupied by the Hungarians and then the Turks in 1524. The Adrianopol peace deal in 1829 removed the town from Turkish control and the new town started construction seven year later with the harbour being built in 1858. The town is laid out with wide streets and right-angle intersections, and many parks with roses give it the name 'City of the Roses'.

Mooring is at the pontoon beside the harbourmaster's office. This is a port of entry and if you choose to stay on the Serbian side of the river and go through the Serbian lock at the Iron Gates then clearance into Romania can be made here. There is a good selection of shops and restaurants in the town.

Here the height above mean sea level is about 48m. Projected for future development is a Ro-Ro terminal.

Km865 to km861

An island at Prahovo splits the river in two with locks on either side. If you have checked out of Serbia you have to go to the Romanian lock on the north side of the island. Use the lock on the south side if you have not checked out of Serbia. The exception to this is if one lock is out of commission for maintenance, in which case you will be advised by an official.

Km864–km863
Portile de Fier 2 (Eiserne Tor 2, Prahovo Lock)
This also incorporates a hydroelectric power station and was completed in 1986.

Contact the lock by Radio on Ch 16 or 10. The lock drops eight metres and takes about one hour to go through. This is a single lock with the same dimensions as one of the Iron Gate locks. There are moorings to tie on to before the lock on the island side. This is not recommended for an overnight stop in case a barge appears. If an overnight stop is required to wait for the lock, there is an anchoring place in a small bay between km866 and km865 close to the Romanian shore and out of the way of the main route into the lock.

On our journey we were directed to the lock on the Serbian side since the Romanian lock was closed for maintenance. At the Serbian side we were reprimanded for not changing the courtesy flag from Romanian to Serbian (a point which hadn't crossed our minds). After this we were given a friendly greeting in perfect English and then found out this worker also spoke Welsh!

There is a small Ro-Ro terminal on the south side of the island between km865 and km864.

Km861
Prahovo
Prahovo on the Serbian side is an industrial town tucked in behind the island and at km859 there is a harbour with 2 cranes. There is a lot of industrial pollution from this town, which is the customs border town with Bulgaria.

Some of Germany's Black Sea fleet was sunk near here to hamper the movement of advancing Soviet forces at the end of the second world war. At extreme low waters, parts of the vessels protrude above the surface.

Km845.5
The River Timok forms the border between Serbia and Bulgaria.

Km851
Gruia
Gruia has one pontoon. The working Ch is 19 and the harbourmaster is Ch 12.
Here you are still 29.14m above the Black Sea.

Km795
Calafat 43°59′.3N 22°55′.0E
River Inspection Ch 82
Harbourmaster Ch 14

Calafat may derive its name from Kalfatern, which means caulking a boat (when caulking cotton was forced into the seams of the hull to make it watertight). There used to be a fortress and shipyards here, but today it is a fairly dirty industrial town. Fresh life will be given to the town when the new bridge from Bulgaria terminates here and it is joined to the European highway system.

There is a ramp for the ferries from Vidin and three cranes, along with four pontoons which are basically old barges and not easy for a pleasure boat to moor on to. They are also busy with local traffic and there is no sign of any recreational boats anywhere. There is an official anchoring place just above the km793 marker.

There are restaurants and shops in the town. The river height above Varna at the Black Sea is 26.68m.

By km777 the river widens and the flow rate decreases.

Km698
At the mouth of the River Girla-Nadeia there is a small commercial port with three specific barges. Apart from this sign of habitation the whole way from Calafat the land is flat; there are no houses, no sign of life, only trees. At night it was difficult to imagine that we were only a few metres from a riverbank as there were no signs of any lights.

Km679
Bechet
River Inspection Ch 22
Harbourmaster Ch 14

There is a pontoon which is used by the ferry to Oriahova, a jetty and two other pontoons. There are also a customs post and shops.

Km630
Corabia
River Inspection Ch 19
Harbourmaster Ch 19

The height here is 20.12m above the Black Sea at Varna.

The chart indicates the navigation channel goes close to the Romanian shore. Storms and floods have changed the course of the river and from the centre of the river it was impossible to go direct into the mooring. This was due to a large deposit of gravel and sand. The entry to the pontoons was to sail downstream and go inshore opposite the church with the golden dome, between km630 and km629 marker posts, and head back upstream close inshore beside the moorings for the barges. There is a pontoon beside a grain silo but it is used for passenger pleasure cruises. We could only stay until the boat was due. There are another two pontoons to the east of the four fuel storage tanks at about km628, but both were full with local boats.

The town is on a raised beach above the river. It looked an interesting place to visit (particularly the church with the golden dome), but due to the lack of a mooring this was not possible.

The town got the name of Corabia since it was first built from the remains of wrecked ships (*corabia* means 'galley').

Warning
The course of the river is constantly changing and the above route may have been changed during the next flood. This applies to all parts of the river: the navigation books can never be completely up to date. One useful tip is to watch where the local boats go.

From here down to the back of Turnu-Magurele is a poverty-stricken swampland.

Km597
Turnu-Magurele
Population 30,187
Harbourmaster Ch 11

There are two pontoons upstream of four cranes. This is in front of a dirty chemical complex, with one chimney belching orange smoke and three belching white smoke, covering the area with toxic fumes and pouring effluent into the river. One of the pontoons is inhabited by the police, who were not keen for us to land and advised that there were no restaurants or bars in the area and if we wanted something like that we should go to Nikopol on the Bulgarian side of the river. It is not a nice place to consider for a stop in any case.

After the town the riverbank is still flat and tree-lined with a lot of artificial planting.

Km564 to km562
Condur Island
At the time of our passage the chart showed the passage to the north of the island with silting to the south, but while we were struggling to find a route round the north a barge passed to the south. There were no marker buoys on the south side of the island; we noted a green one washed onto the riverbank further downstream.

Km554
Zimnicea
Harbourmaster Ch 13
General working Ch 80
Navigation Ch 16

There are 2 pontoons with three cranes but these are located in front of an unattractive tube factory.

There are now dense woods on both sides of the river, with no signs of life.

Km493
Guirgiu
Harbourmaster Ch 11
Guirgiu Radio Ch 22

The authorities requested US$250 to tie up against a pontoon. A barge owner, seeing our plight, offered for us to tie up against his barge close by which cost us a bottle of *tsuika* (Romanian plum brandy).

Guirgiu is the port where large tourist cruise boats that ply between Germany and the Black Sea stop. It is basically a river port with industry surrounding it. The housing complexes are further from the river, but not the most beautiful place to stay or visit.

At the end of the 14th century the town thrived as a customs point, administrative centre, and princely residence for Mircea the Old. In 1420 the area was conquered by the Turks and for the next four centuries was a bridgehead on Romanian land.

Many battles for independence took place in this locality and the town has been in the battle zone until modern times. It was bombed in 1853, 1877, 1916, and 1944. In the first world war it was the only Romanian town to have 80% of its centre destroyed. For this it received the title of 'heroic town' and received the French War Cross.

Technically the town claims many firsts. The first telegraph line, first railway under Romanian administration, first bridge built on a curve in Europe, the first ferry boat, the first commercial sailing ship flying a national flag launched here (*The Marita* in 1834), the first war steam boat (*The Romania* in 1862).

Ion Marinescu High School, established in 1869, is the most distinguished in the county and is associated with many renowned scholars and academics. The clock tower and Teohari Antonescu History Museum are tourist attractions.

Km489
To the east side of the town is the Friendship Bridge which links Romania to Bulgaria by road and rail. The navigation notes and history of the bridge are in the following section for Bulgaria.

Km470 to km464
Lunga Island
During our journey the chart showed the channel to the south, whereas it was to the north.

Km431
This is the entrance to the canal to Bucharest. It was started in 1985 during the Ceaucescu era and would have been the second costliest canal project in Romania's history. The project was to transform the southern part of the Arges River into a 72km navigable canal to provide a direct link from Bucharest to the Danube and hence elsewhere. The project was abandoned shortly afterwards.

Km429
Oltenita
Harbourmaster Ch 13
Navigation Ch 16
Oltenita radio Ch 19

The harbourmaster demanded mooring fees of US$25 per four hours, with a minimum payment of US$75.

We moored free further downstream behind an island and hence did not see Oltenita. The main town of 32,000 people is 3km from the river. There is a shipyard by the river where one boat reported that this was a good place to take down the mast and get some repair work done.

In ancient times it was known as Constantiola and it was the seat of the first bishopric established in Dacia. In the Crimean War the Turks crossed the Danube here and inflicted heavy losses on the Russians.

Km404 to km398
The position of the sandbanks has changed dramatically from the chart, and where the chart shows a route on both sides of Varastic Island the channel to the north was silted up. Similarly, we noted major changes at km384 to km382. Further information on this area is given in the following section for Bulgaria.

Km374
Chiciu (Calarasi)
There is a pontoon here which should not be used. This was a customs post but in 2004 was classified as non-operational.

Km369
This is the entrance to the Bratul–Borcea arm which goes to Calarasi and later rejoins the river. This is considered as an inland waterway; it is not part of the International Waterway and therefore should not be used unless prior permission has been obtained.

This arm is documented at the end of this section for Romania.

Km358 to km356
The passage to the north of Talchia Island on the chart looks narrow and silted. We saw a barge coming through here going upstream. We took this route and did not note a depth less than 3.9m in an area which is shown as silted up.

Km349
On the south bank are the signals for the Bala Canal.

Km348
Izvoarele (Pirjoaia)
Ch 22
This is a large industrial jetty which appeared unused. It could be moored against but it is high. There is a smaller lower jetty to the east.

Km345
This is another entrance into the Bala Arm which goes into the Romanian inland waterways. Here the scenery changes to wooded hills, the river becomes calm and the flow rate decreases.

Km329
The two pontoons shown on the chart do not exist.

Km324
A barge going upstream called us over to advise us of the current situation at km324 to km316. We could have had major problems without their advice. The marker buoy does not exist, and the silting extends further south. At the south of Ceaciru Island there are no entry signs and the channel, which is very narrow, is between Tiu and Ceaciru Island. Silting was in totally different places from those marked on the chart, with the centre of the channel being only 0.9m and the navigable part now being close to the shore north of Ceaciru Island. At km322 the two markers, and also the one at km317, did not exist.

Km313
Rashova
There was a nice-looking restaurant on the waterfront but no place to tie up to so you would have to anchor and go to the riverbank in the tender. Along the shore were many small fishing boats.

The Romans built a series of towers and forts from near here to the Black Sea.

Km308
Cochirleni
Behind the island is the 'ships' graveyard'.

Km300
Cernavoda bridges are the rail and road bridges over the river. For both bridges and in each direction the passage is under the centre span. The air height of the road bridge is 29.99m, and for the rail bridge 30.96m.

The rail bridge, designed by Anghel Saligny, was built in 1895 with French capital. This linked the European rail network to the Black Sea. At the time of its opening it was the longest bridge in Europe at 1.7km.

Km299 to km298
Cernavoda
Harbourmaster and lock keeper Ch 14
Cernavoda Radio Ch 18
We initially tied up in the harbour and did receive a friendly welcome. This was the first harbour to be privatised in Romania and is owned by the company Argos. There is a shipyard here, so presumably some repairs could be carried out.

We reported to the police and customs and they immediately told us to move. They said that they could not guarantee the safety of the boat and that theft in the harbour was rife. Since it was getting dark, and not being familiar with the area, we asked if someone could act as a pilot to show us where they wanted us to go. The chief of police navigated us to the harbourmaster's barge located in the entrance to the canal at 44°20´.44N 28°01´.66E. This is in a fenced-off compound and manned 24 hours so is a good secure mooring. After being introduced to the harbourmaster, who arranged shore power for the boat, the chief of police invited us to join him for a beer in the local pub.

Cernavoda is the port of entry after leaving Bulgaria, so in the morning we visited customs who wished us a pleasant voyage with no other formalities, not even a stamp in the passport.

The town was founded 5,500 years ago and was known as Axiopolis. It has always been an important grain-growing area but it only started to prosper after the harbour was built in 1879. It claims some firsts: 1766 first Romanian school in Dobrouja region, 1860 first Orthodox church and 1868 first mosque.

Cernavoda translates as 'black water' and this is the location of Romania's atomic power station which is based on a Canadian design and began to function in 1995.

The town is drab, with *panalek* buildings but basic facilities are available.

It is a stop for some of the cruise boats.

Downstream from Cernavoda the riverbanks become dense forest and later the east bank has some rock outcrops, becomes hilly and at km279 grassy with a few hamlets.

Km293
Seimeni
Seimeni has a triple-domed church but no pontoon to moor on to.

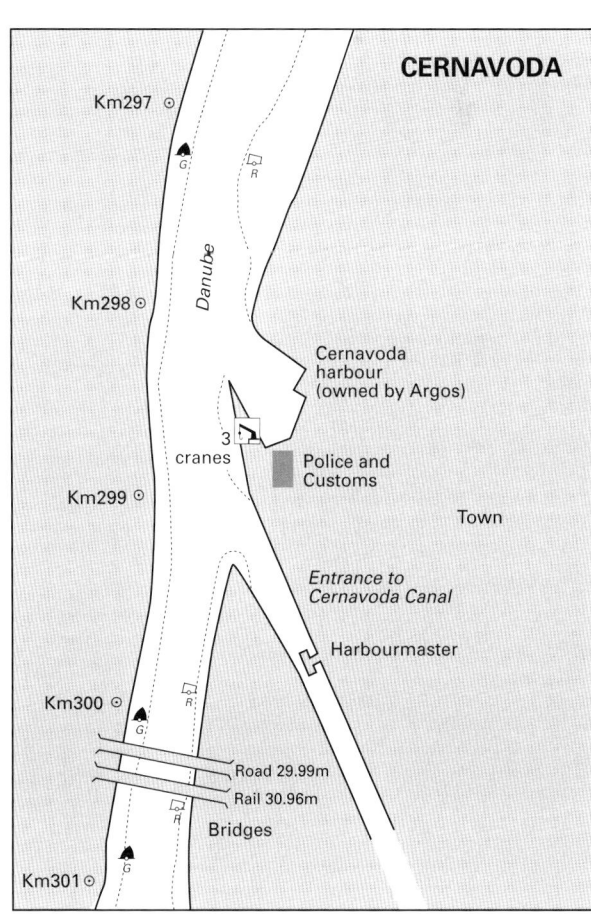

Km274.5
There is a concrete jetty used for loading sand and gravel, which is useful to tie on to, but the area is dirty.

Km272
Topolu
There is only a very small pontoon. The village has a large church with a silver roof and three domes. After the village the scenery changes to woods on both banks.

Km267
Only 10m from the shore we measured a depth of over 20m and further downstream there is an area of whirlpools over a depth of 31m.

Km262
Ghindares
There is only a tiny pontoon suitable for shallow-draught boats. There are many fishing boats in the area. Mooring is achieved by pulling the boats up the riverbank. Ghindares is built on a rocky outcrop and is dominated by a double-domed church with a small steeple.

Km253
Hirsova (Hârsova, Hrsova)
44°40′.83N 27°56′.80E at the harbourmaster's pontoon where you moor

The main office for the harbourmaster is in the building on the other side of the flood defence system from the pontoon. The police pontoon is on the upstream side of this. Restaurants, fuel and shops are available, but see the note below.

There is a harbour and remains of a boatyard. The industry here includes fish processing and a steel-strip mill but during our visit there was no activity at all in the area. Further downstream are a series of pontoons with some pleasure boats and work boats. The town has a rocky outcrop into the Danube and is interesting, with many diverse buildings from traditional small houses to mini *panaleks*. Founded by the Roman Emperor Trajan in AD103, it was called Carsium. It later became a Turkish town where a few ruins from these eras remain on the hill behind the police pontoon. The impressive church with 7 domes is the second highest in Romania.

The harbourmaster did not like the navy 'as it damaged the boats in his harbour'. We were soon to understand why they had this reputation (see km221).

The border police took an interest in our journey and we had a long talk with them. We said we wanted to go to a restaurant to eat, so they drove us in the police car to a restaurant at the main road on the outskirts of town. They asked if we needed fuel and drove us with our cans to the garage. Garages are at either end of town on the main E60 road. Later we were driven to see the church.

Km241
The Borcea Arm rejoins the main river, and the only view is trees.

Km238
Giurgeni
Giurgeni has a pontoon and a bridge, which carries the E60 road that continues to Constanța. The bridge has three spans, with the centre span for downstream navigation giving an air height of 17.7m. The westerly span is for upstream navigation and has an air height

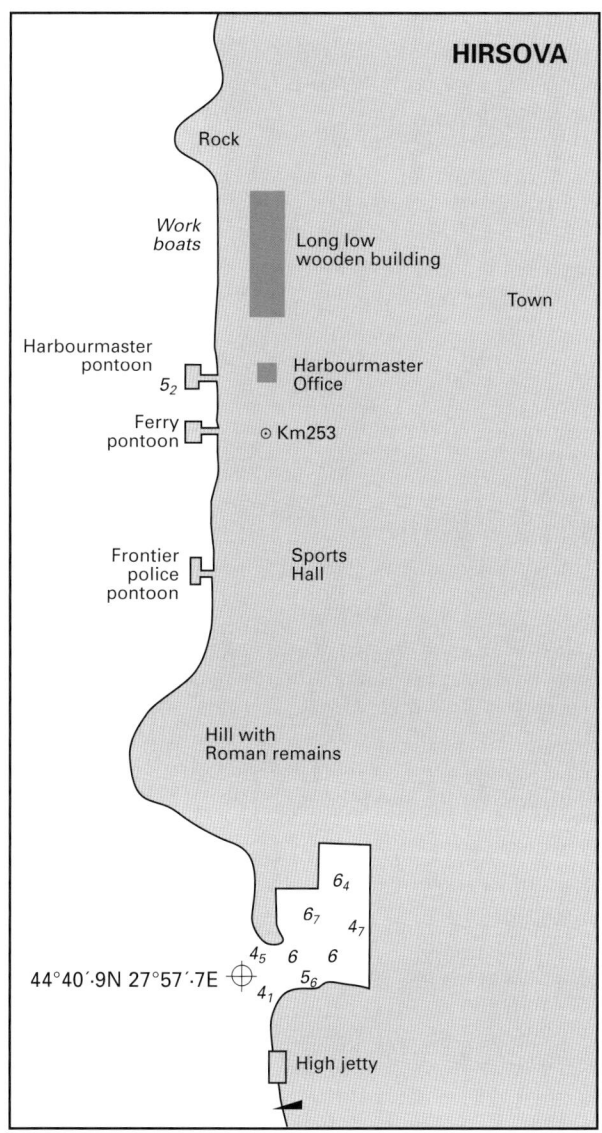

of 15.2m. This was a traditional place to ford the river in ancient times.

Just after the bridge at km237.5 the river divides, with the Dunãrea Veche (Old Danube) (Macin Arm) going to the east and the main Danube, with the navigation channels to the west, until the Macin Arm rejoins the main Danube again at km169; this forms Brăila Island, which is a zoological and botanical reservation.

Km237
The chart shows the route near the south bank, but we saw grass growing in the middle of the river. We noticed a marker buoy near the opposite bank and this is now where the deep water is.

Km225
There is a pontoon here that could be tied on to.

Km221
We tied up for the night against a boat which is partially out of the water. A navy boat like a small frigate came past at an incredible speed causing a tremendous wake in the narrow channel. Our boat and the one we were tied against crashed against each other; fender hooks were ripped out and fenders with hooks disappeared downstream. There was a loud crack of fibreglass breaking and this was the cabin roof

hitting the branch of a tree, which, when the wake subsided, we were unable to reach. This one boat must do more damage to the riverbank than all others put together. Some locals who were fishing nearby complained of the damage to their boats and the small jetty and said the navy justify this by saying 'they are looking for illegal immigrants'. At the speed they were going they would see nothing on the densely wooded riverbanks.

Km215
Almost next to the riverbank the depth was greater than 25m and there were many whirlpools.

Km197
There is a ramp for a car ferry, and for a short stop it could be tied on to at the side.

Km196
Both sides of Lupului Island are navigable. The westerly one is known as the Galeia arm and the numbering system starts again at km10, which is its length before rejoining the main river again.

Km195
The Arm Vilciu, which is a navigable inland waterway arm, rejoins the main river.

Km183
Chiscani
There is a small canal to a power station, noticeable by its two chimneys, water tower, and a dock with 3 cranes.

Km176
Behind Arapu Island is a base for navy boats.

Km174 to km168
Brăila
45°15´.68N 27°58´.25E at the mooring
VHF navigation Ch 16

Brăila is at the head of navigation for small and medium-sized seagoing vessels. It is the country's second largest port, stretching about 6km along the riverbank. There are pontoons for pleasure craft conveniently located near the town centre.

Since there are engineering shops in the town it is assumed that general boat repairs can be carried out. Water is available on some pontoons and on the promenade. Fuel is obtained from a taxi visiting a garage with cans. It is reputed to often have fog in December and January.

The town, originally called Drinago, was founded about 1350 and was referred to as Brayla in 1368 in a transportation and trade licence granted to Brasov merchants. It was occupied by the Turks from 1554 to the end of the Russo-Turkish War and in the peace treaty of Adrianopol in 1829 it was returned to Walachia. At this time it was created a free port and a few years later in 1835 new streets were laid out following the geometric pattern of the old Turkish fortifications. with all streets leading to the Danube.

In the late 1800s and early 1900s many gypsies came here. mainly from the Wallachian Plain, to work in the docks and surrounding area. This gave the town a reputation as 'The gypsy capital of Europe'. Prosperity for the town followed and now it is Romania's tenth largest town, with 217,000 inhabitants. It has large grain-handling and warehousing facilities and is an important industrial centre for metalworking, textiles and food processing.

The reeds which grow in this area are harvested and processed into paper, cardboard, glycerine, xylem, alcohol, fertiliser and briquettes. It imports general cargo, steel and machinery and exports timber, grain and livestock.

Tourists can visit the ethnographic museum, the House of Collections, history museum, theatres and churches.The folk art museum has a display about the local history of fishing. It is home to two old paddle steamers, *Borces* (1914) and *Decebal* (1917), but these are now stored out of the water.

Five kilometres from the town centre tourists visit Lacu Sarat Spa. Surrounded by forest, this salt lake has a high level of salt and is formed from an old course of the Danube. The bottom of the lake is covered by a therapeutic highly mineralised mud that is used for various cures.

Km169
Smirdan
This is on the eastern side of the river opposite Braila. The Old Danube, or Macin Arm of the Danube, which broke off at km237.5 near Giurgeni, rejoins the Danube. Ferries sail between Smirdan and Brăila.

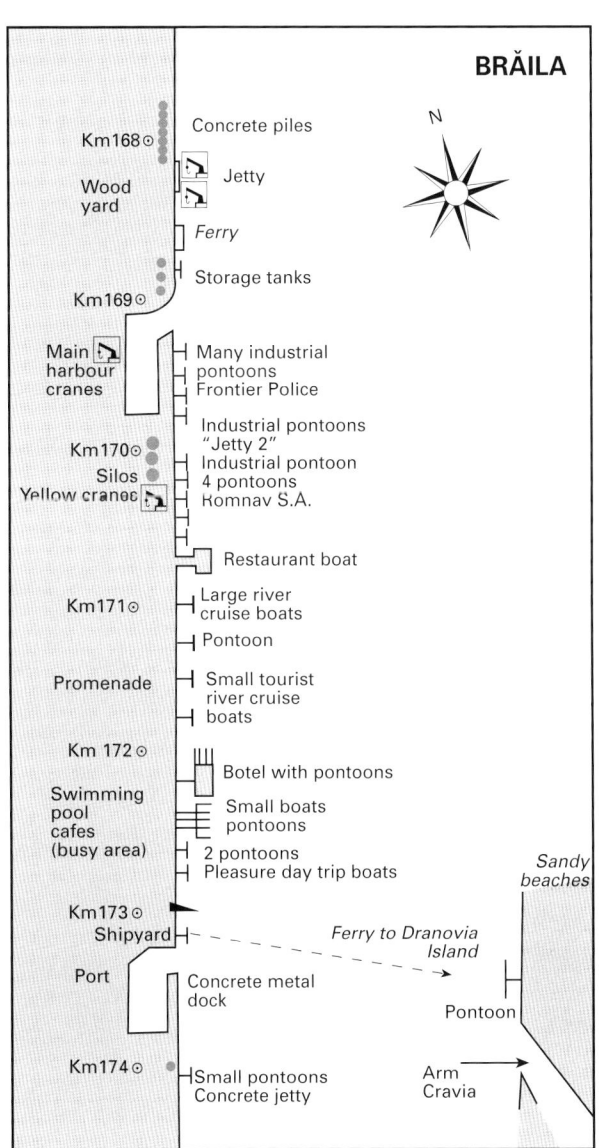

Km155
River Siret
This flows from Moldavia and joins the Danube here.

Km157 to km150 / M80 to M78
Galati (Galatz) 45°25′.3N 28°47′.0E
Navigation Ch 16

This is Romania's major port on the Danube and seventh largest town, with over a quarter of a million people. Here there was initial confusion with the marker posts when they suddenly changed from 150 to 80. It took a little time to realise the marker posts had changed from km to M (nautical miles) because sea-going vessels can reach here.

You have to report to the harbourmaster's office, which is very inconveniently situated at the opposite end of the town away from the river. With the shipyards here it is assumed that boat repairs can be carried out. Water is available at the pontoons and fuel is from garages using taxis and cans. From the Black Sea to here the port is kept open in the winter with icebreakers.

We had planned to meet a local friend who told us by telephone which pontoon to tie up to. There was a fairly cold reception from the local occupants, who were sitting drinking the local wine. Our friend arrived within a few minutes, gathered our passports and disappeared to a building about 100m away. Soon the radio on the pontoons burst into life and so did the inhabitants. The wine was put away, the inhabitants appeared in new clothes, an electric cable with mains power was brought to the boat and a water hose was rigged up. It transpired that this was the pontoon for visiting VIPs!

On the next visit we tied up at the same pontoon, but were told to go away. The same friend talked to the person who had given this instruction, and we were told to wait. Two hours later, when everyone from the pontoon had gone, the same person came back to us and said we could stay and it would cost €50 for a night. We declined his offer and moved to a work barge where two people were working; we gave them two large bottles of beer as our payment to stay the night. They were delighted when we also came back from town with something stronger for them.

Galati has been a port since ancient times, and remains from the 3rd century BC have been discovered. The first written mention of the town is in 1445, and for about 300 years the Turks occupied the town, using it as a navy base until 1829.

By the 19th century it was a major cosmopolitan port exporting grain from Wallachia, fish and caviar to Vienna and Budapest. The coffee houses had newspapers from Vienna so that the local and foreign fishermen and traders were familiar with the news, as well as the fish prices from the outside world. In this era the inhabitants included Germans, Turks, Greeks, Serbs, Tartars, Bulgarians and Georgians.

During the second world war the town was severely damaged by German bombing. During the 1960s there was major reconstruction and expansion, and Romania's largest iron and steel complex was located here. A customer for this product was the country's largest shipyard, which had also grown up in town. The main exports are metal products, timber, cement, chemicals and industrial equipment, and imports are iron ore, coke and grain.

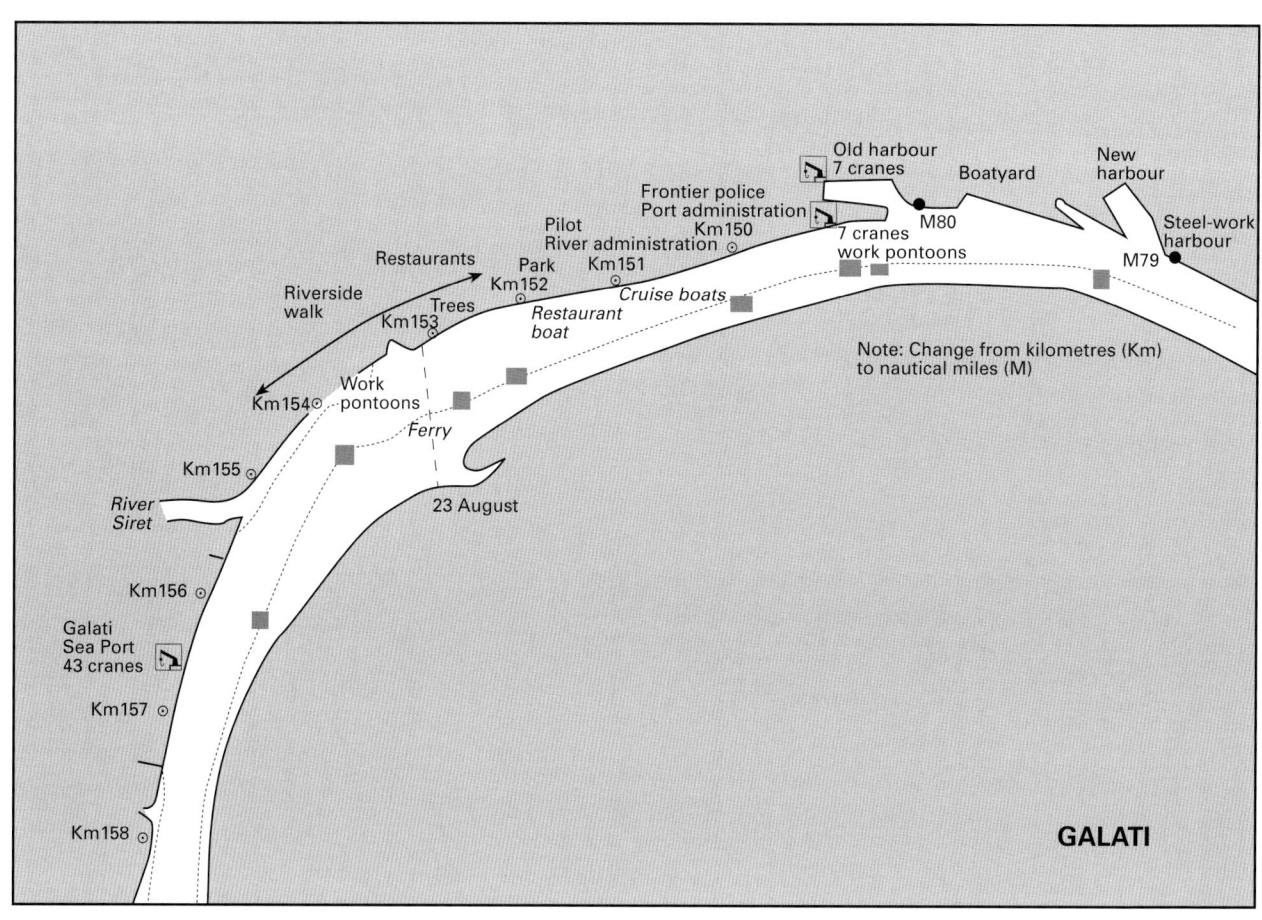

Galati. Cathedral of St George

Galati. The *Tudor Vladmirescu*

The main town is around Boulevard Domneasca where the history museum, council chambers, university, theatres, cinemas, churches and many listed buildings are located. As well as exhibits from the Paleolithic and Neolithic eras, the history museum also has some rare books and letters, including one from Jules Verne. The home of Alexander Ioan Cuza, the first prince of united Romania in 1859, is today an art gallery with over 3,500 exhibits. The zoo, botanical gardens and natural history museum are in the same complex. There is the 17th-century cathedral of St George. Overlooking the river is an old defensive church with galleries for archers and hollow walls for the people to hide in against the Turks. Also from this era many tunnels were dug as escape routes from an invading army. Many still exist under the city and one recently collapsed, with a bus finishing up in the hole. A tree-lined promenade with gardens stretches along the river bank to the TV tower, which has a restaurant at the top. The final mooring of the paddle steamer *Tudor Vladimirescu* (1854) is here. At Barboşi on the outskirts of Galati there are the remains of the Roman frontier town of Tirighina.

M75
Grindu (RHS)
There is a good pontoon here.

We were stopped by a Romanian police boat here to check the papers, since we were nearing Ukraine.

M72.5
Ukraine-Romania Border
The River Prut, which forms the border between Romania and Ukraine and Moldova, is the second longest tributary of the Danube at 950km. It is navigable to Ungheni, which is near Iasi in northeast Romania. Since it forms a state border, recreational use is limited. Apart from the Danube there are only two other rivers in Romania that are navigable, one being the Prut in the east which drains from the Carpathians and in the west the Bega (Bega Canal) which drains the Banat Plain.

From here is the best-buoyed section of the whole Romanian-Bulgarian section of the Danube. The river here is fairly straight, broad and slow-moving, and is the start of the Danube Delta.

For an overview and general information about the Danube Delta see separate section above.

M69 to M67
Reni (Ukraine)
Oil and ore port, with the harbour entrance being at M67, and about 30 cranes surrounding it.

M66
There is a good pontoon on the south bank, but it is inhabited by the Romanian frontier police.

M55
Isaccea
The trees give way here to the town which is on low-lying hills. In a small bay are some industrial moorings at 45°17′.10N 28°27′.17E. The water gauge here indicates that it is less than 1m above sea level.

The Persian King Darius is believed to have crossed the Danube here in 514BC. This is the site of the prosperous Roman town of Noviodunum, built in AD369, and it was a base for their fleet. It has a Celtic name, and was declared to be a *municipium* due to its strategic and commercial importance. It was later occupied by the Turks and called Isac-Kioi. The Turks also used it as a crossing point when going north to fight Christians. Osman II used this crossing point in 1620 when he moved to attack Poland.

M43
45°13′.4N 28°45′.0E

At the confluence of the two rivers are the signals for the entrance of the Chilia Arm to Ismail on the north side. (For notes on the Chilia Arm see below.)

The Sulina Arm international waterway is to the south and is the central of the three main channels. At this junction use navigation Ch 11 or 16. A training wall stretches northwesterly into the river and diverts

THE RIVER DANUBE

Isaccea harbour

some of the water from the Chilia Arm into the Sulina Arm to increase the volume. From this junction to the sea there is a dredged channel carrying about 18% of the volume of the Danube water. The depth of the channel changes due to silting, but is continually dredged to maintain a depth suitable for boats with a draught of 7.32m (width is circa 240–550m), with banks 1 to 2m high.

Signals from M43 to Sulina M0
- The river is marked with red and green buoys (some are very small, many are missing and others are out of place)
- An inverted anchor sign with a red border and line means it is an area where it is forbidden to moor
- M43 A light on a white post 6m high marks the junction of Sulina Arm and Chilia (Kilia) Arm (Kiliyskiy Rukav)
- M38.6 Tulcea: a red triangle flag on the flagstaff of the Danube Inspectorate indicates a strong current at the Tulcea bend and extra care is needed
- M34 A light on a black post 6m high marks the junction of Sulina Arm and St George's Arm
- M21 Gorgova: a blue flag on a flagstaff of the Danube Inspectorate indicates that the canal beyond this point is closed
- M13 Ceamurlia a blue flag on a flagstaff of the Danube Inspectorate indicates that the canal beyond this point is closed
- A blue flag on a dredger indicates the passage is closed while the flag is flying
- A blue flag on the harbour at Reni (Ukraine side) means vessels pass as slowly as possible
- At Sulina old lighthouse the depth in feet over the bar is displayed
- When it is dangerous to enter the Sulina Arm or a large vessel is leaving Sulina for the Black Sea a blue flag is displayed at Sulina Old Lighthouse. When the flag is flying no vessel should enter the channel from the sea.

M41.5 to M40
This is a sharp curve, where only one larger ship is permitted to enter this section at any one time and overtaking is not permitted.

M43
Pătlăgeanca
There is a good pontoon which is used by the ferry, and smaller ones owned by the Tulcea administration.
From here to Tulcea the buoyage system is good.

M40 to M38
Tulcea 45°10′.82N 28°48′.07E at the mooring
Water is available at the promenade, and repairs can be carried out at the shipyard. We got electricity from the barge we were moored on to. The wash from passing ships can be a problem. Icebreakers keep it clear for navigation in the winter but it also suffers from fog, mainly in November and February.

Here was the only place in Romania where the bureaucracy was totally out of control. The authorities came to the boat on several occasions, we had to visit several offices (and some of them several times) up and down the promenade. These included the border police, port movement, harbourmaster and port control. We spent 8 hours 46 minutes dealing with these people over a 2-day period.

In between times we visited the tourist information office, and the office for permission to sail in the Delta, and another permission to visit nature reserves. Romanian Law states that navigation in the Danube Delta with private craft is forbidden by law. The use of such craft is only permitted on the international section of the Danube (Sulina Arm). However, a few permits are issued each year to visit the Delta. They are obtained from the office 'Administraţia Rezervaţiei Biosferei Delta Dunţrii'. This is located at the side door of the information office. For eight days permits cost about €10; they also gave us a list of twelve suggested routes. Not all were practical due to the draught of the boat, as they were designed for travel in one of the small local fishing boats. All visitors to the protected areas in the delta require a permit. The area is closed in the bird-breeding season.

It you intend to rent a boat with a Romanian captain or go with a local fisherman, these permits are available in travel agents and some hotel receptions in Sulina, Murighiol, Uzlina and Crişan. Being caught without a permit involves a fine of about €200. The guides can be arranged at the tourist office or in the harbourmaster's office. Permits for hunting or angling are available from AJVPS (The Association of Sport Hunters and Anglers) at Str Isaccei No10, Tulcea.

Once we had the permit, the border police eventually returned to the boat with our passports. When they saw we had the permission for the delta, which they knew the previous day we were going to ask for, they said we would have to get permission from them too. They disappeared into town to hold another consultation and an hour later came back and announced that permission was granted and we were free to go to the delta.

On the next visit a bureaucrat said to go to one office for a piece of paper, then to another two for more, then bring them to him and he would give us permission to go to the office to get a permit to sail in the delta. We didn't like this idea, so we sent one of the Romanian crew to go to the office to speak Romanian, and he came back with the permit. A nickname for the town is 'Gateway to the Delta', an unfortunate name since it was the only place with restrictions and the gate was almost shut.

In the street parallel to the promenade opposite the Hotel Delta (a square box nine storeys high) is a ship chandler, and on the promenade a shop which repairs and sells outboard motors. A marine electrical shop is located in the street behind the art gallery. Fuel is also

Tulcea: Danube bend

available at the riverside here. In town and floating on the river are a good selection of restaurants and bars. All types of shops are available in the town.

It is a busy port with many ferries to various locations on the Danube, ocean-going ships, shipbuilding and repairs. It is the centre for freezing, canning and manufacturing the fish from the delta, which it exports along with ferro-alloys and aluminium hydroxide. The imports are chemicals in bags, bauxite in bulk, chrome ore and magnesite in bulk.

This was originally a Dacian town, then a Greek fortress, before it became the Roman town of Aegyssus. It has always been an important port, and in the 19th century grain from Wallachia was the main export. The eastern half of the town is dominated by Citadel Hill, with the prominent independence monument in honour of the heroes who fought in the independence war (1877–8).

Tulcea promenade and harbourmaster's office

The history and archaeology museums are just below the monument and built on top of the Roman town of Aegyssus, of which some remains can still be seen. In the town are the ethnographic museum, which includes an exhibition of fishing gear, and the natural history museum and aquarium, which is stocked with River Danube fish and exhibits Delta wildlife.

The oldest Muslim architecture in Romania is the mosque from the 17th century, and it houses the art gallery collection of oriental art. The folk art gallery is near the Hotel Delta. There is a memorial to the local victims of the 1989 revolution in front of the local Orthodox church.

M35
Mila
This is a new tourist complex with 3 good pontoons.

M34
Junction of 2 arms of the River Danube at 45°11′.2N 28°54′.0E.

SULINA ARM

The broadest arm, Saint George's, goes to the south, but the channel to navigate is the narrower northerly one, Sulina Arm. Just inside the arm is a water gauge indicating only 49cm above sea level. Here the scenery is pastoral with trees.

M32
Liganii de Sus
There is a pontoon and nearby a ramp and concrete jetty located beside a thatched cottage.

Here you start to see the real beauty of the Danube Delta.

M31.4
Partizani
On the south bank this has a good pontoon used by ferries and a concrete jetty. This is a small fishing village nestling in amongst the poplar trees.

M31
Another good mooring against a barge which is at right angles to the riverbank and is well marked.

M25
Small pontoons on both banks.

M24
Maliuc
On the north bank; many pontoons and a concrete jetty are located here. The township is popular with tourists, and boat hire is available here. There is a research station, which explores uses for the reeds which grow in the delta. The main processing factory for them is in Braila.

M21
Gorgova
Here there is a large pontoon. This village has no electricity.

M19
Babarada
On the north bank; this has a concrete jetty. Here and at M13 are entrances to the Dunârea Veche (Old Danube), which leads to Mila 23. At Mila 23 there is a fuel barge with diesel, petrol and gas and close by is a small shop and pub. See Dunârea Veche (Old Danube) below.

M14
Lebăda
This village on the north bank has a pontoon which is used by ferries. It is located at an entrance to the Old Danube and opposite the entrance to the Canal Crisan. This leads to Caraorman where they started to build a factory to produce glass using the sand from the river silt, but it was never completed.

M13
There is a statue celebrating the completion of the Sulina Canal, and the Danube Inspectorate building.

M12
Crişan
The main village jetty cannot be moored against as it is regularly used by ferries. The visitors' jetty is nearby but the 'caretaker' of this pontoon wanted almost €4 per hour to moor there. A local fisherman nearby offered his pontoon and after repositioning his boat we shared a few whiskies with him and there was no cost to stay there.

The boat was hammered by the wake of passing boats going too fast, the worst offenders being the police, small ferries, and over-powered fishing boats. The large ocean-going boats caused no problems. Crişan has a modern hotel (Lebăda: The Swan) and near here is a statue from 1894 when King Carol I officially opened the new Sulina Canal. The village is trying to develop tourism based on boat trips, fishing, and wildlife watching. There is a tourist information centre, a small shop, café and bar near the main village jetty

Fishing permit for the Danube Delta

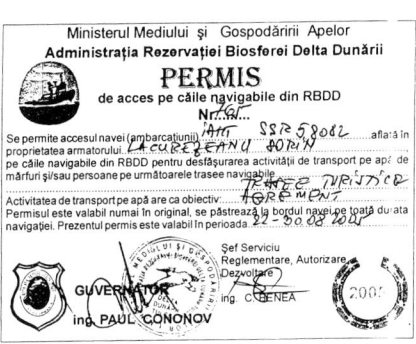

Permit to sail in the Danube Delta

M0
Sulina
45°09'.2N 29°38'.3E

On the southern bank there is a concrete jetty at a sensible height, with plenty of mooring rings running the full length of the town. You are recommended to tie up at the main wharf near the customs which are located in the administration building. They will come to visit the boat.

On this side of the river is the 18.5m high lighthouse dating from 1802, where the depth over the bar is displayed in feet. The currency exchange is at the opposite end of the town and the museum is in between. On the opposite side of the promenade are shops, and one in particular sold almost everything we needed: toiletries next to tools, and films, vegetables next to plastic goods, then more food.

The town consists of six streets parallel to the river with only a soil surface, except for the one at the jetty. Boats appear to be a more popular form of transport than cars for the town's 5,000 inhabitants: the jetty is always busy with water transport.

After months on the River Danube we found an oasis in a low yellow building on the first street near the cathedral. It is the Casa Coral, a bar and restaurant with good food and the best toilets on the Romanian Danube.

By 950 Sulina was a Byzantine port called Sellina and by 1318 it was a Genoese trading post. For a considerable period of its history it had the status of being a free port. After the dredging of the channel, Sulina prospered. When the size of the ships increased Sulina lost its importance and lost out even more when the Constanţa-Cernavoda canal was opened.

After the first world war was a prosperous period when the International Danube Commission had its headquarters in the town and it had the status of being a free port. After the second world war the headquarters were moved to Budapest and Sulina's importance waned. Business was dominated by the Greeks, but they were expelled in 1951.

The graveyard gives an indication of other nations who forged the town's history, with Romanian, Ukranian, Turkish, Greek, Jewish and British graves. The Orthodox church of Santa Maria was visited by the Queen of the Netherlands in 1977 and she was appalled by the dilapidated state it was in, and after the royal visit it was restored at the initiative of the Romanian government.

M0 (out to sea)

The training wall projects over 5 miles out into the Black Sea. Near the end of the wall the volume of water hits the Black Sea and backs up, forming high waves, which carry on well out to sea. South of the entrance we made a depth measurement of 1.9m where on the chart the depth was 10–20m; with the amount of silt the River Danube brings down, changing depths are a permanent problem, and charts cannot always be relied on.

See also *Chapter II The Black Sea. Romania. Navigation notes for entry into the Sulina Canal.*

History of the Sulina Arm

In 1856 the Sulina Arm was less than 3 metres in depth and the other two branches under 2 metres. Shipwrecks were a common occurrence in this era. On one winter night in 1885 a gale swept ashore 24 sailing boats and 60 lighters, and 300 people lost their lives. Sir Charles Hartley was chief engineer for the commission from 1856–1907 and he reported that the mouth at Sulina was a wide-open seabed strewn with wrecks and the only way to navigate here was to avoid the wrecks. The town was regularly flooded if the sea rose by a few centimetres, and the riverbank at this time was covered in tall weeds and reeds.

Sulina-Sfîntu Gheorghe confluence; Sulina Arm to the left

In 1858 Sfîntu Gheorghe channel was the one favoured for canalisation but due to political and economic considerations nothing was done. From 1858 training walls projecting seaward were constructed on the Sulina Arm and these were regularly extended until today they are over 5km long. The 3m depth at the beginning of the project became 6m after completion. In 1855, 36 ships out of 2,928 entering the Sulina Arm were wrecked. Ten years later seven ships were wrecked out of 2,676 entering here, proving the success of this operation.

Between 1857 and 1902 the Sulina Arm was straightened, cutting out 27 bends and reducing the length by 21.9km and forming the Sulina Canal. Dredgers were not only used for maintaining the channel, but for the construction of ports and reclaiming material for dikes to prevent flooding.

To keep the Sulina Canal navigable an estimated 2,100,000m^3 of silt and fine sands have to be dredged annually. The worst time of year is in the spring when the Danube brings down most sediment.

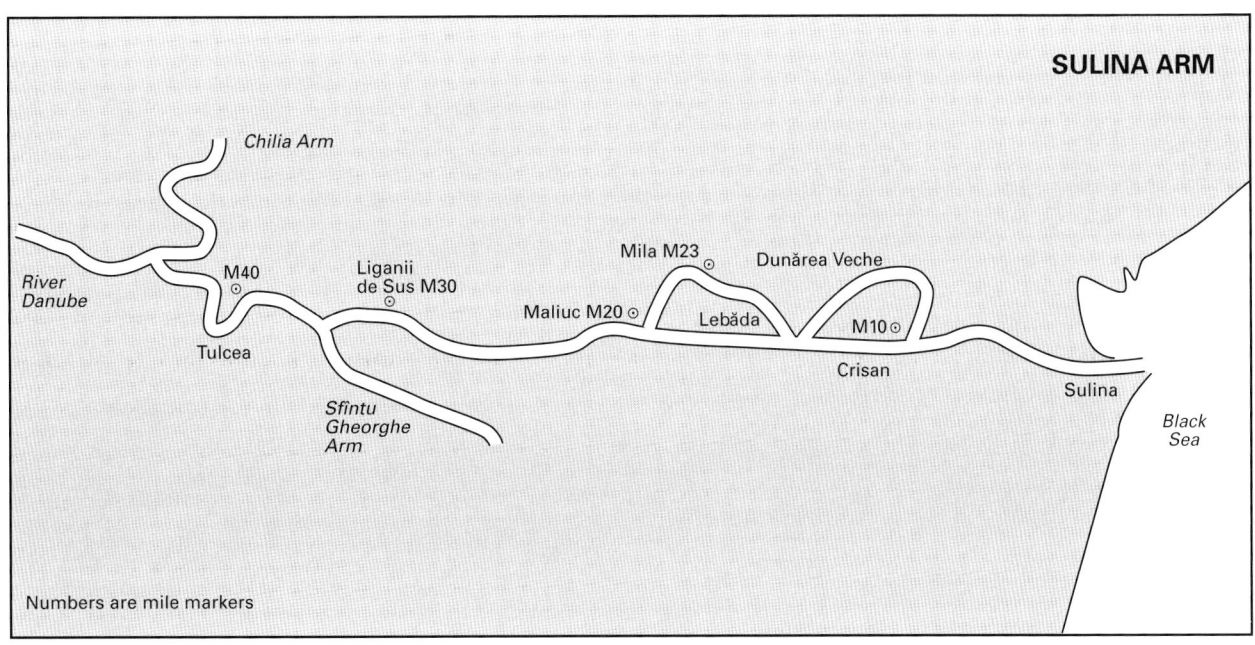

Sulina Arm reeds

There have been many dredgers working on the Danube since the first one became operational in 1895. Today the flagship dredger is the *Dunârea* which was designed specifically for the Lower Danube and is operational up to 20 miles offshore. The hopper capacity is 2,680m³ and can dredge to a depth of 25 metres. It commenced its duties in June 2000 and maintains the vital link between the Danube seaports and the Black Sea.

A boat with a draught of 7.32m, beam 36m and length 225m has sailed on this section of the Lower Danube.

OTHER ARMS OF THE DANUBE RIVER

DUNĀREA VECHE

Dunārea Veche (Old Danube) is now bypassed by the Sulina Canal, but when you enter this backwater the main village is Mila 23. There is a pontoon that sells fuel and gas. Here are the traditional fishermen's cottages, many of which have thatched roofs. The house forms part of the boundary wall and the garden where the vegetables are grown is completely enclosed with wooden fences. The main occupation is fishing and the catch is supposed to go to the fish processing plant at Tulcea, but many of the fish seem to escape this journey and are consumed locally. The village was flooded in the 1960s, causing extensive damage, and much of it had to be rebuilt.

The diversion in the Dunârea Veche

In Tulcea we had arranged the permit to navigate the Delta, and the harbourmaster had arranged for us to meet a guide. The address given was Sai Mila 23, Com Crisan. We headed for Crisan where we spent the night, to discover Mila 23 was a hamlet on the Dunârea Veche, so in the morning we doubled back into the Old Danube.

We would never have found the house if we did not have a Romanian speaker on board. She kept shouting to the people on the riverbank to ask where we could find the family. Eventually we did, and moored on an anchor in the river. Our host collected us in his fishing boat and took us to his small jetty. He explained that he had expected us the previous day and on this day he was going to be busy, but he assured us his son knew the waters well and could act as our guide.

Marian, his son, only spoke Romanian, but through our Romanian crew he discovered the breadth and draught of the boat, so that he knew where he could take us. We were taken through some very narrow waters and sometimes the route looked impenetrable. At one stage we were asked to navigate between two mature trees with only centimetres to spare on both side and branches scraping on the cabin roof, but this soon opened out into a wider channel.

In other cases Marian took us through channels which were so shallow the only indication on the fish finder was 0 and 'SHAL' on the depth-sounder. Measuring the depth at one point with the boat hook we could only have had a centimetre clearance, but we were assured this was enough. After 2 hours of going through the water vegetation, under the canopy of trees, we came out into Lake Fortuna. A flock of pelicans was sitting at the lake side.

We navigated up the lake in the 'deep' channel (that is not more than one metre deep), and were then asked to go into a tiny channel where the boat had to push the reed aside. Eventually we moored and used the dinghy to penetrate even narrower channels between all types of trees, reeds and water vegetation. Our guide wanted to show us the best place to see frogs (there were hundreds of them) and other aquatic life. Without his help we would have had trouble finding our way through the undergrowth and back to the boat.

Through more shallow and narrow channels we reached Lake Baclǎneştii Mari. Here the vegetation changes again. Now it was time for Marian to show us where there were lots of fish. The channel was narrow with huge trees on both sides and branches touching in the middle, giving a shady, eerie atmosphere. The fish finder recorded a depth of 7 metres, but the whole screen was almost black, totally covered with fish icons. We were making our way back to his house through a narrow waterway when a small speed boat came round the corner, obviously not expecting to meet another boat. To avoid collision they had to throw the boat hard over and went through the reeds James Bond-style before rejoining the waterway. (It was the Romanian police, causing a tremendous wake and damaging the tranquil, fragile ecosystem, which they were supposed to be protecting.)

After 8 hours away from civilization we returned back to the house where 'mother' had prepared a meal of four large fish steaks from different types of fish. We asked her how much the meal cost and she says she has no idea about costs. I eventually suggested giving her the same as we paid for the last meal we had in a restaurant. She was embarrassed and said it was too much and she could not accept, so we had to leave the money on the table. We had similar difficulties in paying Marian, our guide. All he wanted was a bungee cord for his bike, since he had never seen one before. We gave him a handful and he was fascinated by them, and did not take too much interest in the money we gave him.

The next day's trip was to Lake Ligheanca and surrounding area, with similar tight manoeuvres being required. On our departure the father suggested a

RIVER DANUBE NAVIGATION: ROMANIA

Dunârea Veche riverbank

route, which started off going through an archway of trees. After about half a mile we thought we must have gone wrong somewhere; however, there was not enough width to turn the boat around and go back. The only option was to continue and eventually leave the trees behind and come into an area of reeds. Once more we reached the Sulina Arm of the River Danube and continued on our way.

For others wanting to explore the Delta, but who don't want to scratch the side of the boat with branches, or have too deep a draught, or don't get a permit to sail in the delta, then the answer is to arrange with one of the local fishermen to take you into the backwaters in their boat. Their local knowledge is invaluable and we would never have ventured into the places we did without our guide. Permits for this type of journey are also required, but are available from tourist offices and hotels. For the less adventurous there are guided tours on boats starting from various locations, and these tours include the permit for a visit to the delta in the price.

On another occasion the River Danube was extremely high. We decided to go exploring the backwaters in the dinghy. On the return to the main river the water flow was getting faster and with the outboard engine on full throttle and two people rowing, we were getting swept backwards further into the wilderness. We made for the riverbank, and took the dinghy out of the water. The walk up the riverbank carrying the dinghy went well for a while, but the trees became denser, and the way was blocked. With the dinghy back in the water, and the engine on full throttle, two people grabbed the trees to assist in pulling us along. Progress was painfully slow, with us making about 200m in an hour. Our luck then changed and a local boat with a very powerful engine came along and towed us back to the main river. With the river being high it was obviously filling up the lakes and backwaters. This was in complete contrast to our previous visit when everything was so calm.

CHILIA (KILIA) ARM (KILIYSKIY RUKAV)

In Ukraine no visa is required for citizens of the European Union, Switzerland, Liechtenstein, Japan, USA, Canada, Romania, Mongolia, Serbia and Montenegro, CIS except Turkmenistan, for a visit of 90 days. Citizens from other countries will need to get a visa in advance before venturing down this arm. The rules are regularly changing so everyone should check on visa requirements before travelling here.

The marker posts here revert from miles back to kilometres. The new canals at the entrance to the Black Sea have a design parameter depth of 6.5m. It was reported from another boat that the navigation channel differs substantially from the chart, although we could not find a chart.

For 115km from M43 four miles north of Tulcea the Chilia Arm is the largest one, draining 60 per cent of the River Danube's water and alluvial deposits. Located on the northern side of the Delta, it forms the border between Ukraine and Romania. It has a meandering course, forming at the mouth a secondary delta where the water flows into the sea through 45 channels.

Km115
Junction with the main River Danube.

Km114
Pătlăgeanca
The pontoon for this village is in the other arm.

Both banks are tree-lined and the villages are hidden behind the dykes.

Km103
Ceatalchioi
Here there is a good pontoon that is used by the ferry. It must be vacated before its arrival at 1000. We were met by an old man who wanted to show us his chickens, pigs, and donkey. Walking down the main street, which is only a dirt track, other old people were herding the cattle, goats and geese back from the fields into the village. They all came over and shook our hands. I ask the Romanian crew what this was all about and was told that until recently it was forbidden for foreign pleasure boats to sail down this arm and we were the first foreign boat to stop here since those people were small children, (probably before the second world war). The shop with the pub had only two tables. We got a similar friendly reception from some younger men who were occupying one of the tables. This was the most primitive place we have been to.

Ceatalchioi: main street

Km101
There is a good pontoon, but it is used by the Romanian frontier police.

Km94
Plauru
There is a good pontoon for the ferry, but it must be vacated when they want to use it. There is a ferry that runs between here and Ismail.

Km93
Ismail (Ukraine)
Ismail radio Ch 16

Some foreign boats report they were not permitted to stop here and could not get clearance even with the use of an agent. Others were successful in stopping here. It is a port of entry. Mooring for visiting pleasure boats is near the passenger terminal near 92km. All services, including repairs, are available.

The trees which have dominated the scenery on this bank since Cernavoda still continue along the riverbank, except at two breaks for the docks.

The Greek town on this site was called Antifilia and it was occupied until the 4th century AD. The Turks called the place Ismail in the 16th century, and the Turkish fort still remains. The Russians occupied it in 1770, 1790, 1811 and from 1877 until 1918, when it was given to the Romanians. In 1944 the Russians got it back again. In the town is the Pokrovsky Cathedral and museums.

Km78
Pardina
There is a pontoon for the ferry but it must be kept clear for their use. From here the river splits into many islands.

Plauru ferry pontoon

Ismail

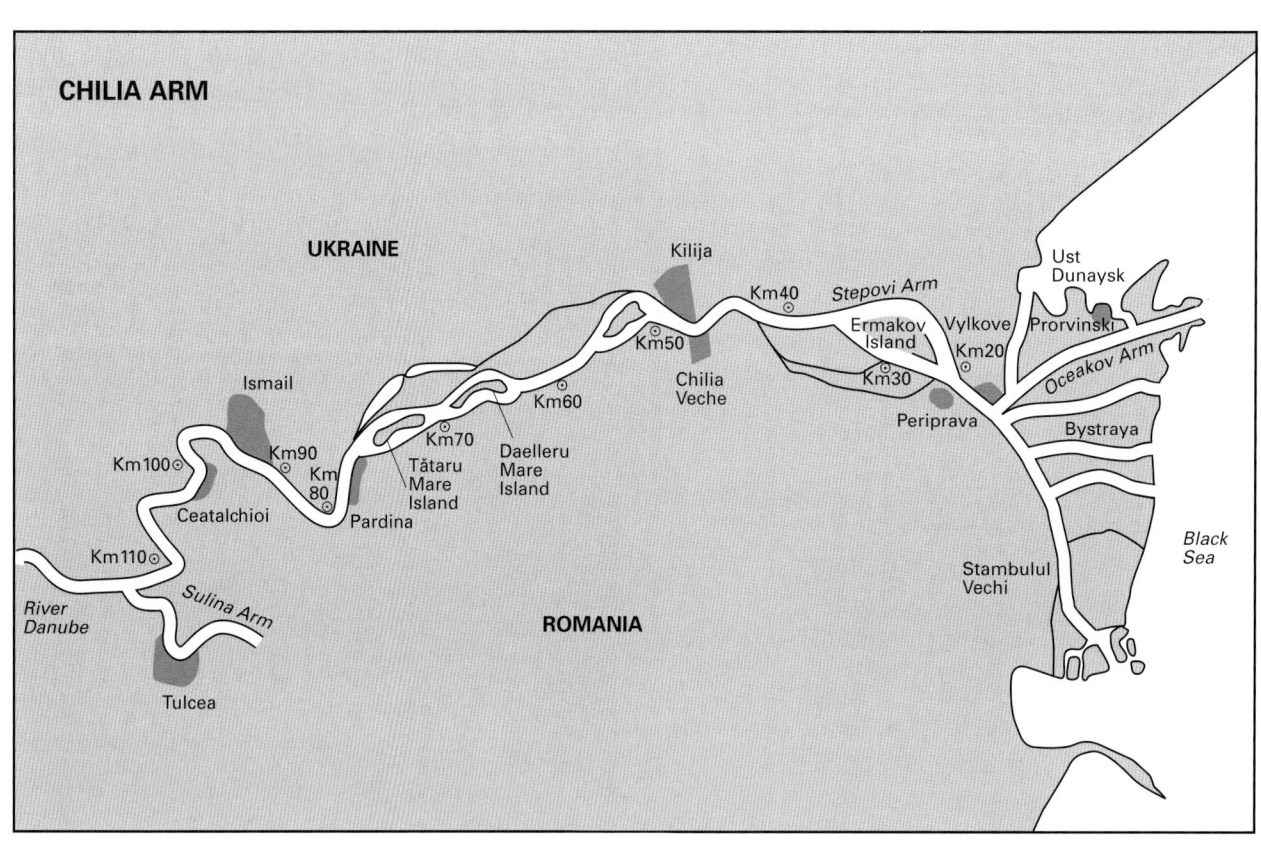

From km75 to km61: navigation is possible on both sides of the islands Tătaru Mare and Dalleru Mare, with the north side being wholly in the Ukraine. The south side has its own kilometre marker posts, starting at 11km.

Km47
Kilija (Chilia) (North Bank: Ukraine)
Ch 17

This is an industrial town with shipbuilding and repairs, and although there has been some reconstruction work, the place looks run down.

Km47
Chilia Veche

This was a suburb of what is now Kilija when it was part of Romania. It is one of the oldest settlements in the Danube Delta, being founded by the Greeks who called it Achillea. The Genoese called the place Licostomo, before the Turks called it Eski-kale (Old Castle). The Moldovians gave it its present name of Chilia. In Greek times it was about 5km from the sea, but today it is over 40km from the sea. A notary, Antonio Di Ponzo, recorded in the 14th century that the town was trading in wine, salt, carpets and 12-year-old slaves. In the 17th century there are records from a monk called Niccolo Barsi of 2,000 sturgeon being caught daily. The town has an impressive church.

Km32 to km22

The northern side of Ermakov island is in the Ukraine. This is known as the Stepovi (Stepovoye) arm and is navigable, with its own km marker posts starting at 12km. The river on the south is the international boundary and is also navigable.

Km24
Periprava (Romania)

Today it is a small fishing village, but in Communist times it had a prison for political prisoners, with a reputation for its brutal treatment.

Km19
Vylkove (Vylkova, Vilovo, Vilkovka) (Ukraine)
Vilkovka radio Ch 11

The navigable channel on the Oceakov Arm (Ochakivs'ke Hyrlo) turns northeast here and is marked with buoys to the sea. From now on the navigable channel is totally in the Ukraine. (The km markers continue on the Stambulul Vechi Arm which heads southwards.) After 7 miles the buoyed channel turns north towards Prorvinskiy. At 45°28′.25N 29°43′.48E there are two options. You can either continue northeast to the sea, or turn west into the channel for Ust Dunaysk. The maximum draught for this channel is quoted as being 2.5m, and there are some severe bends of over 120°.

It is claimed that there are ten navigable channels into the Black Sea, including the new Bystraya Canal. This 13km long canal was used by commercial traffic until 1958 when it was reserved for the Russian navy until the early 1990s. It subsequently silted up, but it has recently been dredged and in August 2004 it reopened with an initial designed depth of 6.5m, later to be 7.3m.

The new Bystraya Canal and the small barren island of Zmiyinyy Ostrov (Serpent's Island) are causing a lot of controversy. Ancient Greeks called the island Leuke (White Island) due to the calcareous rocks. They built

Chilia confluence: Ismail to the left, Tulcea to the right

a temple dedicated to Achilles, which was destroyed in 1837 by Russian sailors who used the stone to construct a lighthouse. The Genoese in the 14th century named it Serpent's Island due to their sailors finding many reptiles in the temple's water reservoirs.

Moldovian and Wallachian (Romanian) princes ruled over the island in medieval times. Serpent's Island's first mention in an international treaty was in the 1878 Berlin Peace Treaty. In August 1944 Red Army troops occupied the island. The Paris Peace Treaty of February 1947 drew the border to the north of the island, leaving it as Romanian territory. Romania agreed to cede it to Soviet Control in February 1948, and a transfer protocol was signed on the island in the May of that year.

From 1967 to 1987 Romania and the Soviet Union unsuccessfully negotiated the limits of the continental shelf. The island as a strategic asset became Ukranian in 1991 with the collapse of the Soviet Union. A 1997 treaty agreed Ukraine would deploy no aggressive weapons on Serpent's Island and would consider it uninhabited. Ukraine has since manned the island and deployed weapons there, and constructed an air traffic control system, which covers the Black Sea and Mediterranean as far as Libya. A radio monitoring and jamming station, a patrol ship, two submarines and a military garrison are based here. Over 20 meetings between the two sides have produced no results.

Romania claims the Bystraya canal will be used to put pressure on them to give up territorial rights for the continental shelf. The canal gives Ukraine another access to the River Danube and they have stated they will charge less in transit fees than Romania does for the use of the Sulina Arm, causing Romania substantial financial losses. The stakes over the island and canal are even higher now since oil and gas have been discovered around it. Romania has joined NATO, but Ukraine is not a member, so the entrance to the River Danube is now even more strategically important.

SAINT GEORGE'S ARM (GURU STÂNTUL GHEORGHE, BRATUL SFÎNTU GHEORGHE)

The marking here reverts back from miles to kilometres.

This is the most southerly arm and it carries about 22% of the water to the Black Sea. It meanders for 106km from M34 to Sfîntu Gheorghe on the Black Sea coast. It is not dredged as regularly as the Sulina Canal, and reliable figures for its depth are not available. When the river was high we typically measured minimum depths of over 3m over the whole length. It must be emphasised that silting can change the depth of the river dramatically. Between 1857 and 1886 some cuttings were made to get rid of sharp bends, and without dredging this deepens this arm. However, in recent years some of the biggest meanders have been sectioned in order to reduce the navigation course and increase the water speed and consequently the depth.

Km105
Between the junction with the Sulina Arm and Nufăru are 2 restaurant barges.

Located in the poplar and willow tree woodland are the following townships.

Km104
Nufăru
There is a car ferry across the river, but no pontoon. This is the Roman town of Talamorium where they built a citadel, later to become the castle of Perislava in the 10–14th centuries.

Km100.5
There is an excellent jetty but unfortunately it is for the military and is a restricted area, and stopping is not permitted.

Nufăru

Km100
Victoria
There are traces of a prehistoric settlement in this village which is a short distance from the river. The scenery to the south of the river is now hills.

Km97
Băltenii de Sus
Located on a rocky outcrop, it has no pontoon and the fishing boats are dragged up on the shore.

Km94
Băltenii de Jos
Here there are two good pontoons.

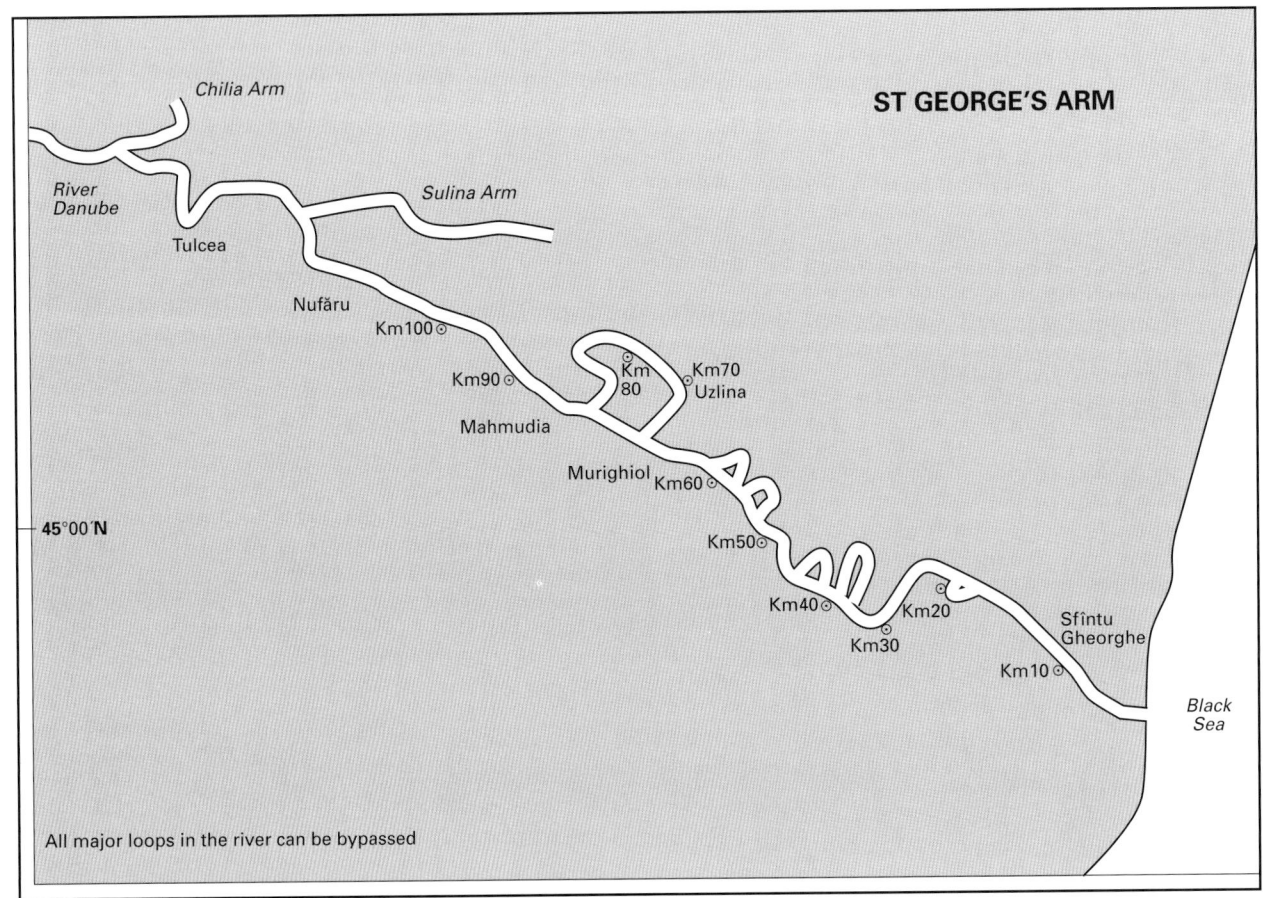

Km88
Mahmudia

(Called Independența in the Communist era.) It is not a tourist-friendly town. There is a new 3-star hotel and a 4-star hotel with pontoons, and also the official Port Mahmudia pontoon, but none of them would permit us to tie onto them. (We were welcome to tie up alongside a floating crane.) There are several local bars and a few shops. In the main street, at right-angles to the river, is a shop that sells gas, and at the end of the street on the outskirts of the town a garage. Unfortunately there are no taxis in town to bring the fuel to the boat.

On the hill with the flat top to the west of the town was the fortress of Salsovia, built on the site of a Romano-Byzantine fortress. The pagan Emperor Licinius controlled the eastern empire in 313 until he quarrelled with Constantine and lost all his European empire except Thrace. Licinius started to persecute the Christians but was defeated in battle by Constantine at Adrianople and Chrysopolis in 324. Constantine banished Licinius and finally ordered his execution in Salsovia.

Mahmudia Lipovenian church exterior

Mahmudia. Car, horse and cart ferry

Uzlina – tourist villas

Km77
Uzlina

There is an excellent pontoon here and it is free to be used since the big ferry no longer calls here. Today this is a modern tourist complex with hotels, pensions, villas and restaurants, but no shops. The hotel has a fuel store for its own boats and it may be possible to get some in an emergency. Boats are available for hire, but only with a boatman. These can tour the small canals or lakes, or be used for fishing. Also at the complex there is water-skiing, horse riding, bike hire, and helicopter trips can be arranged. In the area are many idiotic people in fast power-boats and much vigilance is needed. If you want to stop and stay off the boat at the hotel it is €65 per night including breakfast. Here there are the offices of the Delta Dunarii Biosphere Reservation. Jacques Cousteau also assisted in the setting up of an education and research foundation here in the early 1990s.

Km65
Murighiol

This is a popular fishing village with a good pontoon and a restaurant ship.

There are traces of a Romano-Byzantine fortress from the 4th–6th century.

After here the trees on the riverbank give way to reeds, grass and less dense woodland. There is no sign of life until Sfîntu Gheorghe.

The chart shows the distance from Mahmudia to the sea to be 90km. This is the marking on the old Danube, but some canals have been constructed to cut out the bends and this can reduce the journey to about 35km.

Km0
Sfîntu Gheorghe 44°53′.71N 29°35′.56E at the mooring in the small harbour

There are two pontoons here, but the ferry stops overnight at one of them. The ferry from Tulcea delivers all the supplies here, and there is only one vehicle in town, and this is the frontier police. The roads are all sand. There are a few tractors, and the main mode of transport is by donkey and cart.

To the east of the town are some new tourist facilities, but they will not serve alcohol unless you buy a meal. The bars in town are very basic and the shops only have minimal stock. The frontier policeman noted

THE RIVER DANUBE

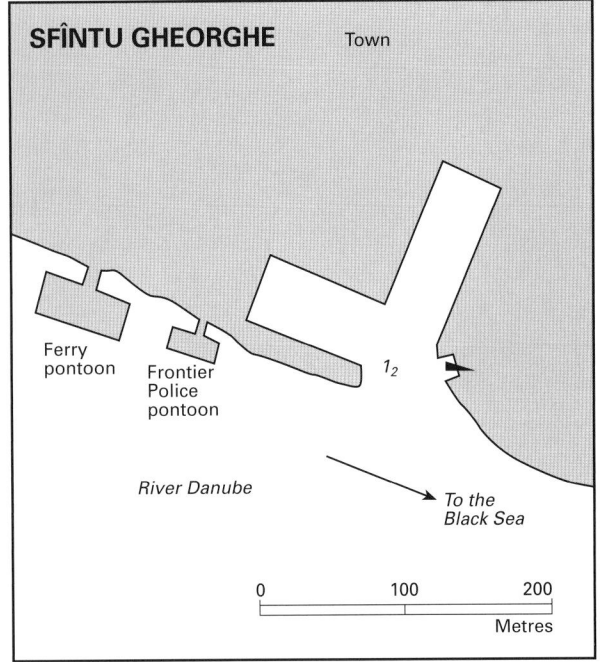

the name of the boat and our passport numbers in his notebook and then advised that we were the first foreign tourist boat that he had seen here.

In the town's tourist literature it claims to be at 045° north, making it exactly halfway between the equator and the North Pole. (By the GPS it is 7 miles further south.)

Saint George is the patron saint of the Danube Delta. The town of Sfîntu Gheorghe was first recorded in 1318. In January it hosts the International Festival of Amateur Theatre, and in February the Secular Winter Customs Festival. It has always been dependent on fishing and in the Black Sea, up to 5 miles offshore and for substantial distances on both sides of the river mouth, are fixed fishing nets which are generally very poorly marked.

At its mouth it forms the Sacalin Islands. In ancient times this was claimed to be the largest mouth of the River Danube and was called Hieron Stoma (The Sacred or Holy Mouth).

Sfintu Gheorghe harbour

The sediment from this channel forms the longshore drift in front of Lake Razim and stretches south to Constanţa. The discharge has been known to reach Nos Kaliakra.

THE BORCEA ARM

If the use of this arm was permitted the journey would be 22km shorter than by the International Waterway which is to the east. It is believed that it is also deeper than the International Waterway.

The Borcea Arm starts a new system for the km markers starting at 100km. At 98km is the entrance to the canal which 4km later terminates at Calarasi Industrial Harbour complete with the cranes for unloading the barges. The Calarasi Commercial Port is located between km94 and km93. Calarasi was first documented in 1593 during the reign of Michael the Brave (Mihai Viteazul). Today the industry is food processing (fish), flour milling, pulp and paper-making from reed from the local swamplands.

Unaware that we were not permitted to use this channel, since it is considered as a Romanian inland waterway, we proceeded to Calarasi. We received a friendly reception with people helping us to moor while the customs explained this was only for Romanians. Later a customs officer who spoke excellent English explained about this arm being an inland waterway and said we should sail in the arm to the east which is the international waterway.

It is unfortunate that foreigners could not officially sail here since 8km from the main Danube people were swimming, playing football, in canoes, fishing and there were two people with a tractor and trailer with rakes cleaning the beach. It looked a nice holiday place. After passing such a long length without seeing people, this was an interesting and exciting area with friendly people.

EU residents will be able to sail this arm now that Romania is in the European Union. However, we met one boat who, when at Russe in Bulgaria, was advised that the international arm was unnavigable due to low water. The boat club contacted the Romanian authorities and obtained permission for the boat to sail instead in this arm, which had sufficient water for navigation.

The Borcea Arm has a series of small townships along the riverbank as follows.

Km92
Magureni

Km88
Cadina

Km80
Goslogeni

Km76
Dichiseni (Discheni)
A former Roman settlement.

Km67
Junction of Bala Canal
This is a 10km long canal connecting the Borcea arm with the main Danube.

Km57
Pietrouil

Km42
Fetesti 44°N 27°E
This is located on the main road and the head of the rail bridge to Constanța. Its industry is food processing, livestock raising, growing grapes and cereals.

Km26
Bordusani

Km18
Facaeni

Km4
The last 3km of the Fruhere Arm to the west are closed to navigation and to rejoin the main Danube the eastern route has to be taken. This has the continuation of the kilometre marker posts from the main Danube to km250 and the main river is rejoined at km241.

Behind Calarasi and the Borcea arm lies the Baragan Steppe, a treeless, waterless, wilderness covered in thistles. It was to this wilderness, with cold winters and the highest recorded summer temperatures in Romania, that many Banatar Swabians were deported. Their former home on the Serbian border was surrounded by military and government officials on the eve of 17 June 1951. Those who were considered to be landowners, or connected with political affairs, were rounded up, and with a few possessions and animals were loaded onto boxcars and the freight train deposited them here. The Swabians are descendants of Non-Commissioned Officers who were Germans who stayed behind to give a German presence in the Banat. After the peace of Passarowitz Duke Karl Alexander of Wurttemberg sent a ship with 150 Bavarian and Swabian girls, so that the men could increase there presence there. This vessel was known as the *Moidle-Schiff* (merry vessel).

Today it is a cereal-growing area.

Bulgaria

Km845.5
The River Timok forms the border between Serbia and Bulgaria.

Km794 to km785
Vidin
43°58'.6N 22°52'.5E
Population 64,000 (approx.)

Km794
There is a huge crane and a Ro-Ro terminal. For use of the crane, arrangements are made in the administration building.

Km790.5
Harbourmaster Ch 11
Transit information Ch 16
There are five pontoons and we were instructed to moor against pontoon No.5 and later moved to No.3. (The Bulgarian definition of a 'pontoon' might be an old barge moored to the riverbank.)

The customs, harbourmaster, border police and other officials are located in the white building opposite pontoon No.3. The border police spoke English and were very efficient; however, all other authorities were exactly the opposite. Nothing prepared us for the bureaucracy that was to follow, we had to visit many offices and collect about 40 rubber stamps on a mountain of paperwork.

The authorities issue a permit for a $20 note (no other currency is acceptable). This permit is the permission to stop at other ports on the Danube.

During our four-day stint of form-filling a Swedish boat claimed their proof of ownership was their insurance policy, since you cannot insure something that does not belong to you. Entry to Bulgaria was refused to them and when we met them further downstream a few days later, they advised that their solution was to sail down the Romanian side of the river.

Between pontoon 5 and 6 there is the restaurant Vidom on a pontoon, which has four 'real' pontoon moorings for visitors to the restaurant. There are many good restaurants in the town and water available near the pontoons. There are other jetties and cranes at the east end of the town.

A ferry runs from here to Calafat in Romania.

The Celts occupied this area before the Romans came along and built the town of Bononia in the first

---

John Neale gives his account of this area in *Practical Boat Owner* June 2004, which corroborates our experience. 'We were soon stopped by a Bulgarian gunboat whose crew told us to clear into their country at Vidin 30 miles away. The buoyage was barely adequate and we reached there in the dark, tying up to an old jetty. At 2300, no less than seven officials arrived to tell us we could not remain there and must check in further downstream. After they attempted to move us against a three knot current, I protested, saying it was too dangerous. After much discussion, they agreed to let us stay where we were, with the memorable words: 'Welcome to Bulgaria – don't come ashore'. In the morning we went down the river to the customs pontoon in Vidin, to be charged $40 agent's fees for filling in lots of forms in triplicate for ship's manifest (cargo), crew list, ships documents and owner's documents.'

century AD. When the Romans left, the Bulgars occupied the area and named it Bidin. The Hungarians enlarged the fort and in the 14th century and it became the capital of the independent northwest Bulgarian kingdom under Ivan Sratismir. In 1391 the Turks occupied Vidin and stayed there until the 19th century, except for a few brief periods.

One exception was 1794–1807 when Osman Pazvantoglu was leader of Vidin District. He was backed by Napoleon who had wanted to expand his influence in the area and supplied engineers who strengthened the fort. In 1878 Vidin again returned to Bulgaria, and in 1885 Serbia's attempt to take over the town was defeated. This fortress from the 10th century that dominates the town and the river had the nickname Baba Vida (Grandmother Vida). Other old buildings include several mosques, old churches, synagogues and a bazaar. There is a very interesting flood defence barrier, which runs the length of the town along the riverbank. Normally the metal barricade lies flat and can be used as a walkway, but in times of potential flood, can be raised. Today Vidin is a market town for the outlying farms and is famous for its wine and ceramics.

Vidin is looking forward to future prosperity with a European Union project known as Pan-European Transport Corridor Four, which aims to create a major north–south transport route linking Greece and Western Europe through Bulgaria and Romania. The new bridge will cross the Danube between Vidin and Calafat in about 2008.

Km774
Botevo
Here the river widens out and the flow rate slows down.

Km770
Artchar
Artchar, beside the river of the same name, was at one time the Roman capital of Upper Thrace and called Ratiaris. This was fortified, as were many other towns along the Danube, by Trajan on his Dacian Campaign. Here the altitude above the Black Sea at Varna is 24m.

Vidin

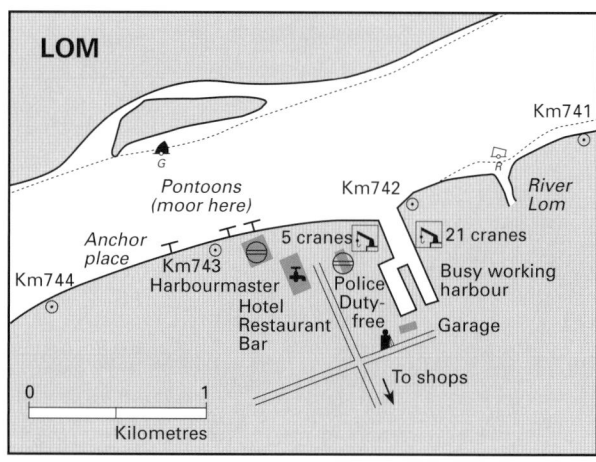

Km744 to km740
Lom 43°49'.5 23°13'.3E
River inspection Ch 20
Harbourmaster Ch 12
Lom Radio Ch 16

We moored at pontoon 3. The harbourmaster and customs arrived immediately, asked for two copies of the crew list and checked the papers we had collected at Vidin. (They are located in a single-storey building on the river bank opposite pontoon No. 2.) It is a very user-friendly area with a hotel, bar, restaurant, water, and duty-free. Gas and fuel can be obtained from a garage on the road parallel to the river about half a kilometre from the pontoon. It is to the east, located behind the cranes.

Lom has run-down *panalek* blocks and many derelict buildings not a pretty tourist sight, but the people give one of the friendliest welcomes you will get anywhere. There are ample shops and a market in the town. Lom is a busy port and one company loads huge barge convoys with lorries which are transported to Germany, taking literally thousands of lorries off the road.

Lom is the site of the Roman town of Almus.

Km718
Dolni–Tzibar
There is a semi-derelict jetty. It is used by small fishing boats and not very suitable for pleasure craft.

Km703
Kozloduy
The officials at Vidin indicated by sign language that we must not go to Kozloduy or we would be jailed. This is the site of the Bulgarian atomic power stations.

The Bulgarian national hero Hristo Botev (born in 1848 in Kalofer), at the age of 20 met the Bulgarian revolutionary Vassil Levski, who Bulgarians consider their 'apostle of liberty'. They stayed together in an abandoned mill near Bucharest in Romania. Botev was then a teacher in various locations and contributed to and started revolutionary newspapers such as *Word of the Bulgarian Emigrants*, *Freedom* and *Independence*.

In the spring of 1876 the Revolutionary Committee divided the country into four revolutionary districts and the planned uprising was to start on 1 May, but in effect in one area it started on 20 April.

On 16 May Botev with some of his rebels embarked on the Austrian steamship *Radetzky* and further rebels, numbering about 200, joined at other ports so that they did not attract attention. On 17 May the rebels

Steamship *Radetzky*

Radetzky was built in 1851 at Obuda shipyard in Budapest. Several proposals were put forward to save the ship and bring it back to Bulgarian waters, but these all failed. The ship was decommissioned in 1918 and scrapped by the Austrian Ship Society in 1924.

In 1964 a Mrs Lozanova opened a bank account with 2.50 leva (€1.5) and campaigned for the school children to raise funds. 1,200,000 children raised enough funds to rebuild the *Radetzky* in honor of Botev's 90th anniversary.

The original inventory book was found at the shipyard and a substantial contribution was received from a Mr Kirali Josef, who was 84 at the time but had kept a full album of his time working on the boat from 1906 to 1918.

The specification for the replica is 57.4m long and 17.5m wide, draught 1.15m, steam-driven with side paddle wheels, to produce a speed upstream of 8kph and downstream 12kph, carrying 300 passengers. The vessel was delivered to Kozloduy on 30 May 1966.

The exhibition on the ship today has many original items from its predecessor and preserves the memory of Botev's heroism.

hijacked the ship and forced it to moor at Kozolduy. The diary of Captain Englender survives and he writes that he was impressed with Botev, by his correctness, power and temperament. Botev with his rebel *cheta* fought Turkish posses and reached the Vratza Mountain, but did not get any support from the local revolutionary committee. On May 20 the revolutionary poet Botev was killed and the rebels split into small groups, with many of them being killed by the Turks and a few escaping to Romania and Serbia.

The 120km route of from Kozloduy to Vratza is marked by 68 stones and 6 remembrance memorials and a broad alley of trees on either side.

Km678

Oriahovo 43°44'3N 23°56'4E
Harbourmaster Ch 13
River inspection Ch 18

There is a real pontoon with bollards here, not just an old barge. There is a sign at the pontoon for water but the tap area is all broken up. There are two garages for fuel 1km and 3km west of the village. On the east side of the village is the ferry terminal, which transports vehicles to Bechet in Romania. This area is fenced off and under customs control. As requested we tried to report to the officials who were located in the compound. Security asked us if we had a lorry, and since we had a boat we were turned away, so there is no bureaucracy here.

The town by the river is totally derelict and the buildings are only shells. This could be the backdrop for a film after an atomic bomb has dropped. The only restaurant we found was at the entrance to the ferry terminal. This is the business centre for the prostitutes, who have plenty of lorry drivers as customers when they are held up waiting for their customs papers to be processed.

Km641

Baikal

Although there is a pontoon marked on the chart, there is no suitable place to stop.

Km637

The river Isker joins the Danube and at 368km this is the longest of Bulgaria's 526 rivers which are longer than 2.3km. Near the mouth of the river are remains of the Roman town of Oescus where some foundations can still be observed.

Km625

Zagrjden

There is a jetty here, but it has sloping sides and is not easy to tie on to.

Km608

Somovit
Harbourmaster Ch 13

Here there are good pontoons in front of a railway goods yard and beside two cranes. There are the small, picturesque Turkish houses scattered up the hillside with a limited number of shops up the hill.

Km598

Nikopol 43°21'.2N 24°53'.3E
Harbourmaster Ch 14
River inspection Ch 20

There are good pontoons at the west end of the town. In front of the pontoons there is a park with a garage on the opposite side where fuel and water can be obtained. There are a number of shops near the pontoons. One small one was crammed with every imaginable thing from shoes, clothes, food, booze, electrical products, toys and many other items. Our cooker was faulty earlier in the day, and it was here that we purchased a 2-ring gas cooker for about €12 as a temporary replacement for the one on board. There are numerous cafés and restaurants, not of a very high standard, but adequate. The town appears run down but this is compensated for by friendly people.

At one time the fort here was the most important on the Danube, having been originally built by the Roman Trajan. He gave the town the name Nikopolis which means 'the city of victory'. It was strengthened and enlarged by various occupiers of the town.

During the Turkish occupation there was a crusade against them by a multinational force led by Sigismund of Hungary. The River Danube was the route taken to attack the Turks here. but the Crusaders were lured into a trap and the horses got entangled on stakes, and many were slaughtered by Sultan Bajazet's army, with the rest fleeing. The Russo-Bulgarian army freed the town from the Turks in 1878.

Km564 to km562

The island of Condur. The chart shows the channel to be on the north side, but this was silted up and the channel ran between this island and Belene Island.

Km576 to km560

Belene Island

Although the marker buoys are few and far between and many are out of position, this is one area that is well marked with 'no entry' signs. The biggest prison in Bulgaria is sited here. Construction of an atomic power station started here but was never completed; now there are reports of the work recommencing again.

Around this area the riverbanks are low and tree-lined with a lot of artificial planting. Belene Island, along with 9 smaller ones in the area covering a 16km stretch of the Danube, has been declared a RAMSAR site. The islands are a good example of natural riverine wetland, hosting several species of rare plants, and 5 globally threatened bird species: pigmy cormorant, ferruginous duck, white-tailed eagle, corncrake and aquatic warbler. It is also an important breeding ground for many other birds, as well as a stopover for 20 migratory species.

Km560
There is a small canal up to Belene town but this is a no-go area for pleasure craft. However, on the main river at km559 there is a small harbour identified by 3 cranes, with water available.

Km554
Svintov (Svištov, Svistova)
43°37′.2N 25°21′.1E
Harbourmaster Ch 12
River inspection Ch 19

There are 2 pontoons together in front of a large yellow building on to which recreational craft can tie. We were directed to pontoon No. 2 and asked to moor on the downstream side with the bow into the pontoon. Here there was mains power and a cable TV antenna on the pontoon. Water is obtained from the large yellow building. The bureaucrat's questionnaire was probably the longest one ever, with not only the usual questions like length, draught, engine size, but also the make of radio and GPS, how many bunks, and many other irrelevant questions.

Here is the most southerly town on the Bulgarian Danube. It is more upmarket than most and has a lively night life, with all types of shops, cafés, bars, disco, and tequila bar. It is also a busy port with 13 cranes and was noisy with barges being loaded all through the night. Today it is still busy as a stopping point for cruise boats.

Since Roman times it has been a crossing point for many nationalities, including 1916 when the Bulgarians and Germans crossed here to attack Romania.

Dimitar Apostalov Tsenov who was a 19th-century philanthropist and humanist was born here in 1852. He was an entrepreneur, merchant, stock owner, and ardent patriot. He bequeathed his fortune to the citizens of Svintov to endow an economic institute which is now the D A Tsenov Economic Academy. He wrote, 'people should constantly follow the road of cultural growth in order to achieve its ideas'.

Km498 to km489
Rousse (Ruse, Russe, Ruscuk, Rushchuk, Rustschunk, Runuek)
43°51′.3N 25°57′.3E
Population 192,000
Harbourmaster Ch 14
Rousse Radio Ch

The Romans built a fort here and named it Sexanta Prista, meaning 'the city of 60 ships', and it was their largest harbour on the river. Today it is the largest Bulgarian harbour on the river. The town is a cultural

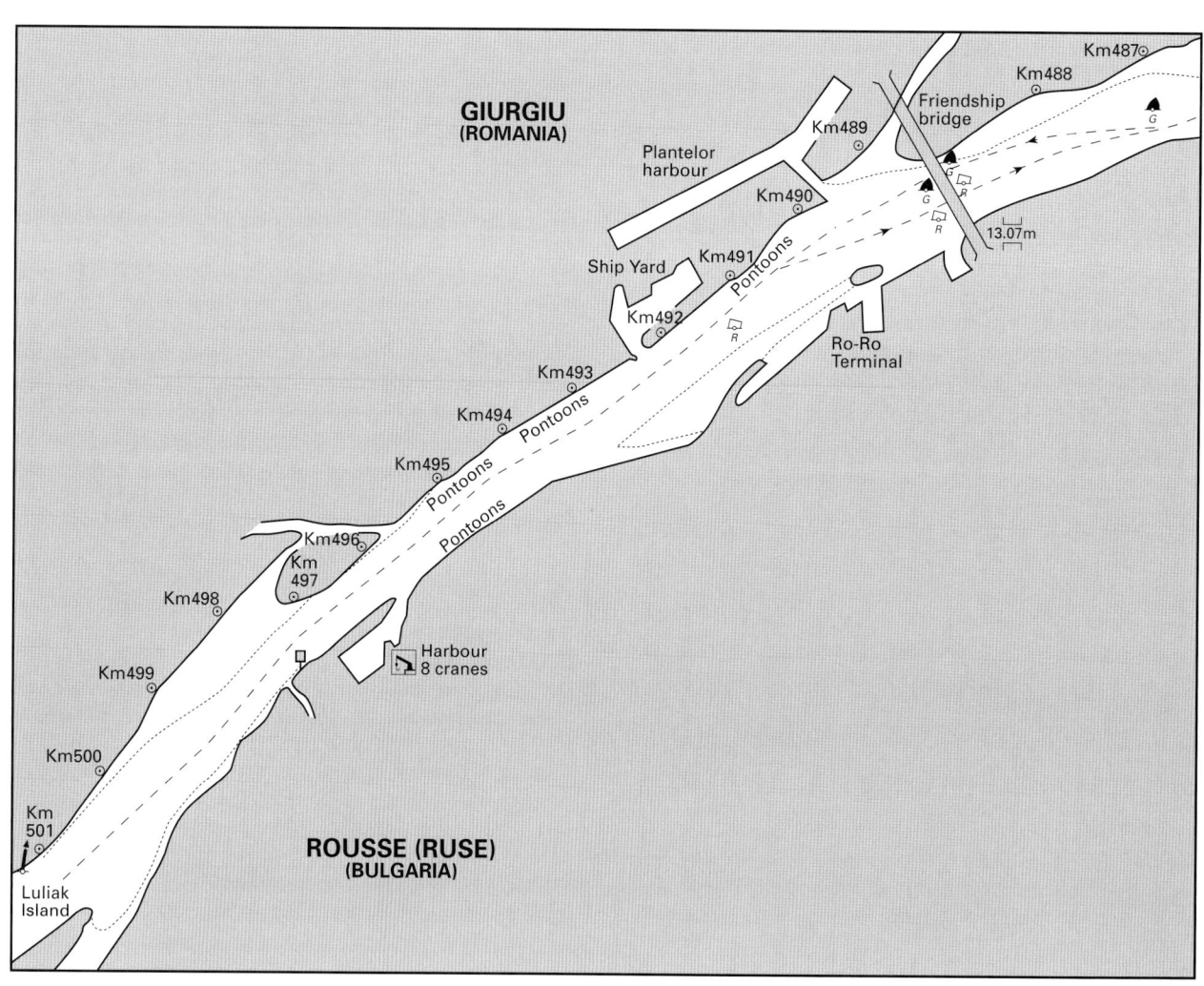

centre with a university, art gallery, opera, theatre and museums. Before the second world war Rousse was the richest city in Bulgaria. About 200 buildings are listed in the architectural and historic heritage of Bulgaria. Many are based on the same plans as Viennese buildings and this gives some areas the look of a Central European town. The most important of these are the 1908 Liberation Monument, the Drama Theatre, High School of Music, Chamber of Commerce and Industry, Dohodnoto Zdanie, the Kaliopa house, as well as merchants' houses. It earned the nickname Little Bucharest, which in turn was called Little Paris, or Paris of the East. Places of interest are the Leventabia Fort, Kyuntukapa Gate, the 1632 Holy Trinity Church, and the Mahmoud column. Baba Tonka (Granny Tonka) used her house to store supplies for Bulgarian rebels. She also acted as a navigator through the adjacent swamplands when they went on raids. All her five sons and two daughters were hanged by the Turks for their subversive activities. The skull of one of the rebel leaders, Stefan Karadzha, is still on display in her house, which is now a museum.

Sights to see nearby are the large Lipnik Park, and the ruins of the 10th-century town of Cherven. High up in the Roussenki Lom river valley is the Ivanovo Rock monastery, churches, chapels and caves with murals and frescoes, which were built between the 12th–14th century.

Km489
The Friendship Bridge
The central span is higher and narrower than the adjacent spans. For traffic going downstream the route is under the wider span to the south of the centre span. The air height above normal river level is 13.07m. Vessels travelling upstream use the span to the North of the centre span which has an air height of 13.13m. The bridge, which connects Bulgaria and Romania, is 2,224m in length, is the longest across the Danube, and claims to be the second longest in Europe after the bridge crossing the Tagus in Lisbon. Being the only bridge between the two countries it is normal for there to be huge queues and delays. Truck drivers typically faced a border delay of 10 days there, and earned it the nickname 'bottleneck bridge'. The two-level box girder bridge carrying the road on top and railway underneath was completed in 1954, and had a major reconstruction in 2003.

Km470 to km464
At Lunga Island the channel on the chart is on the Bulgarian side but in fact it is on the narrower Romanian side.

Km466
Riachovo
Pontoon.

Km458
Two pontoons behind Michka Island.

Km433
Toutrakan 44°03'.0N 26°36'.4E
Harbourmaster Ch 12
Toutrakan radio Ch 18
This looks like a picturesque place with red-roofed buildings in the trees going up a hillside around a church. On the skyline are *panalek* buildings and a tower. But when you go ashore you find the place is semi-derelict, and there are no decent cafés or restaurants; there was also no sign of a garage.

Km403
Popina
Small pontoon.

Km404 to km398
The navigation channel has deviated considerably from the chart.

Km395
Vetren
Vetren, between here and Silistra is where, just inland, is the Srebarna (Silver) Lake, which was connected to the River Danube until 1949 when a dam was built. After the annual flooding stopped, the level of the lake fell and it was reconnected to the River Danube in 1994. In 1983 it was added to the UNESCO list of monuments of world cultural and nature sites. The lake is a eutrophic wetland, densely overgrown with emergent and submergent aquatic vegetation, sustaining representative and rare wetland habitats. As a natural protected zone, it is home to 260 bird species of which about 100 types breed here. It is the only Bulgarian nesting site for a colony of Dalmatian pelicans and home for white-fronted geese, glossy ibis, great cormorant, European herons, and many other interesting species. These Danubian wetlands are on the important migration bird route Via Pontica, between Northern Europe and Central Africa, and are the winter home for some species like the white-fronted and greylag geese. The lake is overgrown with reeds and other water plants, representing 67 species, some of which are rarely found in Europe. It is home to 39 mammals and 21 reptiles and amphibians as well as many fish species.

Km376
Silistra
Harbourmaster Ch 70
Radio Ch 80
The harbourmaster is in the building at the east side of the square behind the pontoon. The customs and other officials are based at the road crossing point at the opposite side of town. It was impossible to contact the harbourmaster and we later found out that in his office he had the radio on another channel and used it only to chat to his friends.

They claimed that UN Convention No. 518, which states that the River Danube is an international waterway, does not exist. They invented their own rules. The RYA International Certificate for Operator of Pleasure Craft was of no use since the word 'captain' did not appear on it, even though it conformed with United Nations Resolution No. 40 of the working party on inland transit. The crew list, which was completed identical to the one at the previous port, was not acceptable and had to be done another way. One customs officer kept pushing the certificate of British Registry in our faces for two days and screaming that the document was false since it had no rubber stamp on it. The home port written on one form was different from the registration (which in Britain is centralised in Swansea) and they claimed this was impossible. The crew had no seaman's papers or official documents stating that they were qualified crew. All lockers were tipped out and lists had to be made for each individual item of drink and food on the boat. Telephones were examined for all calls made and received in Bulgaria. The video camera was checked for what film had been shot in Bulgaria. The passports were removed for two days and the British Embassy was calling the fiasco a diplomatic incident, although they were no help in solving the problem.

A local contact we knew advised that customs had now determined that, due to incorrect paperwork, we were the biggest criminals they had ever come across. The papers were passed to the town magistrate and finally to the court. The result was (without a hearing or a trial) that a fine of 2,000 leva (about €1,000) was imposed. This took 4 days before we could move again.

Silistra is a clean town. The central pedestrian way is paved with nice flagstones and has cafés and restaurants. There is a restaurant ship on a pontoon in front of the large industrial building. There was also one at the side of the harbourmaster's office but neither of them were working when we were there.

There was a sign for electric power with a long oblong socket, but it was not working. There was a sign for water in a metal case, but the bolts were rusted up and it could not be opened, water was obtained from the harbourmaster's office. There are two garages for fuel in town, one at the road crossing point and one behind the multi-storey flats.

Silistra was a Thracian township before being occupied by the Romans, who called the place Durostorum; was one of a chain of fortresses along the Danube. The only remains from Emperor Trajan's era is a tomb, and from the Turkish era a tower and some walls. (The remains from the Communist era are the bureaucrats!)

In the Middle Ages when the name changed to Drustur it was an important military, trade and cultural centre and a bishop's and patriach's seat during the years of the first Bulgarian kingdom. The town was a strong fortress under Tsar Simeon (second Bulgarian kingdom). Between 1913 and 1940 the town was in Romanian territory. The historical sites that still exist are the fortress Medzhit Tabiya dating from 1841–53 and Saint Peter and Paul's church from 1862. There is a Thracian vaulted sepulchre with rich mural decorations.

Km375

End of border with Romania.

APPENDIX

BOOKS

Navigation
CEVNI European Waterways Regulations Tom Murrell (RYA). The CEVNI rules explained
List of Lights and Fog Signals. Mediterranean, Black and Red Seas Vol E NP78 (Admiralty)
The Danube, A River Guide Rod Heikell (Imray Laurie Norie and Wilson)

Guidebooks
Blue Guide Bulgaria James Pettifer (A & C Black (Publishers) Ltd)
Blue Guide Romania Caroline Juler (A & C Black (Publishers) Ltd)
Bulgaria (2005) Richard Watkins, Tom Masters (Lonely Planet Publications)
Romania & Moldova Steve Kokker, Cathryn Kemp (Lonely Planet Publications)
Rough Guide to Bulgaria Jonathan Bousfield, Dan Richardson (Rough Guides)
Rough Guide to Romania Tim Burford, Norm Longby (Rough Guides)
Traveller's Bulgaria Lindsay and Tim Bennett (Thomas Cook Publishing)

General interest
The Jason Voyage (The Quest for the Golden Fleece) Tim Severin (Hutchinson & Co Ltd)
The Ulysses Voyage (Sea Search for the Odyssey) Tim Severin (Hutchinson & Co Ltd)
Black Sea, The Birth Place of Civilisation & Barbarism Neal Ascherson

History
Romania. An Illustrated History Nicolae Klepper (Hippocrene Books Inc)
A Concise History of Bulgaria R J Crompton (Cambridge University Press)
The Black Sea, A History Charles King (Oxford University Press)

Children's
Welcome to Romania Grace Pundyk (Franklin Watts)
Boxes

APPENDIX

GLOSSARY OF WORDS USED ON CHARTS

English	Bulgarian (phonetic)	Romanian	Turkish
Bank	Plitchina	Tarm,-ul	Şiğlik
Bay	Zaliv	Sin de Mare	Bük, Bükü, Körfez, Ormos (Om)
Cape, Point, Promontory	Nos	Cap-ul,-u	Burun, Burnu (Br); Akra, Akrotirion (Ak)
Farm	Ferma	Ierma	Çiftlik, Çiftligi
Gulf	Zaliv	Golf,-ul	Kolpos (Kp)
Green	Zelen	Verdeata	Yesil, Ham
Hill, Peak	Hulm, Vruh	Deal,-ul; Dimb,ul	Tepe, Tepesti (T)
Hill, Mound	Mogila	Juiuk, Juk	
Island	Ostrov	Ostrov,-ul, Insul,-a,-a	Ada, Adasi (Ad); Nísos (N)
Islet	Ostrovche	Ostrov,u, -ul	Adacik (Adc); Nisís (Nis)
Jetty, Pier Quay; Wharf	Kei Pristanishte	Dig,-ul Chei,-ul Splaiu,-l	Iskele Rihtim
Lake	Ezero	Ghiol,-ul; Lac,ul,-u	Gol
Lighthouse	Far	Far,-ul	Fener Kulesi
Marine Farm	Talyan	Pescarie	Balik Çiftlikleri
Mountain	Planina	Munte,-le	Oros, Orosi (O)
Obscured	Zatamnen		Karanlik (Obscd)
Peninsula	Poluostrov	Peninsul,a,a	Yarimada (Yad)
Port, Harbour	Pristanishte	Liman,-ul; Port,-ul	Liman, Limin, Limani
Prohibited area	Zabranena zone	Zona interzisa	Yasak Saha
Prohibited area for diving	Zabranena zone za Pluvanc	Interzis scufunda rilor	Dalisa Yasak Sahalar
Red	Cherven	Ros-Rosu	Kirmizi
Ridge	Rid	Creasta	Sirt(t)
Rock, Rocky.	Skala, Skalist	Stinc,-a,-a	Vrahos, Vraho (Vos)
Ruin	Ruini	Ruina	Harabe (Ru)
Saint	Sveti	Sfantul; Sfînt,-a,ul	Ayios, Aiya, Ayion (Ay)
Shoal	Plitko	Scazut,a,a	Şiğlik
Straight	Tochno	Strimtoare	Boğaz, Boğazi
Stream, Small river	Reka, Potok	Girl,-a,-a; Riu,-l, Pirau,-l	Dere, Deresi, Derecik (D)
Tower	Kula	Turn,-ul	Kule
Tumulus	Grobnica	Tumulus	Huyuk
Village	Selo	Catun; Sat,-ul	Koy, Koyu
Visibility	Vidimo	Vizibilitate	Gorunus, Acisi
White	Byal	Alb,-a	Beyaz (W)
North	Sever	Nord,-ul	Kuzey
South	Ug	Sud,-ul	Guney
East	Iztok	Est,-ul	Dogu
West	Zapad	Apus,-ul; Vest,-ul	Bati

INDEX

Agigea, 63, 64
Ahtopol, 26
Akheloy, 40
Albena, 13
Altiman Bay, 28
anchors and anchoring, 5, 6, 71
Arkutino Bay, 30
Artchar, 98
Atiya Bay (Zaliv), 33

Babarada, 88
Bahna River, 77
Baikal, 99
Bala Canal, 81, 96
Balchik (Baltchik, Baltjik), 13, 54-5
Bălteniii de Jos, 94
Bălteniii de Sus, 94
Baragan Steppe, 97
Basarabi, 64
Bay of the Birds (Taukliman Bay), 58
Beautiful Headland (Nos Kaliakra), 57-8, 59
Bechet, 79
Beğendik Br, 22, 24
Belene Island, 99-100
Beliyat Bryag (White Coast, Laguna, Bialiata), 56
birds, 58, 73, 74, 100
Black Sea, 18-67
boating, 15
Bolata, 58
books and guides, 103
Borcea Arm (Bratul Borcea), 80, 82, 96-7
border police, 9-10
Bordusani, 97
Bosporus, 18, 21
Botevo, 98
Bourgaski Mineralni Bani, 12
Brăila, 83
Brăila Island, 82
Bratul Borcea (Borcea Arm), 80, 82, 89, 96-7
Bratul Sfîntu Gheorghe (Guru Stântul Gheorghe, St George's Arm), 67, 73, 87, 94-6
Bulgaria, 8-13
  Black Sea coast, 18-20, 25-59
  River Danube, 97-102
Buna 1 and 2, 56
Bunata Yacht Club (Nessebar), 42
buoyage, 6, 69
Burgas Bay, 31-44
Burgas East, 36
Burgas Marina, 36-7
Burgas West, 36
Butamyata Bay, 26
Byala, 45-6
Bystraya Canal, 93

Cadina, 96
Calafat, 79, 97
Calarasi (Chichiu), 80, 96

canals, 80, 81
  Bystraya, 93
  Calarasi, 96
  Midia, 63
  Poarto Alba-Midia-Navodari, 64
  River Danube-Black Sea, 63-4
  Sulina, 67
Cape Tuzla, 62
Carevo (Tzarevo), 27-8
Castrich (Kastrič), 26
The Cauldrons (Cazanele), 69, 76
caves, 59
Cazanele Mari & Mici (The Cauldrons), 76
Ceamurlia, 86
Ceariru Island, 81
Ceatalchioi, 91
Cerna, River, 76
Cernavoda, 63, 64, 81
certificates, 3
charts, 2, 8, 14, 69
  glossary, 104
Chernomorets, 32, 34
Chichiu (Calarasi), 80
Chilia (Kilija), 93
  Arm (Kiliyskiy Rukav), 73, 85, 86, 91-3
Chilia Veche, 93
Chiscani, 83
Çilingoz Koyu, 21, 22, 23
Clashing Rocks, 21
Claudia (Kladovo), 78
clothing, 15
cloud, 20
Cochirleni, 81
commercial traffic (Danube), 71
communications, 8, 14
Condur Island, 80, 99
Constanța, 62, 64-6
Corabia, 79
Costinesti, 62
Cranevo (Kranevo), 54
credit cards, 3
crew lists, 3
crime, 9
Crişan, 88
currents, 18, 69, 71
customs and traditions, 11, 16, 74

Dalyan Burnu, 21
Danube, Delta (Delta Dunarii), 68, 73-4, 86-90
  Biosphere Reserve Authority, 74
Danube, River, 18, 68-102
  Danube Commission, 68, 69, 72
  Danube Convention, 71
  Sulina Arm, 68, 73, 85-6, 87-90
  other arms, 90-7
declarations, 3
Delfin (Dolfin) Marina, 52
depths (Danube), 68, 69
Dichiseni (Discheni), 96
diving, 59

Djerdap Power Station (Iron Gates), 77
Dobra, 78
Dobreta Turnu Severin, 78
documentation, 3, 10, 15-16, 68, 71
Dolfin (Delfin) Marina, 52
Dolni-Tzibar, 98
Donji Milanovac (Donli Mianovic, Majdanpek), 78
Drenkova, 76
Druzhba (St Konstantin and St Elena, Drojuba), 13, 51
Dubova, 76
Dunârea Veche (Old Danube) (Macin Arm), 82, 83, 90-1
Dune (Duni, Dyuni, Djuni, Dunes Holiday Village), 30

Eiserne Tor 2 (Portile de Fier 2, Prahovo Lock), 79
electricity, 4, 9, 15
emergency telephone numbers, 8, 14
engine cooling water intake, 4
engine specifications, 3
equipment, 4-5
Eşilnița, 76
Evksinograd, 50-1

Facaeni, 97
fenders, 5
festivals, 11, 16
Fetesti, 97
fishing
  Black Sea, 18-19
  Danube Delta, 73-4
flags, 2
fog (Black Sea), 20
food and drink, 7, 11-12, 16-17
formalities, 3, 9 11, 15-16, 68, 71
Foros Bay (Zaliv), 33, 36
Friendship Bridge, 80, 101
Fruhere Arm, 97
fuel, 4

Galati (Galatz), 84-5
Galeia Arm, 83
gas, 4
Ghindares, 82
gifts, 3
Girla-Nadeia, River, 79
Giurgeni, 82
glossary, 104
Golden Sands (Zlatni Pjasaci, Zlatni Pyasatsi), 13, 53
Golubac (Golubex), 78
Gorgova, 86, 88
Goslogeni, 96
Grindu, 85
Gruia, 79
Guirgiu, 80
Guru Stântul Gheorghe (Bratul Sfîntu Gheorghe, St George's Arm), 67, 73, 87, 89, 94-6

CRUISING BULGARIA AND ROMANIA 105

INDEX

health, 5, 9, 15
Hirsova (Hârsova, Hrsova), 82
history, 13, 17, 71-2
hotels, 9

ice, 20, 71
ice supplies, 32
Iğneada, 21, 24
insurance, 3
international waterway signs, 70
internet, 6, 8, 14
Iron Gates (Portile de Fier), 69, 77-8
  Lock, 77
Iron Gates 2 (Portile de Fier 2, Eiserne Tor 2, Prahovo Lock), 79
Isaccea, 85
Isker, River, 99
Ismail, 92
Izvoarele (Pirjoaia), 81

Kabakum Bisser Beach (Pisatel), 52
Kaliakra reserve, 58
Kamchia, 46
Kamchiya, River, 45
Karaburun, 21, 22
Kasatura Koyu, 21, 23
KastriäË (Castrich), 26
Kavarna, 56-7
Kilija (Chilia), 93
  Arm (Kiliyskiy Rukav), 73, 85, 86, 91-3
Kilyos (Kumköy), 21
Kiten, 28
Kiyiköy (Midye), 21, 23
Kladovo (Claudia), 78
Korabostroitelnitzy, 33, 36
Kozloduy, 98-9
Kranevo (Cranevo), 54
Krapets, 59
Kraymorie, 33, 36
Kumköy (Kilyos), 21

Lacu Sarat Spa, 83
Laguna (Beliyat Bryag), 56
languages, 8, 14
  glossary, 104
Large Cauldron (Cazanele Mari), 76
Lebăda, 88
Lepenski Vir, 78
Liganii de Sus, 87
lights, 6, 18, 19
Listi, 26
Lom, 98
Lukoil Marina, 35
Lukoil oil terminal (Rossenetz oil terminal), 33
Luminita, 64
Lunga Island, 80
Lupului Island, 83

Macin Arm (Dunâ,rea Veche, Old Danube), 82, 83, 90-1
Magureni, 96
Mahmudia, 95
Majdanpek (Donji Milanovac), 78
Maliuc, 88
Mamaia, 66
Mangalia, 60-1
Medgidia, 63, 64
medicines and health, 5, 9, 15
Mermaid (Rusalka, Roussalka, Russalka, Rousalka), 58
Midia Canal, 63

Midye (Kiyiköy), 23
Mila, 87
mineral waters, 12-13
mobile phones, 8
Moldova Veche, 75
money, 3, 8-9, 14-15
mooring and anchoring, 5, 6, 71
Murighiol, 95

National Sports Academy (NSA) Marina, 40, 41
nature reserves, 58, 73-4, 86
navigational information, 6-7
  River Danube, 68-71
Navodari, 64
Navtex, 6
Nera, River, 75
Nesebărski Zaliv (Nessebar Bay), 43
Nessebar, 41-3
night navigation (Danube), 71
Nikopol, 80, 99
Nos Atiya, 32-3
Nos Atkin, 32
Nos Chukalyata, 33, 36
Nos Emenie, 44, 45
Nos Foros, 33
Nos Galata (Varna Bay), 45
Nos Kaliakra (Beautiful Headland), 57-8, 59
Nos Khrisosotira, 32
Nos Shabla, 58-9
Nos Sveti Dimitur, 51
Nos Sveti Georgi, 50
Nos Talasakra, 32
Nufăru, 94

Oceakov Arm (Ochakivs'ke Hyrlo), 93
Old Danube (Dunârea Veche) (Macin Arm), 82, 83, 90-1
Oltenita, 80
Oriahovo, 99
Orsova Town, 76-7
Otmanli, 33, 35-6
Ovidiu, 64

paperwork, 3, 9-11, 15-16, 68, 71
Pardina, 92
Partizani, 88
passports, 9, 15
Pătlăgeanca, 86, 91
Pearl Beach, 29
Periprava, 93
pets, 10, 16
photography, 15
Pietrouil, 96
Pirjoaia (Izvoarele), 81
Pisatel (Kabakum Bisser Beach), 52
place-names, 7
Plauru, 92
Poarto Alba-Midia-Navodari Canal, 64
Pomorie, 13, 38-40
Pomorie Boat Club, 39
Pomorski Lake, 38
Popina, 101
Port Mangalia, 60-1
Port Midia, 64, 66
Port Tomis Marina, 64-6
Portile de Fier (Iron Gates), 69, 77-8
  Lock, 77
Portile de Fier 2 (Eiserne Tor 2, Prahovo Lock), 79

Portita (Portitei), 66-7
ports of entry, 9-10, 15-16
Prahovo, 79
  Lock (Portile de Fier 2, Eiserne Tor 2), 79
Primorsko, 28-9
Prorvinskiy, 93
Prut, River, 85
public holidays, 11, 16

qualifications, 3

Radetzky (steamship), 98-9
radio (Danube), 69
radio licence, 3
RAMSAR Convention, 74, 100
Rashova, 81
Ravda Bay, 40, 41
refrigerators, 5
registration documents, 3
religion, 11, 16
Reni, 85, 86
repairs, 4
rescue services, 6
restaurants, 7
Rezovska, River, 22, 25
Riachovo, 101
Ribarski Pristan Bay (Zaliv), 36
right of way (Danube), 69
River Bahna, 77
River Cerna, 76
River Danube *see* Danube, River
River Danube-Black Sea Canal, 63-4
River Girla-Nadeia, 79
River Isker, 99
River Kamchiya, 45
River Nera, 75
River Prut, 85
River Rezovska, 22, 25
River Siret, 84
River Timok, 97
Riviera, 13, 52, 53
Romania, 14-17
  Black Sea coast, 18-20, 60-7
  River Danube, 75-97
Romanian Sailing Federation, 15
Ropotamo, 30
Rossenetz oil terminal (Lukoil oil terminal), 33
Rousse (Ruse, Russe, Ruscuk, Rushchuk, Rustschunk, Runuek), 100-1
rubber stamp, 3
Rusalka (Roussalka, Russalka, Rousalka) (Mermaid), 58

Sacalin Islands, 96
sailing season, 6
St Elena *see* St Konstantin and St Elena
St George (town) *see* Sfintu Gheorghe
St George'ís Arm (Guru Stantul/Bratul Sfintu Gheorghe), 67, 73, 87, 89, 94-6
St Konstantin and St Elena (Drojuba, Druzhba), 7, 13, 51
St Paraskeva Bay (Zaliv Sveta Paraskeva), 29
St Toma Island (Snake Island), 30
salt, 44, 83
Sandal Br, 21, 24
Sarafovo, 38, 39

sea level, 19
sea and weather, 18-20
seamanship, 7
security, 9
Seimeni, 81
Serbia, 68, 69, 77, 78, 79, 97
Serpent's Island (Zmiyinyy Ostrov), 93
service and spares, 4
Sfîntu Gheorghe (town of St George), 67, 95-6
 see also St George's Arm
Shabla, 59
ship chandlers, 4, 37, 47
showers, 5
signs (Danube), 69, 70
Silistar, 26
Silistra, 101-2
Sinemorets, 26
Siret, River, 84
Slănchev Den (Sunny Day), 52
Slunchev Bryag (Sunny Beach), 43-4
Small Cauldron (Cazanele Mici), 76
Smirdan, 83
Snake Island (St Toma Island), 30
Somovit, 99
Sozopol, 31-2
Sozopolski Zaliv (Sozopol Bay), 32-4
spares, 4
spas, 12-13, 83
Stambulul Vechi Arm, 93
Stepovi (Stepovoye) Arm, 93
Strandja coast, 25-7
Sulina, 86, 88-9
Sulina Arm, 68, 73, 85-6, 87-90
Sulina Canal, 67
Sunny Beach (Slunchev Bryag), 43-4
Sunny Day (Slănchev Den), 52
Sveta Anastasia Island, 33, 34, 35
Sveti Vlas, 44
Svintov (Sviötov, Svistova), 100
swimming, 7

Taekjip (Tekjip, Tekija), 78
Taukliman Bay (Bay of the Birds), 58
taxis, 9, 15
Tekjip (Tekija, Taekjip), 78
telephones, 8, 14
temperatures, seaside, 20
Thrace (Turkey), Black Sea coast, 18-24
time, 8, 14
Timok, River, 97
tipping, 9, 15
toilets, 5, 9, 15
Topolu, 82
Toutrakan, 101
traditions and customs, 11, 16, 74
trailer-sailers, 6-7
Trajan's Tablet, 78
Trakata, 50, 51
transit log, 10-11, 16
Tulcea, 86, 91
Turkey (Thrace), Black Sea coast, 18-24
Turnu Severin (Dobreta Turnu Severin), 78
Turnu-Magurele, 79-80
Tzarevo (Carevo), 27-8

Ukraine, 68, 69, 85, 91-3
Ukraine-Romania Border, 85
UNESCO National Biosphere Reserve, 74
United Nations Danube Convention, 71, 101
Uzlina, 95

Vama Veche, 60
Varna, 13, 46-9
Varna Bay, 45
Varna East, 46
Varvara, 26-7
Veliko Gradiste, 75
Veterani Cave, 76
Vetren, 101
Victoria, 94
Vidin, 97-8
Vilciu Arm, 83
Vilova (Vilkova, Vylkove, Vylkova), 93
visas, 2, 9, 15
Vramos Bay (Zaliv), 32
Vylkove (Vylkova, Vilova, Vilkova), 93

water supplies, 4
waterway signs, 70
weather, 8, 14
 Black Sea, 20
 Danube, 71
weather forecasts, 6
websites, 6
White Coast (Beliyat Bryag), 56
winch, 5
winds (Black Sea), 19
wine, 12, 16

Yaliköy, 21, 22

Zagrjden, 99
Zaliv Atiya (Bay), 33
Zaliv Foros (Bay), 33, 36
Zaliv Ribarski Pristan (Bay), 36
Zaliv Sveta Paraskeva (St Paraskeva Bay), 29
Zaliv Vramos (Bay), 32
Zaton, 66
Zimnicea, 80
Zlatni Pjasaci (Zlatni Pyasatsi) (Golden Sands), 13, 53
Zmiyinyy Ostrov (Serpent's Island), 93